THE DAY THE
EARTH
STANDS
STILL

UNMASKING THE OLD GODS BEHIND ETs, UFOs, & THE OFFICIAL DISCLOSURE MOVEMENT

DEREK P. GILBERT & JOSH PECK

FOREWORD BY DR. THOMAS HORN

DEFENDER

CRANE, MO

*The Day the Earth Stands Still: Unmasking the Old Gods behind ETs, UFOs, &
the Official Disclosure Movement*
Josh Peck & Derek P. Gilbert

Defender Crane, MO 65633 ©2017 by Thomas Horn. All rights reserved.
Published 2017. Printed in the United States of America.

ISBN: 978-0-9991894-8-1

A CIP catalog record of this book is available from the Library of Congress.

Cover illustration and design by Jeffrey Mardis.

All Scripture quotations from the King James Version; in cases of academic
comparison, those instances are noted.

*This book is dedicated to my
amazing wife, Christina Peck,
and our three beautiful children,
Jakie, Nathan, and Adam.*
—Josh Peck

࿎

*In memory of my dad, Paul Bailey Gilbert (1935–2005),
who read* Chariots of the Gods *and decided that
believing von Däniken required more
faith than believing the apostles.*
—Derek P. Gilbert

CONTENTS

ACKNOWLEDGMENTS

I have way too many people to thank and acknowledge. The reason for me stating that is not to complain, but to marvel in the blessings within my life. God has brought so many wonderful people in my life, all of whom have contributed in some way to my growth and learning; there is no way I could list them all here. That being said, I must apologize to those I will inevitably leave out, as I will try and keep this section short. First, as corny and clichéd as it might be for a Christian to do this in beginning of his acknowledgments section, I thank my Lord and Savior Jesus Christ, without whom I would be nothing. I also thank my beautiful family for providing the encouragement, support, and prayer throughout the writing process. A huge thank you goes out to my coauthor, Derek Gilbert, for his dedication, hard work, and brilliance in his writing, both in content and style. I also thank Derek and his wife, Sharon, for their ongoing friendship, mentorship, and loyalty to my family and me.

A very special thank you goes out to Dr. Michael Heiser, from whom I have learned more in the past two years than throughout the rest of my years before. Mike's work in bringing solid theology to the mainstream and fringe Church has been an incredible blessing to me and my family, and frankly, there are no words to describe what his work has done for us. Not only that, but I consider Mike a great and personal friend. I must also thank Joe Horn, my best friend in the world (apart from my wife, of course), for the countless efforts he has put forth in order to provide time for me to write, even when it meant taking on extra work for himself. I thank my publisher, mentor, and most importantly, friend, Tom Horn, for far more reasons than I could ever list in an entire book—let alone in only an acknowledgments section. Last, but certainly not least, I thank my amazing audience who has been there for me through the years providing support, comfort, prayer, and celebration when necessary. The Lord has blessed me richly with these and other phenomenal people in my life, and I am eternally grateful for them all.

—Josh Peck

This book wouldn't exist without the support and encouragement of my wonderful, beautiful, and loving wife, Sharon K. Gilbert, who convinced me that I can, in fact, write.

Special thanks to Tom Horn, CEO of Defender Publishing and Sky-WatchTV—first, for agreeing to let Josh and me take a crack at this topic, but mainly for giving us and our best friends, our wives, the opportunity to research, write, and speak about the awe-inspiring wonder of God's creation. Tom's faith in us is a real honor, and we are blessed to serve our King in this way.

I echo Josh in my praise for Dr. Michael S. Heiser, whose name you will see more than a few times in this book. Mike's research on the Divine Council, and his willingness to share it, has guided and informed our understanding of theology.

Thanks are also due to several brothers in Christ who have likewise blazed trails with their ministries: Guy Malone, our missionary to Roswell for more than a decade and the organizer of the paradigm-shaking Ancient of Days Bible UFO Conferences; Joe Jordan, cofounder and president of CE4 Research Group; and Chris White of Chris White Ministries, writer/producer of the excellent *Ancient Aliens Debunked*, a three-hour "debunkumentary" featuring Dr. Heiser. The film absolutely destroys the claims of the ancient alien/astronaut believers, and by so doing it demolishes the foundation on which the case for "official disclosure" is built.

I owe a special thanks to my coauthor, Josh Peck. It's an honor to share credit with him for this book. Josh and his wife, Christina, who, like Josh, is a coworker at SkyWatchTV, are a joy to be around and a true inspiration, a living testimony to the power of God. That may sound like an exaggeration, but it's not. Look up their testimonies on the Web sometime. Besides that, they're both brilliant.

Finally, all credit for anything I get right in this book goes to our Lord and Savior, Jesus Christ. I'm just trying to use what He's blessed me with for His glory. So, if you like this book or find it helpful in any way, don't thank me—thank Him.

—Derek P. Gilbert

FOREWORD

Dr. Thomas R. Horn

ALMOST A DECADE ago, following the release of the book *Nephilim Stargates: The Year 2012 and the Return of the Watchers,* I did a series of televised shows with J. R. Church and Gary Stearman for their *Prophecy in the News* broadcast, in which we discussed the idea of supernatural "portals, doorways, and openings." The concept is actually an ancient one—that gateways between our world and other dimensions exist or can be created through which those entities some describe as UFOs can pass. At one point, the programs with Church and Stearman (available online at You-Tube.com[1]) focused on a theory I had briefly raised in *Nephilim Stargates* involving infamous occultist Aleister Crowley, Jet Propulsion Laboratory founder Jack Parsons, and Church of Scientology founder L. Ron Hubbard. A portion of that original material reads:

> As is referenced in chapter 2, in 1918 famed occultist Aleister Crowley attempted to create a dimensional vortex that would bridge the gap between the world of the seen and the unseen.

The ritual was called the Amalantrah Working and according to Crowley became successful when a presence manifested itself through the rift. He called the being "Lam" and drew a portrait of it. The startling image, detailed almost ninety years ago, bears powerful similarity with "Alien Greys" of later pop culture.

L. Ron Hubbard and Jack Parsons attempted to do this very thing by inviting the spirit of Babylon [their magical working was called *Babalon*] through a portal during a sex ritual. Their hope was to incarnate the whore of Babylon—a demon child or Gibborim. Parsons wrote that the ritual was successful and that at one point a brownish/yellow light came through the doorway. At the same moment he said he was struck by something invisible, and a candle was knocked out of his hand.

It is interesting that following Crowley's magic portal (which produced the alien-looking LAM) and Hubbard and Parson's Babalon Working ritual, Crowley died in 1947—the same year as the Roswell crash and the same year Kenneth Arnold [a friend of Parsons] saw his flying saucers and sightings of "aliens" increased around the world. Was a portal indeed opened by these men's invitations?[2]

J. R. Church was very interested in the idea that men heavily involved in the occult with a strange UFO-alien twist and covertly connected with segments of this government's aerospace endeavors might actually have opened a portal allowing the increase into our world of powerful demonic influences.

Several years after *Nephilim Stargates* was published and the *Prophecy in the News* shows aired, a book by Nick Redfern titled *Final Events* was released that repeated the basic outline of my work, but this time around reportedly had the backing of a secret government group commissioned to get to the bottom of the UFO phenomenon. The group ultimately concluded that the mysterious manifestations are demonic and directly connected to Parsons and company and their Babalon Workings. According to Redfern, they are called the "Collins Elite."

Initially skeptical of the *Final Events* outline and sensing that somebody somewhere had simply repeated to Redfern what I had said and extrapolated it into a full-blown fabrication, I decided to talk to him on the phone and then conduct a follow-up Q & A over email, which is published in the bestselling book *Exo-Vaticana* and essentially verifies Redfern's story.

Meanwhile, my sources in the United States—which extend from U.S. military intelligence to national defense employees with both Department of Defense, Pentagon, and intel top-secret security clearances—came back empty-handed. This included our friend Col. Steve Bauer, who served longer as a U.S. government military aide than anyone in the history of the White House under five American presidents—Nixon, Ford, Carter, Reagan, and Bush. Bauer had never heard of the "Collins Elite" and couldn't locate a single intelligence resource that otherwise would substantiate Redfern's claims. But I knew, having said that, that this didn't mean the story as detailed in *Final Events* was untrue. Counterintelligence, Majestic 12-level compartmentalization, and official denial is a well-established part of the government's past and present protocols when handling questions concerning UFOs and so-called alien abduction activity—a fact that every significant investigator into this phenomenon has run into when trying to separate fact from fiction. So I moved on and checked with another of my international contacts—former director of Britain's Military of Defense's department for UFO research, Nick Pope—and was surprised when he cautioned against disbelief and even confirmed the existence of a Collins Elite-like group among Britain's aristocracy. Following this, I reached out to Gregory Richford, a Ball Aerospace contact who works with advanced systems and technologies for Space Control & Special Missions. He, too, cautioned against doubting the Collins reality and sent me a four-page document outlining their main points of operation. Yet it was not until now, with the release of *The Day the Earth Stands Still,* that a work has satisfied an authoritative answer for my deepest queries—the power operating behind unusual aerial phenomena and connected to a coming official-disclosure moment is synonymous with those illegal spirits the New Testament calls "demons." Authors Derek P. Gilbert and Josh Peck have bravely gone where no volume has gone before in authoring a persuasive stream of history—past, present, and future.

INTRODUCTION

MORE AMERICANS BELIEVE in ETs than in God.

I wish I were exaggerating. Okay—maybe I am a little, so let me unwrap that a bit to explain what I mean.

Recent surveys show that American adults are more likely to believe that extraterrestrials are visiting Earth than to believe in God as He's revealed Himself to us in the Bible.

Again, I wish I were exaggerating, but I'm not.

A 2012 study commissioned by the National Geographic Channel found that 36 percent of Americans believe that UFOs exist. The same percentage said they believed that aliens have visited Earth. Seventy-seven percent said there is evidence that Earth has been visited, regardless of whether they'd made up their minds on the question one way or the other.[3]

To compare, the Barna Group found in 2017 that while 73 percent of American adults call themselves "Christian,"[4] only 10 percent have a biblical worldview.[5]

That may seem surprisingly low to you, but it was a slight improvement over their 2009 survey. The prophet Hosea would feel at home on the streets of America today. God's people are truly being destroyed for lack of knowledge.

Some Christians believe we're wasting time on UFOs that's better spent preaching the gospel. We've been criticized by some for helping to spread the ET meme. With all due respect, it's time to wake up and smell the ozone. That ship has sailed.

It's simple math: A third of America's adult population—about eighty-one million people—believe ET has been phoning home from a domestic area code, and only 10 percent of us—about twenty-four million—believe in God as He is described in His book. In other words, doctrinally sound, Bible-believing Christians are outnumbered in America by ET believers three to one.

Christians should be disturbed by this. Something has changed in our culture since the end of World War II. Hollywood and the media have pushed the idea that visitors from the stars make Earth a regular vacation spot. The messaging has been effective. Popular science fiction has become, as Dr. Michael S. Heiser terms it, "televangelism for the ET religion."

There is another aspect to the phenomenon that we'll discuss in this book. Every four years, ETI (ExtraTerrestrial Intelligence) disclosure activists—yes, that is a thing—get excited that an outgoing or incoming American presidential administration might finally open the books on the government's secret UFO investigations. The idea that "official disclosure" of the existence of extraterrestrial intelligence would happen in 2016 was ignited by the role of John Podesta as chair of Hillary Clinton's campaign. Podesta, an adviser in the Clinton and Obama administrations, is known to be a believer in the existence of ETIs, and emails from Podesta's Gmail account released by WikiLeaks added fuel to the fire. The UFO research community was stunned to learn that a former NASA astronaut reached out to Podesta more than once to arrange a meeting with President Obama about "nonviolent ETI from the contiguous universe."[6]

That didn't happen, but it raises an important question: What if Fox News breaks into its programming one day next week to announce that an extraterrestrial craft has just landed on the White House lawn? Setting aside the military questions (like, how it got past our air defenses), Christians need to be prepared to respond to such a report.

Why? Because the media beats the UFO meme like a two-year-old with a new toy drum. The public is being primed to accept the arrival of ETs, and the propaganda pushed by Hollywood and the media includes the idea that we'd need to rewrite the Bible as soon as the saucer lands. We'd be told that the crazy-haired guy on cable was right all along[7]—our distant ancestors weren't visited by God and His angels, you see; they were just too primitive to see advanced ETIs and their technology for what they were.

The truth is just the opposite: Westerners, indoctrinated by the cult of scientism, don't recognize divine imagery from the ancient world for what *it* is. We see a UFO where Mesopotamians of 2,600 years ago would instantly recognize a royal throne and its divine guardians.

Hardly a day goes by without a news site somewhere serving up click-bait of a fuzzy UFO video or an out-of-place "artifact on Mars." Nothing is ever proved, but it keeps the flickering flame of hope aglow. This Chinese water-torture approach to ETI disclosure is frustrating for UFO believers, but it's effective. See the statistics above—one in three Americans believe, and with far less evidence than we have—in the life, death, and resurrection of Jesus.

Even the Vatican is hedging its bets to stay ahead of the disclosure meme. In 2014, Pope Francis indicated his willingness to baptize an ET if one landed in St. Peter's Square and expressed that wish.[8]

Please understand that we're not saying we believe evidence of alien contact exists. We do not. As Christians trying to emulate the example of the people of Berea, who listened to Paul and then carefully compared his words against Scripture, we should be discerning in all things with the Word of God as the final authority. And His Word gives us a theological framework to accept a disclosure event without deleting a single jot or tittle—even if, as we believe, such a "disclosure" will be a lie.

You see, your status on this planet and in the universe is not affected by a green-skinned entity in a silver jumpsuit suddenly appearing on the White House lawn—or an angel of light manifesting on the Temple Mount, for that matter.

You are created in the image of God. In this book, we'll explain what that really means and why it matters in this context.

When we compare God's silence on the possibility of extraterrestrial life to the volumes written by the prophets and apostles about powerful, dangerous entities who already share the planet with us, it's clear that Christians should pay less attention to theoretical ETIs and pay more attention to the all-too-real principalities, powers, thrones, and dominions that Paul warned us about—especially since the latter are working very hard to persuade us that they're the former.

To that end, in this book we'll follow a chain of evidence and suggest, for the first time anywhere to the best of our knowledge, that the modern, "ancient alien" gospel has its roots in a very old supernatural source—and we'll name the entities involved. This enemy has tried to claim the Earth and all that lives on it literally for thousands of years.

The enemy is not extraterrestrial, although it's part of their deception to convince the world, like Baudelaire's generous gambler, that they don't exist—at least not in the way they're described in the Bible.

Demonic? Oh, no. It's much darker than that.

The modern preachers of their false gospel probably don't recognize it for what it is. That's by design. To these otherworldly entities, humans are at best useful idiots. At worst—well, when they tell contactees that their only desire is to serve man, just remember: That might be the title of their cookbook.

chapter one

THE WORLD IS PRIMED
FOR ET DISCLOSURE

THE WORLD IS ready to welcome ET. This is especially true in America, which has clearly moved into a post-Christian era. Some argue it's already gone beyond that into openly anti-Christian territory, which isn't hard to believe if you pay attention to the news. So, in a nation that has rejected the concepts of sin and salvation as obsolete, a belief system that offers salvation without sin, or the stress and effort of defending it, is perfect. The ET gospel sells because guilt feels bad, thinking is hard, and the only sin in a postmodern world is telling someone else that his or her worldview is flawed.

Doctrine in this ET religion is built on scraps of evidence, some of it contradictory, and since there is no central office to enforce orthodoxy, believers are free to read into their "gods" just about anything they want.

Christians, on the other hand, believe in a Deity who told His followers to love God with all their hearts, souls, and *minds*.

5

Surprising Statistics of ET Believers and Christians

We need to unpack some of the data we shared in the introduction. To repeat, about a third of American adults believe it's "somewhat" or "very" likely that we've been visited by an ETI,[9] while only 10 percent of us have a biblical worldview.

This would be just another topic for talk-show conversation if it wasn't for one critical fact: The UFO phenomenon isn't scientific, it's spiritual. What's truly distressing, though, is that most of the people who *think* they have a biblical worldview really don't. According to Barna's 2017 survey, "only 17 percent of Christians who consider their faith important and attend church regularly actually have a biblical worldview."[10]

In other words, 83 percent of regular churchgoers don't believe all the key tenets of the Christian faith. To them, Christianity is a sort of spiritual buffet where you can load up on the things you like and ignore the things you don't.

It's important that we define our terms, especially when we're dealing with what people believe about eternity. There are huge gaps, spiritual sinkholes, between what people say and what they actually believe and do. For example, when people were asked if they had a "biblical worldview," 46 percent of Americans said "yes."[11]

So what *is* a biblical worldview? According to Barna:

A "biblical worldview" was defined as believing that absolute moral truth exists; the Bible is totally accurate in all of the principles it teaches; Satan is considered to be a real being or force, not merely symbolic; a person cannot earn their way into Heaven by trying to be good or do good works; Jesus Christ lived a sinless life on earth; and God is the all-knowing, all-powerful creator of the world who still rules the universe today. In the research, anyone who held all of those beliefs was said to have a biblical worldview.[12]

In other words, basic Christian doctrine. Christianity 101. But digging deeper into Barna's findings over the last decade or so is eye-opening for serious Christians. For example:

- 61 percent agree with ideas rooted in New Spirituality [i.e., New Age teachings].
- 54 percent resonate with postmodernist views.
- 36 percent accept ideas associated with Marxism.
- 29 percent believe ideas based on secularism.[13]

Among the concepts drawn from New Spirituality that have entered the Church, Barna found that about a third of American Christians strongly agree that "if you do good, you will receive good; if you do bad, you will receive bad." More than a quarter (28 percent) strongly agree with the statement that "all people pray to the same god or spirit, no matter what name they use for that spiritual being."[14]

Now, we're not into the Sacred Name nonsense (the idea that if you don't call God by His correct name, you're praying to a pagan deity), but the percentage of practicing Christians who agree with that statement should be zero.

The influence of postmodernism is reflected in the finding that 23 percent of America's practicing Christians strongly agree that "what is morally right or wrong depends on what an individual believes."[15]

Really? Even for Stalin, Pol Pot, and Hitler?

Worse, Millennials and Generation X-ers are up to eight times more likely to accept these competing worldviews than their elders. Men, who should be the spiritual heads of their households, are twice as likely to be open to these views as women.[16]

Consider this: Donald J. Trump was elected president at least in part because of his platform to address border security and unrestricted immigration, especially from Islamic nations. Conservative Christians are aware of the potential conflict that could erupt from importing millions of Muslims into a predominantly (if only in name) Christian nation.[17]

As of this writing, Muslims make up slightly more than 1 percent of the American population. Imagine the outcry if one of every three people you saw on the street believed a religion that was completely alien to the gospel of Jesus Christ!

Oh, wait—they already do.

But because the face of this faith is an ETI, which can be almost anything believers want it to be, rather than Ayatollah Khameini or Abu Bakr al-Baghdadi, the church ignores it. Most pastors and Bible teachers don't even acknowledge it. It's weird. It's "woo." It's harmless.

Except that it isn't.

The Religion of UFO Phenomena

If you doubt that the UFO phenomenon is a religion, check out one of the major UFO festivals sometime. People travel great distances to Roswell, New Mexico; McMinnville, Oregon; Kecksburg, Pennsylvania; and other places hosting festivals and conferences to celebrate the possibility of ETI contact. You'll generally find a heavy New Age presence at these gatherings. Besides the tarot card readings and healing crystals, a strong desire to meet our "space brothers" is evident among many of the pilgrims who've made the journey.

In short, you encounter people searching for answers to the big questions that have haunted humanity since very early in our history: Where do we come from, why are we here, and where do we go when we die?

What you won't find at these festivals—at least, not to our knowledge—are seminars on astrophysics, aerospace engineering, or advanced mathematics. If the point of these conferences is to explore whether we've been contacted, what the ETIs want, and ways to visit Zeta Reticuli, shouldn't the *how* of all this be part of the discussion? Wouldn't NASA or some of the big defense contractors have booths to recruit promising young talent?

Instead, it seems that ETs' presence on Earth is a given, the potential threat of a hostile ETI is downplayed (in spite of the abduction accounts of Betty and Barney Hill, Travis Walton, and others), and the main question on everyone's mind is when the United States government will stop playing coy and show the world what's stashed at Area 51 and Wright-Patterson Air Force Base. Because then we'll finally *know*.

Know what, exactly?

To listen to the evangelists of the ancient alien gospel, who have been preaching regularly on American cable television networks for more than a decade, we'll finally know where we came from, why we're here, and where we go when we die.

In other words, the answers we Christians hold in our hands every time we pick up a Bible. Why aren't UFO seekers looking there?

∽

We shouldn't be surprised that belief in ETs has been growing in America over the last seventy years. For at least twice that long, most of our leading thinkers in the secular realm have embraced modernist and postmodernist thought. We'll deal with the implications of these philosophies in an upcoming chapter, but in a nutshell: Modernists believe that science is the only reliable tool for finding truth, while postmodernists, on the other hand, believe truth is unknowable.

You can see why neither of those philosophies is friendly to a Christian worldview. We believe in an invisible God who spoke the universe into being. As a supernatural being, He defies observation and measurement through natural means. And a God who defines objective truth—as in, "I am *the* truth"—is anathema to postmodernists.

We Americans have been soaking in postmodern philosophy since about the 1930s. Thanks to the influence of this self-refuting philosophy on our education system, most of us are unprepared to demand actual evidence for extraordinary claims like, "We're being visited by ETIs."[18] Instead, we're content to ignore a belief system that's lured in a third of our friends and family members, which is something we'd never do if the face of ET featured horns and a goatee.

Thanks to postmodernism, which has taught too many of us that our beliefs are wrong if they hurt someone else's feelings, we let the claims of UFO believers slide by without critical examination. After all, we've been conditioned to believe truth is relative, filtered through personal experience and shaped by our culture. So your humble authors, as Anglo-Saxon American males, have a different set of "truths" than, say, a woman from Tibet.

Eh…hold it. Not so fast. Christian apologist Ravi Zacharias tells the story of a college professor who argued that, unlike in the West, salvation in India is not an either-or thing. Either-or logic is Western, you see. In India, this scholar insisted, salvation is not *either* Christ *or* nothing else, it's both-and—*both* in Christ *and* other ways.

Zacharias ended the debate with a simple question: "Are you saying that when I'm in India, I must use either the 'both-and logic'—or nothing else?"

The professor thought for a moment. "The either-or does seem to emerge, doesn't it."

Zacharias replied, "Yes, even in India we look both ways before we cross the street because it is either me or the bus, not both of us!"[19]

A physicist friend recently encountered a more extreme example of postmodernist thought. While teaching a college physics class, an African-American student responded to Newton's Law of Universal Gravitation by saying it didn't apply to him because it was a *white* man's law. Once our friend, who doesn't suffer fools gladly, realized the young man wasn't kidding, he invited the budding scientist to join him on the roof of the four-story building to put his theory to the test. By jumping.

For his remark, our friend was compelled to endure several sessions of sensitivity training. But you get the point—we can't be content to dismiss the UFO phenomenon by saying, "Jesus works for me, but all others have to find their own path to God."

Propositional truth—claims that can be tested on the strength of logic and evidence—exists. Christianity is based on propositional truth. Example: Jesus is God.[20] Since Jesus said no one comes to the Father except through Him, then there are no other paths to God. This being true, following the ET highway to its final destination can have eternal consequences.

And if a third of America believes ET is out there, and three-quarters of us believe there's evidence of ETI contact, then the odds are at least one person in your church buys into the ETI gospel.

Since the mid-1980s, conferences have become an integral part of the UFO phenomenon. Every year, major cons bring thousands of truth-seekers from across the United States and the world to hear experts on the phenomenon discuss the reasons we're being visited, accounts of contactees and abductees, and the evidence thereof.

Major events on the annual calendar include the Roswell UFO Festival, of course. The 1947 crash of something in the desert northwest of the town caused a stir at the time, but the incident was more or less forgotten until about thirty years later. At least some of the residents of the city shared their belief with the authors at the 2017 festival that the current interest in the Roswell UFO crash was the result of city leaders in the '70s looking for a way to save a town that was dying a slow death. The 1967 closure of Walker Air Force Base, located just three miles south of the central business district, had an enormous impact on the local economy. Seven thousand of the city's thirty-nine thousand people moved away and about four thousand homes flooded the local real estate market.[21] One can understand the desperation of local business owners to find something to draw people to a dusty desert town located about two hundred miles south of Albuquerque.

Other major conferences are held in Scottsdale, Arizona; McMinnville, Oregon; Eureka Springs, Arkansas; Joshua Tree, California; and other places with gatherings whose organizers may take offense at being left off this list. The point is not to catalog the events, but to illustrate that conferences bringing together hundreds or thousands of people to discuss the hows and whys of ET visitation are happening all over the country.

They're promoted by nationally syndicated radio and television programs and facilitated by the ease of Internet communication.

The question is why? What motivates people to travel across the country to sit through lectures when they could just as easily find the information in books or on YouTube? We suspect it's for the same reasons people travel to Bible prophecy conferences, something we can speak to from personal experience: The journey is worthwhile because it's about something transcendent. The expense and inconvenience of getting to an event is a small price for the joy that comes from being around others who understand, who *get it*. The sense of belonging to a community is something UFO believers don't experience at church (and likewise for far too many believers in Bible prophecy), work, or home. And deep down, they feel a nagging sense of something missing—something they might just find at the next UFO conference.

A former trauma doctor who's become the father of the official disclosure movement, Steven Greer, isn't shy about connecting ETIs to the world's spiritual health:

> It is hard to imagine why someone with a wife and four kids leaves a half-million-dollar-a-year job until you understand that, in Greer's view, extraterrestrials are nothing less than an answer to a spiritual crisis. Why save one life in an emergency room when you can save an entire planet?...
>
> On his 18th birthday, he climbed up onto a fire tower to meditate. Again, he saw a disc materialize. Feeling a tap on the shoulder, he turned to behold a small creature with "beautiful eyes." Greer felt himself flying as the creature beamed him onto a spaceship. Time stood still. He felt connected to everyone and everything.
>
> After that experience, he continued to "connect with a pure, universal love." Every night he meditated. And every night the aliens came.[22]

Pure, universal love. For many believers, this is the promise of the UFO phenomenon—transcendence. Something bigger and more beautiful than the grubby, noisy world they inhabit. And Dr. Steven Greer is the voice crying out in the wilderness to make straight the way of ET.

This is the reason presentation topics at UFO conferences are rarely, if ever, about logistics—how exactly the ETIs solved the huge problems of energy consumption, radiation exposure, food storage, and simple mechanical reliability needed to cross the vast emptiness of space. With few exceptions, regular speakers at these events focus on the spiritual implications of ET visits than on the science of how they got here.

This is not by accident.

Even though a handful of well-known cases suggest a darker purpose to their visits, the attitude towards our alleged space brothers is generally positive. With a few notable exceptions, experts in the field generally avoid lingering too long on the idea that something dark and deceptive might be at the heart of the UFO phenomenon. We suggest that this, too, is not an accident.

chapter two

THE MEDIA AND HOLLYWOOD

THE MEDIA HAS played a key role in promoting this new faith. Without the reach of the Internet, cable television, and Hollywood, it's doubtful that the gospel of ET would have spread as far and as fast as it has.

They probably wouldn't characterize themselves this way, but the regulars on cable TV alien hunter shows are essentially, as Dr. Michael Heiser calls them, televangelists for the ET religion. *Ancient Aliens* is, incredibly, now in its twelfth season on the History Channel.

The *History* Channel! Do you remember when the History Channel still broadcast programs about *history?* Sadly, actual history is as popular on cable as it was in high school. So programmers turned to so-called reality shows, rehashing old cases about UFOs and alien contact, and they found gold in them thar thrills.

We humans love a mystery, and other cable networks have followed the History Channel's lead over the last decade with varying degrees of success. Programs about the paranormal and unexplained are featured on National Geographic, SyFy, Animal Planet, and the Travel Channel.

Mystery sells. And nothing is more mysterious than the unexplained lights in the sky and persistent stories of those who claim to have been aboard the ships.

Ancient Aliens and Clones

The most popular and influential program on cable catering to the hunger for the ET gospel is undoubtedly *Ancient Aliens*. It was launched by the History Channel in 2010 as a successor to *UFO Hunters*, which aired in 2008 and 2009. A number of other programs featuring the UFO pheno- menon have come and gone since the turn of the century—*UFO Chasers*, *UFOs Declassified*, *UFO Files*, *Hangar 1*, and *Unsealed: Alien Files* to name a few—but *Ancient Aliens* is plugging along in 2017, a top-ten cable show with about 1.2 million adult viewers in its Friday-night time slot.[23] By the time you read this, 130 episodes of *Ancient Aliens* will have delivered the subtle message that the Bible's account of where humanity came from was incomplete.

In retrospect, the shift from UFOs to "ancient aliens" was a brilli- ant programming decision. There are only so many ways to make jittery mobile phone videos of blurry lights in the night sky look interesting. Famous cases like Roswell, Kecksburg, and the Phoenix Lights have been analyzed as often as the Kennedy assassination. Without new information on old events, which isn't likely, or spectacular new cases to investigate, the UFO phenomenon runs out of material pretty quickly—at least as far as what can be turned into entertaining television.

By tying the UFO phenomenon to unsolved mysteries of the past, the producers of *Ancient Aliens* opened a gold mine of material. Everything from the pyramids to cults and mystery religions were suddenly fair game. Borrowing heavily from the work of Erich von Däniken and Zecharia Sitchin, *Ancient Aliens* has linked ETIs to ancient Sumer, the cyclopean architecture of the Americas, and Freemasonry.

And, of course, the Bible. This, too, is no accident. Researcher and author Jason Colavito observed that "*Ancient Aliens* stopped being about space aliens years ago and is now a sort of propaganda arm for New Age religion, which explains why it is so much more interested in the mystery of consciousness than actual evidence for the existence of space aliens.... Over the years *Ancient Aliens* has become *Theosophy: The Series.*"[24]

Exactly right.

The beauty of this approach is that the producers of *Ancient Aliens* don't have to prove a thing. A medieval painting, an inscription from the ancient Near East, or an odd-looking prehistoric petroglyph is all they need to build another episode. Host Giorgio Tsoukalos begins so many statements with, "Could it be…" or, "Is it possible…" that the show has become a parody of itself.

A classic example is the fascination ancient astronaut believers have with Ezekiel's wheel:

> As I looked, behold, a stormy wind came out of the north, and a great cloud, with brightness around it, and fire flashing forth continually, and in the midst of the fire, as it were gleaming metal….
>
> Now as I looked at the living creatures, I saw a wheel on the earth beside the living creatures, one for each of the four of them. As for the appearance of the wheels and their construction: their appearance was like the gleaming of beryl. And the four had the same likeness, their appearance and construction being as it were a wheel within a wheel. When they went, they went in any of their four directions without turning as they went. And their rims were tall and awesome, and the rims of all four were full of eyes all around. And when the living creatures went, the wheels went beside them; and when the living creatures rose from the earth, the wheels rose. Wherever the spirit wanted to go, they went, and the wheels rose along with them, for the spirit of the living creatures was in the wheels. When those went, these went; and when those stood, these stood; and when those rose from the earth, the wheels rose along with them, for the spirit of the living creatures was in the wheels. (Ezekiel 1:4, 15–21, ESV)

The analysis by Tsoukalos? "It reads much more like an encounter with some type of extraterrestrial craft that was misinterpreted as some type of a divine event."[25]

Well, yeah, if you're not a Mesopotamian living 2,600 years ago. That type of imagery was common back then. Believe it or not, the subjects of Nebuchadnezzar would have known exactly what they were seeing—a royal throne and its divine guardians.

The UFO interpretation is modern, but it isn't new. *The Spaceships of Ezekiel*, a 1974 book by Josef P. Blumrich, capitalized on the growing popularity of von Däniken's *Chariots of the Gods*, with the added marketing appeal that Blumrich wrote the book while he was "chief of NASA's systems layout branch of the program development office at the Marshall Space Flight Center."

Except that he wasn't:

One of the reasons so many people have (and still do) think Blumrich's book is worth referencing is that he claimed (and so his followers are fond of repeating) that he was a NASA engineer. He wasn't. As Jason Colavito demonstrated a long time ago, documentation exists from the U.S. State Department that shows the State Department could find no evidence that Blumrich was affiliated with NASA. Frankly, it wouldn't matter if Blumrich was an engineer. His ideas are based on desperate and uninformed misreadings of the biblical text anyway. We know what Ezekiel saw because his descriptions mirror ancient Babylonian iconography that we can look at today because of archaeologists. The imagery is no mystery, nor is its meaning.

So, once again, the uncritical thinkers in the ancient astronaut orbit (and I do mean orbit) were duped by a "researcher" that lied to them. You have to wonder how many times this has to happen before some of these folks wake up. The ancient astronaut theory is primarily supported by industrious but duplicitous researchers offering fraudulent research to an emotionally and psychologically primed audience. It's actually pretty sad.[26]

So Blumrich was a fake and Tsoukalos got things backwards. We think Ezekiel saw a UFO because our twenty-first century worldview misinterprets divine imagery from the sixth century B.C. Sadly, people who say they take the Bible seriously aren't any better prepared to understand what the prophet saw than Giorgio Tsoukalos. Those who've studied Ezekiel usually haven't read up on Mesopotamian religious imagery. Evangelists of the ET religion disregard what the ancient Mesopotamians believed because—well, because aliens.

That's behind the continued popularity of the work of the late Zecharia Sitchin. In a nutshell, Sitchin, who passed away in 2010, claimed that Mesopotamian iconography showed the existence of a forgotten planet called Nibiru beyond Neptune. This planet, Sitchin claimed, follows a highly elliptical orbit into the inner solar system about every 3,600 years with catastrophic consequences. Sitchin also equated the Anunnaki, the gods of Sumer, with the biblical Nephilim, and claimed that they arrived on Earth some 450,000 years ago to mine gold in Africa.

Sitchin's theories are behind much of the Planet X angst that clogs up the Internet. Biblical scholar Dr. Michael S. Heiser, who reads Sumerian, has thoroughly debunked Sitchin's theories, even going so far as to post his personal tax returns to show that he wasn't trying to profit by publicly challenging Sitchin.[27] That hasn't stopped Sitchinites from continuing to spread the idea that the gods of the ancient world were actually astronauts from outside the solar system looking for wealth, riches, or just some R & R on Sol III.

All manner of ancient mysteries are explained away with, "Well, we don't know—so aliens." For example, one of the more convincing stories we're told about our ancestors is that they couldn't possibly have moved the stones used to build the pyramids, the temple at Baalbek, or Machu Picchu because our modern cranes can't lift that kind of weight today.

What we're *not* told is that between 1768 and 1770, the Russians trans-ported the heaviest stone ever moved by humans, the 1,500-ton Thunder Stone, nearly four miles overland to the center of St. Petersburg without animal or machine power.

Think about that. While the American colonies slowly marched toward their war for independence, four hundred Russians with rope, timber, and a bunch of six-inch-diameter bronze spheres moved a block of granite that weighed as much as sixty-five fully loaded tractor-trailers across six kilometers of dry land in nine months. So just because we don't know exactly how people moved big blocks of stone four thousand years ago, it doesn't follow that it must have been aliens.

Yet as factually void as the show is, people still watch *Ancient Aliens.* And the lack of response from the church to the ancient alien meme isn't helping. Ignoring the UFO phenomenon hasn't made it go away. To repeat: A third of Americans believe we're being visited by ET. Only 10 percent believe in God as He's described in the Bible.

Why do we keep coming back to those numbers? Because we're in the middle of an information war, and pop culture is on the side of the aliens.

Popularity of Science Fiction Films and Television

Science fiction is popular entertainment. Five of the twenty highest-gros-sing movies of all time (adjusted for inflation) are from the *Star Wars* series (two of which were the top-grossing films of 2015 and 2016), and *E.T.: The Extraterrestrial* is number four.[28] Other films from the last ten years like *Star Trek: Beyond; X-Men: Apocalypse; Transformers: Age of Extinc-tion; Guardians of the Galaxy; Star Trek Into Darkness; Thor: The Dark World; MIB 3; Transformers: Dark of the Moon; Thor; Avatar; Transformers: Revenge of the Fallen; Star Trek;* and *Indiana Jones and the Kingdom of the Crystal Skull* were all among the top twenty films for their year of release, and all incorporated alien contact in one way or another.

In the early years of sci-fi cinema, *The Day the Earth Stood Still* (which obviously influenced the title of the book you're reading now) featured

Gort, a robot with lasers in his eyes, and an iconic flying saucer that set the table for modern UFO iconography.

On television, of course, we've been entertained over the last half a century by *Star Trek* and its spinoffs; *Doctor Who; The X-Files; Babylon 5; Stargate SG-1* and its spinoffs (which featured a strong "the old gods were ancient aliens" theme); and anthology series that often featured ETIs like *The Twilight Zone* and *The Outer Limits*.

The ETs weren't all friendly, but the theme of alien contact has been a Hollywood staple for more than sixty years. Thanks to Hollywood, we know what aliens are supposed to look like, the type of craft they fly, and the role of government in covering it all up. It's been repeated and rehashed so often that the tropes have taken on lives of their own.

No wonder so many of us take the existence of extraterrestrial intelligence as a given. We've been conditioned to accept it as reality for a very long time.

chapter three

THE RISE OF MYSTICAL SCIENTISM

HOW DID WE get here? How has such a thriving cottage industry developed from so little physical evidence? It says more about America's philosophical and religious state than it does about the number of times strange
lights in the sky have been seen by credible witnesses.

A Fresh Look at the Tower of Babel

Humans have wondered about the stars since forever. That's understanda-
ble; they're beautiful and mysterious, as out of reach as mountain peaks.
And perhaps for the same reasons, the earliest speculation about the stars
revolved around gods, not extraterrestrials.

As with mountains, humans have associated stars with deities since
the beginning of human history. Three of the most important gods in the
ancient Near East, from Sumer to Israel and its neighbors, were the sun,
moon, and the planet Venus. To the Sumerians they were the deities Utu,
Nanna, and the goddess Inanna; later, in Babylon, they were Shamash,

Sîn, and Ishtar. The Amorites worshiped Sapash, Yarikh, and Astarte (who was also the god Attar when Venus was the morning star—and here you thought gender fluidity was new).

God not only recognized that the nations worshiped these small-g gods, He allotted the nations to them as their inheritance—punishment for the Tower of Babel incident.

> When the Most High agave to the nations their inheritance, when he divided mankind, he fixed the borders of the peoples according to the number of the sons of God.[29]

> And beware lest you raise your eyes to heaven, and when you see the sun and the moon and the stars, all the host of heaven, you be drawn away and bow down to them and serve them, things that the LORD your God has allotted to all the peoples under the whole heaven.[30]

In other words, God placed the nations of the world under small-g "gods" represented by the sun, moon, and stars, but He reserved Israel for Himself. The descendants of Abraham, Isaac, and Jacob were to remain faithful to YHWH alone, and through Israel He would bring forth a Savior.

But the gods YHWH allotted to the nations went rogue. That earned them a death sentence.

> God has taken his place in the divine council;
> In the midst of the gods he holds judgment:
> "How long will you judge unjustly
> and show partiality to the wicked? *Selah*...
> I said, "You are gods,
> sons of the Most High, all of you;
> nevertheless, like men you shall die,
> and fall like any prince."[31]

To be absolutely clear: Those small-g gods are not to be confused with the capital-G God, YHWH, Creator of all things including those "sons of the Most High." We know the consensus view among Christians is to treat the gods of Psalm 82 as humans, usually described as corrupt Israelite kings or judges. With all due respect to the scholars who hold that view, they're wrong. The most obvious error in their view is that verse 7—"nevertheless, like men you shall die"—makes no sense if God is addressing a human audience.

No. When the Bible says "gods" it means gods.

There are other, more technical reasons to view the Divine Council as a heavenly royal court. We direct you to Dr. Michael S. Heiser's excellent website, www.TheDivineCouncil.com, for accessible, scholarly, biblical support for this view.

Seriously, go there and read. Understanding the divine council view is critical to really grasping what's going on with the UFO phenomenon. (And why the world is still such a mess, for that matter.) There are supernatural beings who have exercised the free will they were created with to rebel against their Creator. As Christians, this should be our default view. After all, Paul spelled it out:

> For we do not wrestle against flesh and blood, but against the rulers, against the authorities, against the cosmic powers over this present darkness, against the spiritual forces of evil in the heavenly places.[32]

Rulers, authorities, cosmic powers, spiritual forces of evil. Those aren't concepts, ideas, or random acts of misfortune. Paul was warning us about supernatural evil intelligences who want to destroy us. And guess what? At least some of them are "in the heavenly places."

We'll refer to that verse many times in this book. Ephesians 6:12 is key. As our friend Pastor Carl Gallups likes to say, spiritual warfare is a lot more than finding the willpower to pass up a second bowl of ice cream.

How the Fallen Have Guided Humanity

Why this detour though the Bible? Two reasons. First, to document that humanity has looked to the stars as gods for at least the last five thousand years, as far as Babel and probably beyond. And second, to set the stage for what we believe official disclosure is really about—the return of the old gods.

You see, the Enemy has been playing a very long game. Once upon a time, Western civilization—Christendom, if you will—generally held a biblical worldview. While the influence of the spirit realm on our lives wasn't perfectly understood, at least it was acknowledged. And while the Church of Rome can be fairly criticized for keeping the Bible out of the hands of laypeople for nearly a thousand years, at least the learned scholars and theologians of the Church made a fair effort to interpret their world through a biblical filter.

Admittedly, this is speculation, but it seems consistent with history: It appears that the principalities and powers have nudged and prodded humanity through the Enlightenment, then Modernism, and into Postmodernism to move modern man from a supernatural worldview to one that could believe in an external creator—ancient aliens—while denying the existence of a *supernatural* Creator.

In other words, to accept our ET creator/ancestors we first had to reject the biblical God. In 1973, British science fiction author Arthur C. Clarke wrote, "Any sufficiently advanced technology is indistinguishable from magic." By substituting advanced science for the supernatural, ancient alien evangelists are spreading a sci-fi religion for the twenty-first century. It offers mystery, transcendence, and answers to those nagging Big Questions. And best of all, ETI believers don't need to change the way they think or act—except maybe to promise to live peacefully with our neighbors in the contiguous universe.

Greek Philosophers

This view found fertile intellectual soil in areas influenced by Greek philosophy. It's beyond the scope of this book to examine why that's so, but the evidence is compelling that the rise and spread of Greek thought has run parallel with the belief in life among the stars.

A pause here for a big "thank you" to author and artist Jeffrey W. Mardis. His excellent book *What Dwells Beyond: The Bible Believer's Handbook to Understanding Life in the Universe*[33] was very helpful in guiding our thoughts as we planned this project. Rather than rewrite his work, however, we'll summarize here the emergence of cosmic pluralism, the concept that intelligent life exists elsewhere in the universe, and then suggest you get a copy of *What Dwells Beyond* for your personal reference library.

The idea that there are more inhabited worlds in the universe than just our own isn't new. It dates to six centuries before the birth of Jesus, about the time Nebuchadnezzar led the army of Babylon across the ancient Near East to conquer, among other nations, the kingdom of Judah. A Greek philosopher, mathematician, and engineer named Thales of Miletus (c. 620 B.C.—c. 546 B.C.) is credited with being the father of the scientific method. According to later philosophers, Thales was the first to reject religious cosmology in favor of a naturalistic approach to understanding the world. Among his theories was the belief that the stars in the night sky were other planets, some of which were inhabited.

The influence of Thales is felt even today. While there are benefits to searching for the natural causes of, say, earthquakes rather than attributing them to the temper of Zeus, denying the influence of the supernatural altogether has blinded science in many fields of inquiry. For example, researchers into the effects of prayer tend to focus on the physiological benefits. It reduces stress and makes you "nicer."[34]

Well and good, but since prayer is a direct hotline to the Creator of all things, could there be more behind the benefits of prayer than just sitting quietly? Is it possible that people who pray are nicer and more relaxed because they've tapped into what the apostle Paul called "the peace of God, which surpasses all understanding"?[35]

To a scientist with a naturalist bias, the answer is, "Of course not." Since God can't be observed and quantified, He must not exist. And so extra "niceness" is a result of what *can* be observed—the physical act of talking to (in their minds, an imaginary) God.

The intellectual descendants of Thales included influential thinkers such as Pythagoras, who in turn influenced Plato, as well as Democritus and Leucippus, who developed the theory that everything is composed of atoms. Epicurus, building on the teaching of Democritus, proposed that atoms moved under their own power, and that they, through random chance, clumped together to form, well, everything—matter, consciousness, and even the gods themselves, whom Epicurus believed were neutral parties who didn't interfere in the lives of humans.

It's clear that Epicurus and his followers have had quite an influence on modern thought.

Interestingly, about three hundred years after the death of Epicurus, Paul encountered some Epicureans (and their philosophical rivals, the Stoics) on Mars Hill in Athens. Epicurus, cited by the early Christian author Lactantius, is credited with posing what's called the Problem of Evil:

> "God," he says, "either wants to eliminate bad things and cannot, or can but does not want to, or neither wishes to nor can, or both wants to and can. If he wants to and cannot, then he is weak— and this does not apply to God. If he can but does not want to, then he is spiteful—which is equally foreign to God's nature. If he neither wants to nor can, he is both weak and spiteful, and so not a god. If he wants to and can, which is the only thing fitting for a god, where then do bad things come from? Or why does he not eliminate them?"
>
> I know that most of the philosophers who defend [divine] providence are commonly shaken by this argument and against

their wills are almost driven to admit that God does not care, which is exactly what Epicurus is looking for.[36]

You can see why the Epicureans wanted to tangle with a preacher of the gospel of Jesus Christ. They must have thought Paul would be an easy target. Ha!

Of course, this so-called problem is often presented as "proof" that God doesn't exist. Epicurus' thought exercise assumes that there is only one god (and the authors believe there is, in fact, only one capital-G God, YHWH, but the Bible clearly names multiple small-g gods who have rebelled against their Creator) who is responsible for everything, good and bad, that happens in the world. In other words, to satisfy the Epicureans, free will would be eliminated for every being in creation except the Creator, because to eliminate bad things requires eliminating the power to do them.

And yet, in spite of this logical disconnect, the philosophy of Epicurus—that everything is the product of natural processes, even the supernatural—is the foundation of the worldview of most people in Western societies, even though it's a safe bet that most people have never heard of Epicurus. The work of the late Dr. Edgar Mitchell—Apollo astronaut, sixth man to walk on the moon, and cofounder of the Institute of Noetic Sciences, a parapsychological research group "dedicated to supporting individual and collective transformation"[37]—was consistent with the teachings of Epicurus. More on Dr. Mitchell elsewhere in this book.

It's no coincidence that the influence of the Greek philosophers faded with the spread of Christianity. The materialistic bias of Greek thought was pushed back for a time by the supernatural power and message of the gospel. To be blunt, when you follow materialist philosophy to its logical end, you're left with the worldview of Epicurus: The only goal in life is to pursue pleasure and avoid pain.

Why? What's the point? How would Epicurus answer the Big Questions? In short, the Epicureans' view of life is depressingly bleak: We come from nothing through random natural processes; our purpose in life is to avoid being hurt; and we go nowhere when we die because our souls cease to exist.

Nothing, nothing, and nothing. That's what a materialist worldview offers.

And yet it came storming back after more than a thousand years underground with the dawn of the so-called Age of Reason, the Enlightenment. Ironically, the emergence of Islam in the seventh century may be partly responsible for holding back the influence of Greek philosophy in the West. After the first great wave of Muslim expansion wiped out Christianity in northern Africa, travel from the Eastern Roman Empire to Western Europe became more difficult as travel across the Mediterranean was no longer safe. It was only after the fall of Constantinople in 1453 and the resulting wave of refugees bearing what copies they could carry of the works of ancient Greek thinkers that the Enlightenment took root. And those ideas are blooming now in the twenty-first century.

Emanuel Swedenborg

The materialist ideals of the Greeks manifested in the rejection of a supernatural source for the Bible. And if those books were not inspired, then the words in them were free to be reinterpreted or discarded based on human reason. Likewise, supernatural experiences were open to interpretation based on human wisdom, without being filtered through comparison to the Word of God. This resulted in the odd mix of science and spiritism that is the legacy of Emanuel Swedenborg, an eighteenth-century Swedish scientist, philosopher, and mystic. He was undoubtedly brilliant, but sometimes the brilliant are blinded by their own light.

Swedenborg's theology encompasses the following concepts:

- The Bible is the Word of God; however, its true meaning differs greatly from its obvious meaning. Furthermore, He and only He, via the help of angels, was in the position to shed light upon the true meaning and message of the Scriptures.

- Swedenborg believed that the world of matter is a laboratory for the soul, where the material is used to "force-refine" the spiritual.
- In many ways, Swedenborg was quite universal in his concepts, for he believed that all religious systems have their divine duty and purpose, and that this is not the sole virtue of Christianity.
- Swedenborg believed that the mission of the Church is absolutely necessary inasmuch as, left to its own devices, humanity simply cannot work out its relationship to God.
- He saw the real power of Christ's life in the example it gave to others and vehemently rejected the concept of Christian atonement and original sin.[38]

Emanuel Swedenborg

Swedenborg believed the angels who contacted him lived elsewhere in the solar system. To this day, the Swedenborg Foundation offers a modern translation of the mystic's 1758 work, *Life on Other Planets*, a book that "details Swedenborg's conversations with spirits from Jupiter, Mars, Mercury, Saturn, Venus, and the moon, who discuss their lives on other planets and how their cultures differed from those of earthly life."[39] Swedenborg's teachings on spiritism and angelic ETIs are still around, although rebranded as the New Church. (Maybe Swedenborgianism didn't test well in focus groups.) It's a small sect, with maybe ten thousand worldwide, but is the idea of angels on Jupiter communicating through visions any stranger than ETIs from "the contiguous universe" sending messages for the president of the United States through a retired NASA astronaut?

No, it is not. And we will discuss that astronaut later in this book.

Joseph Smith and Mormonism

Of course, Swedenborg, who died in 1772, wasn't the last word in the rise of mystic scientism. Others with a belief in the link between humanity and life from the stars included Joseph Smith, who founded Mormonism about fifty years after Swedenborg's death. The cosmology developed by Smith included the existence of many worlds. God, to Smith, was flesh and blood,[40] formerly a mortal man who'd earned godhood and, apparently, the right to create multiple earths.

[29] And [Moses] beheld many lands; and each land was called earth, and there were inhabitants on the face thereof.

[30] And it came to pass that Moses called upon God, saying: Tell me, I pray thee, why these things are so, and by what thou madest them?

[31] And behold, the glory of the Lord was upon Moses, so that Moses stood in the presence of God, and talked with him face to face. And the Lord God said unto Moses: For mine own purpose have I made these things. Here is wisdom and it remaineth in me.

[32] And by the word of my power, have I created them, which is mine Only Begotten Son, who is full of grace and truth.

[33] And worlds without number have I created; and I also created them for mine own purpose; and by the Son I created them, which is mine Only Begotten.

[34] And the first man of all men have I called Adam, which is many.[41]

A full analysis of the Church of Latter-Day Saints is more than we can tackle in this book, but just consider: A two-hundred-year-old religion that claims fifteen million adherents—one of whom, Mitt Romney, might have been president of the United States—officially teaches that there are many inhabited earths scattered throughout the universe. As we'll see, the Mormon church isn't the only one that blends its theology with a belief in extraterrestrial life.

The Fox Sisters and Spiritism

Beginning with the Second Great Awakening in the 1790s, which was itself a reaction to the rationalism and deism of the Enlightenment, nineteenth-century America saw successive waves of spiritual movements roll across the United States, spreading from east to west like supernatural tsunamis. A series of revivals, cults, and camp meetings followed European settlers westward as the country grew and prospered. The raw, unspoiled nature of the frontier contributed to a desire to restore Christianity to a purer form, free from the formality and hierarchy of the churches of Europe.

The Second Great Awakening, which swelled the numbers of Baptists and Methodists especially, peaked by the middle of the nineteenth century, but other spiritual movements followed close behind. The spi-

Kate and Margaret Fox

ritualist movement, which emerged from the same region of western New York state that produced Joseph Smith and the Church of Latter-Day Saints, the so-called Burned-over District, first appeared in the late 1840s. Sisters Kate and Margaret Fox, ages 12 and 15, claimed to communicate with spirits through coded knocks or "rappings." They convinced their 17-year-old sister, Leah (or brought her in on the gag), who took charge of the younger two and managed their careers for years.

The Fox sisters not only enjoyed long careers as mediums, they left a legacy that continues to this day in the work of television mediums like John Edward, Theresa Caputo, and Tyler Henry. In fact, as we'll discuss in a later chapter, communications from disembodied spirits is a much larger part of the modern UFO movement than serious researchers are comfortable with. And this, despite the fact that Margaret and Kate admitted in 1888 that they'd invented the whole thing:

> That I have been chiefly instrumental in perpetrating the fraud of Spiritualism upon a too-confiding public, most of you doubtless know. The greatest sorrow in my life has been that this is true, and though it has come late in my day, I am now prepared to tell the truth, the whole truth, and nothing but the truth, so help me God!... I am here tonight as one of the founders of Spiritualism to denounce it as an absolute falsehood from beginning to end, as the flimsiest of superstitions, the most wicked blasphemy known to the world.[42]

The Fox sisters used a variety of techniques to produce the sounds that fooled gullible audiences into believing that spirits answered their questions, one of which was simply cracking their toe joints.[43] But even after their confession was published by a New York City newspaper, the spiritualist movement never skipped a beat. To this day, "many accounts of the Fox sisters leave out their confession of fraud and present the rappings as genuine manifestations of the spirit world."[44]

In other words, the movement lives on even though its founders admitted their act was as real as professional wrestling.

Why were Americans and Brits, who likewise flocked to stage shows featuring mediums and psychics, so eager to believe? Scholars speculate that the Industrial Revolution led people to explore spiritual frontiers to find meaning in rapidly changing lives.[45] Its quick adoption by prominent Quakers in New York tied the Spiritualist movement to several radical religious causes, including abolition (which may be why it never caught on widely in the South) and women's rights.

Whatever the cause of its popularity, the Spiritualist movement continued into the twentieth century and attracted some well-known believers. Sir Arthur Conan Doyle, the creator of *Sherlock Holmes*, was one; in fact, Doyle wrote *The History of Spiritualism* in 1926, and he pegged March 31, 1848—the very first time Kate and Margaret Fox claimed to hear from spirits—as the date the movement began.

Helena Blavatsky and Theosophy

By the fourth quarter of the nineteenth century, the Spiritualist movement was joined on the spiritual scene by the new Theosophist movement, a

blend of Eastern and Western mystical traditions that found fertile ground among urban elites. Following the lead of their founder, Theosophists saw Spiritualism as unsophisticated and provincial. For their part, "Spiritualists rejected Theosophy as unscientific occultism."[46]

The founder of Theosophy, Helena Petrovna Blavatsky, is an enigmatic character, partly because it's difficult to confirm much of what she said and wrote about herself. According to the official histories, she was the daughter of a Russian-German noble-

Helena Petrovna Blavatsky

man who traveled widely across Europe and Asia in the 1850s and 1860s. By cobbling together traditions cribbed from Eastern sources, Blavatsky laid the foundation for the modern UFO phenomenon and ET disclosure movement.

Entire books have been devoted to the life and claims of Madame Blavatsky, and we don't have time or space here to dig deeply into the material.

There's a lot of ground to cover before we get to the index, so we're only going to scratch enough of the surface to show why Blavatsky's strain of spiritual thought is important to the modern UFO phenomenon.

Blavatsky acknowledged the existence of Spiritualist phenomena, but denied that mediums were contacting spirits of the dead. Madame Blavatsky taught that God is a "Universal Divine Principle, the root of All, from which all proceeds, and within which all shall be absorbed at the end of the great cycle of Being."[47] If you catch the Eastern flavor of her teachings, you're right—Madame Blavatsky wove Hindu and Buddhist concepts into her philosophy, and it's claimed that she and Henry Steel Olcott, with whom she founded the Theosophical Society in New York City in 1875, were the first Western converts to Buddhism. The success of Theosophy in the U.S. and U.K. did much to spread Eastern mysticism in the West, and the New Age Movement owes a debt to Helena Blavatsky.

Through her most famous books, *Isis Unveiled*, published in 1877, and her magnum opus, *The Secret Doctrine*, published in 1888, Blavatsky attracted international attention to her society and its goal of uniting the world in brotherhood by blending the philosophies of East and West through the study of comparative religion, philosophy, and science.[48]

In *The Secret Doctrine*, which Blavatsky claimed was channeled from a prehistoric work called *The Book of Dzyan* (which critics accused her of cribbing without credit from a number of sources, including the Sanskrit Rigveda), she wrote:

> Lemuria was the homeland of humanity, the place of the first creation. Further, there were to be seven Root Races ruling the Earth in succession, of which humanity today was only the fifth. The fourth of these races were the Atlanteans, who were destroyed by black magic. Lemuria would rise and fall to spawn new races until the Seventh Root Race, perfect in every way, would take its rightful place as master of the world.[49]

Who, you ask, were the Atlanteans, and what is Lemuria? In the nineteenth century, this odd marriage of Spiritualism and Modernism gave rise to competing claims that the human race was either evolving or devolving. Spiritualists accepted Darwinian evolution because it supported their belief in the continued development of the spirit after death. Blavatsky and her followers, on the other hand, believed that humanity had left behind a golden age that collapsed when Atlantis fell beneath the waves.

Lemuria, like Atlantis, was another lost continent that was believed to be submerged somewhere in the Pacific or Indian Oceans. It got its name in 1864 when zoologist Philip Sclater noticed that certain primate fossils existed in Madagascar and India, but not in Africa or the Middle East. Sclater postulated a lost continent that connected Madagascar and India to account for the lemur fossils—hence Lemuria. No kidding.

While the possible existence of Lemuria was dropped by the scientific community when plate tectonics and continental drift caught on, the lost continent was kept alive by the imagination and teachings of pseudoscientists and spiritual leaders like Helena Blavatsky.

Mysterious symbols, tragic history, and memories of a glorious, golden past transmitted by disembodied Masters via "astral clairvoyance" to Blavatsky (and later Theosophists like C. W. Leadbeater) apparently stirred something in the hearts of those who read *The Secret Doctrine*. With nothing but the force of her powerful will, Madame Helena Blavatsky convinced thousands that the history they'd been taught was a lie, and that humanity's future was to return to the golden age that was lost when Atlantis slipped beneath the waves.

To put it simply, in Theosophy, Helena Blavatsky gave the world a religious faith in human evolution as an integral part of cosmic evolution. The ultimate goal was perfection and conscious participation in the evolutionary process—self-directed evolution, a concept that spurred the Eugenics movement of the late nineteenth and early twentieth centuries (and, although they don't admit it, the Transhumanist movement today). Blavatsky taught that this process was overseen by the Masters of the Ancient Wisdom, a hierarchy of spiritual beings who'd been guiding humanity's development for millennia.

From a Christian perspective, it's easy to recognize the deception embodied by the doctrines of Theosophy. While Blavatsky's critics accused her of inventing her faith out of whole cloth, a discerning follower of Jesus Christ can recognize some common lies: Humanity is the product of random evolutionary chance; we once enjoyed a golden age when we lived like gods; and our destiny is to regain that exalted status through proper spiritual discipline, ultimately to become one with God and the cosmos. This describes a common belief system that Dr. Peter Jones calls "one-ism."[50]

Obviously, this is fundamentally at odds with the Christian faith, which recognizes above all that we are most definitely not God. But the idea that we contain within us the spark of divinity is appealing. It's a good lie. In fact, it's literally the oldest lie in the Book: "Ye shall be as gods."

And as this book develops, even though it may not be obvious now, we'll show how this old lie is at the heart of the modern ET disclosure movement.

chapter four

CROWLEY AND CTHULHU

HOWARD PHILLIPS LOVECRAFT (1890–1937) is one of the giants of twentieth-century literature, although he wasn't recognized as such until after his death. And because he wrote horror fiction, he wasn't the kind of writer who got invited to fancy society parties. Lovecraft and his friends, most of whom he knew through volumes of letters—by one estimate, one hundred thousand of them[51]—that some believe were more influential than his published work, wrote to entertain, usually by crafting terrifying tales and conjuring monstrous images of overpowering, inhuman evil.

H. P. Lovecraft was a sickly child who missed so much school in his youth that he was basically self-educated. He never completed high school, giving up on his dream of becoming an astronomer, because of what he later called a "nervous breakdown." It's possible that whatever intellectual gift Lovecraft was given came at the expense of social skills. It's also possible that he was tormented by the same demons—psychological or spiritual—that led both of his parents to spend the last years of their lives in an asylum. Lovecraft lived as isolated an existence as he could manage

H. P. Lovecraft

most of his life, and he admitted that "most people only make me nervous" and "that only by accident, and in extremely small quantities, would I ever be likely to come across people who wouldn't."[52]

As a child, Lovecraft was tormented by night terrors. Beginning at age 6, young Howard was visited by what he called night-gaunts—faceless humanoids with black, rubbery skin, bat-like wings, and barbed tails, who carried off their victims to Dreamland. The nocturnal visitors were so terrifying that Howard remembered trying desperately to stay awake every night during this period of his life. It's believed that these dreams, which haunted him for more than a year, had a powerful influence on his fiction.[53]

From a Christian perspective, it's a shame that Lovecraft's mother, who raised Howard with his aunts after his father was committed to a psychiatric hospital when Howard was only three, failed to recognize the phenomenon for what it was—demonic oppression of her only child. But by the late nineteenth century, the technologically advanced West didn't have room in its scientific worldview for such things. In fact, Lovecraft claimed to be a staunch atheist throughout his life.

Ironically, in spite of his disbelief, the fiction of H. P. Lovecraft has been adapted and adopted by occultists around the world after his death. The man who died a pauper not only found an audience over the last eighty years, he inspired an army of authors who have preserved and expanded the nightmarish universe that sprang from Lovecraft's tortured dreams.[54]

Although Lovecraft claimed he didn't believe in the supernatural, he was more than happy to use the spirit realm as grist for his writing mill. Lovecraft apparently saw potential in the doctrines of Blavatsky for stories that would sell. They did, but mostly after his death. During his lifetime, Lovecraft was barely known outside the readership of pulp magazines, the type of publication called a "penny dreadful" a couple of generations earlier in England.

While Lovecraft may have rejected the idea of a lost continent or two as the now-forgotten motherland of humanity, the concept served him well as an author. The notion that certain humans gifted (or cursed) with the ability to see beyond the veil were communicating with intelligences vastly greater than our own also made for compelling horror. Lovecraft viewed the universe as a cold, unfeeling place, so in his fiction those intelligences, unlike the kindly ascended masters of Blavatsky's world, had no use for humanity—except, perhaps, as slaves or sacrifices. The horror of discovering oneself at the mercy of immense, ancient beings incapable of mercy is a common theme in Lovecraft's tales, and he gave those ideas flesh and bone with carefully crafted prose that infused them with a sense of dread not easily or often distilled onto the printed page.

It's fair to say that Lovecraft's style of gothic horror has had a powerful influence on horror fiction and film over the last seventy-five years. Stephen King, Roger Corman, John Carpenter, and Ridley Scott, among others, drew on his style if not his Cthulhu mythos directly. Maybe that's not the kind of legacy left by Ernest Hemingway or F. Scott Fitzgerald, but compare the number of people who have seen *The Thing*, *Alien*, or any movie based on a King novel (*The Shining*, *The Stand*, *It*, etc.) to the number of people who've read Hemingway or Fitzgerald. (Not *claimed* to read them, but actually sat down and *read* them.) Even though H. P. Lovecraft was basically unknown during his lifetime, he's had far greater influence on pop culture than the literary greats who were his contemporaries.

And, as we'll see, the influence of the staunch atheist Lovecraft has bled over into the metaphysical realm. Maybe it's fitting that the principalities and powers aligned against their Creator would find an atheist a most useful tool.

While Lovecraft was beginning his career as a writer, across the ocean another man fascinated with arcana and the influence of old gods on our world was hearing voices from beyond. Edward Alexander "Aleister"

Crowley, born 1875 in Warwickshire, England, traveled to Cairo in 1904 with his new bride, Rose Kelly. While there, Crowley, who'd been a member of the Order of the Golden Dawn about five years earlier, set up a temple room in their apartment and began performing rituals to invoke Egyptian deities. Eventually, something calling itself Aiwass, the messenger of Hoor-Paar-Kraat (known to the Greeks as an aspect of Horus, Harpocrates, the god of silence), answered. Over a period of three days, April 8–10, 1904, Crowley transcribed what he heard from the voice of Aiwass.

> The Voice of Aiwass came apparently from over my left shoulder, from the furthest corner of the room....
>
> I had a strong impression that the speaker was actually in the corner where he seemed to be, in a body of "fine matter," transparent as a veil of gauze, or a cloud of incense-smoke. He seemed to be a tall, dark man in his thirties, well-knit, active and strong, with the face of a savage king, and eyes veiled lest their gaze should destroy what they saw. The dress was not Arab; it suggested Assyria or Persia, but very vaguely. I took little note of it, for to me at that time Aiwass and an "angel" such as I had often seen in visions, a being purely astral.
>
> I now incline to believe that Aiwass is not only the God or Demon or Devil once held holy in Sumer, and mine own Guardian Angel, but also a man as I am, insofar as He uses a human body to make His magical link with Mankind, whom He loves.[55]

That eventually became the central text for Crowley's new religion, Thelema,[56] which in turn is the basis for Ordo Templi Orientis. The OTO is a secret society similar to Freemasonry that, like Blavatsky's Theosophical Society and the Freemasons, believes in universal brotherhood. The primary difference between Thelema and Theosophy is in the nature of the entities sending messages from beyond. Blavatsky claimed to hear from ascended masters who were shepherding humanity's evolution; Crowley claimed to be guided by gods from the Egyptian pantheon: Nuit, Hadit, and Ra-Hoor-Khuit.[57]

Aleister Crowley in OTO garb

The irony of all this is that Lovecraft, who denied the existence of Crowley's gods and Blavatsky's mahatmas, may have drawn his inspiration from the same well.

A key thread woven through the fiction of H. P. Lovecraft was a fictional grimoire, or book of witchcraft, called the *Necronomicon*. The book, according to the Lovecraft canon, was written in the eighth century A.D. by the "Mad Arab," Abdul Alhazred (Lovecraft's childhood nickname because of his love for the book *1001 Arabian Nights*). Perhaps significantly, inspiration for the invented grimoire came to Lovecraft in a dream,[58] and through his many letters to friends and colleagues, he encouraged others to incorporate the mysterious tome in their works. Over time, references to the *Necronomicon* by a growing number of authors creating Lovecraftian fiction led to a growing belief that the book was, in fact, real. Significantly, one of those who believed in the book was occultist Kenneth Grant.

Grant was an English ceremonial magician and an acolyte of Crowley, serving as Crowley's personal secretary toward the end of his life. After Crowley's death, Grant was named head of the OTO in Britain by Crowley's successor, Karl Germer. However, Grant's promotion of an extraterrestrial "Sirius/Set current" in Crowley's work infuriated Germer, who expelled Grant from the organization for heresy.[59]

Lovecraft's fiction inspired some of Grant's innovations to Thelema. Grant said Lovecraft "snatched from nightmare-space his lurid dream-readings of the *Necronomicon*." Instead of attributing the *Necronomicon* to

Lovecraft's imagination, Grant took it as evidence of the tome's existence as an astral book.[60] Furthermore, Grant believed others, including Crowley and Blavatsky, had "glimpsed the Akashic *Necronomicon*"[61]—a reference to the Akashic records, a Thesophist concept describing a collection of all human thoughts, deeds, and emotions that exists on another plane of reality accessed only through proper spiritual discipline.

Kenneth Grant was perhaps the first to notice the strange parallels between the writings of H. P. Lovecraft and Aleister Crowley. In *The Dark Lord*, an extensive analysis of Grant's magickal system and Lovecraft's influence on it, researcher and author Peter Levenda documented a number of these similarities.

> In 1907, Crowley was writing some of the works that became seminal to the doctrines of Thelema, known as The Holy Books. These include *Liber Liberi vel Lapidus Lazuli, Liber Cordis Cincti Serpente*, and other works written between October 30 and November 1 of that year, and *Liber Arcanorum* and *Liber Carcerorum*, written between December 5th and 14th that same year. Lovecraft would have had no knowledge of this, as he was only a seventeen-year old recluse living at home on Angell Street in Providence, Rhode Island, dreaming of the stars.
>
> Instead, he later would write of an orgiastic ritual taking place that year in the bayous outside New Orleans, Louisiana, and on the very same day that Crowley was writing the books enumerated above. The story Lovecraft wrote is entitled "The Call of Cthulhu" and is arguably his most famous work. He wrote the story in 1926, in late August or early September, but placed the action in New Orleans in 1907 and later in Providence in 1925.
>
> How is this relevant? Lovecraft's placement of the orgiastic ritual in honor of the high priest of the Great Old Ones, Cthulhu, and the discovery of a statue of Cthulhu by the New Orleans police on Halloween, 1907 coincides precisely with Crowley's fevered writing of his own gothic prose. In the *Liber Liberi vel*

Lapidus Lazuli, for instance, Crowley writes the word "Tutulu" for the first time. He claims not to know what this word means, or where it came from. As the name of Lovecraft's fictional alien god can be pronounced "Kutulu," it seems more than coincidental, as Kenneth Grant himself noted.

However, this is only the tip of an eldritch iceberg. In Crowley's *Liber Cordis Cincti Serpente*—or "The Book of the Heart Girt with a Serpent"— there are numerous references to the "Abyss of the Great Deep," to Typhon, Python, and the appearance of an "old gnarled fish" with tentacles...all descriptions that match Lovecraft's imagined Cthulhu perfectly. Not approximately, but perfectly. Crowley's volume was written on November 1, 1907. The ritual for Cthulhu in New Orleans took place on the same day, month and year.[62]

Now, this could be nothing more than a strange coincidence. Your authors, however, are not coincidence theorists. Levenda, an excellent researcher and a gifted author (and more on just how gifted shortly), and Kenneth Grant before him, also concluded otherwise.

Both men—the American author and the English magician— were dealing with the same subject matter, and indeed Lovecraft had dated the first appearance of the Cthulhu statue to the same year, month and day that Crowley began writing these sections of the Holy Books. There is no hard evidence that either man knew of the other, although the author believes that references to an English satanist in Lovecraft's "The Thing on the Doorstep" could be an allusion to Crowley. In any event, to suggest that these two men cooperated or collaborated in any deliberate way would be the height (or depth!) of conspiracy theory.

It may actually be more logical to suggest— as an explanation for some of these coincidences— that darker forces were at work. In fact, it is possible that the same forces of which Lovecraft himself writes—the telepathic communication between followers of Cthulhu and the Great Old Ones—was what prompted him to write these fictional accounts of real events. Either Lovecraft was in some kind of telepathic communication with Crowley, or both men were in telepathic communication with ... Something Else.

As Christians, your authors are inclined to go with the supernatural explanation. If the apostle Paul knew his theology, and he did, then we must consider the influence of principalities and powers on our natural world. And that's the most likely source of the odd, highly improbable Crowley-Cthulhu connection.

In the early 1970s, Grant would break with the American OTO and form his own Thelemic organization, the Typhonian OTO. The "Sirius/ Set current" that Grant identified in the '50s referred to the Egyptian deity Set, god of the desert, storms, foreigners, violence, and chaos. To grasp the significance of Grant's innovation to Crowley's religion, a brief history of Set is in order.

Set—sometimes called Seth, Sheth, or Sutekh—is one of the oldest gods in the Egyptian pantheon. There is evidence he was worshiped long before the pharaohs, in the pre-dynastic era called Naqada I, which may date as far back as 3750 B.C.[63] To put that into context, this author (Derek Gilbert) estimates that the Tower of Babel incident probably occurred between 3500 B.C. and 3100 B.C.[64] Writing wasn't invented in Sumer until about 3000 B.C., around the time of the first pharaoh, Narmer (whom some researchers identify as Nimrod).[65]

Set was originally one of the good guys. He protected Ra's solar boat, defending it from the evil chaos serpent Apep (or Apophis), who tried to eat the sun every night as it dropped below the horizon. During the Second Intermediate Period, roughly 1750 B.C. to 1550 B.C., Semitic people called the Hyksos—actually Amorites[66]—equated Set with Ba`al, the Canaanite storm-god,[67] and scholars have concluded that Ba`al-Set was the lord of Avaris, the Hyksos capital. But the worship of Ba`al-Set continued even after the Hyksos were driven out of Egypt. Two centuries after Moses led the Israelites to Canaan, three hundred years after the Hyksos expulsion, Ramesses the Great erected a memorial called the Year 400 Stela to honor the four hundredth year of Set's arrival in Egypt. In fact, Ramesses' father was named Seti, which literally means "man of Set."

Set didn't acquire his evil reputation until the Third Intermediate Period, during which Egypt was overrun by successive waves of foreign invaders. After being conquered by Nubia, Assyria, and Persia, one after another between 728 B.C. and 525 B.C., the god of foreigners 'was no longer welcome around the pyramids.[68] No longer was Set the dangerous rabble-rouser whose appetite for destruction kept Apophis from eating the sun; now Set was the evil god who murdered his brother, Osiris, and the sworn enemy of Osiris' son, Horus.

By the time of Persia's rise, Greek civilization was beginning to flower, and they identified Set with Typhon, their terrifying, powerful serpentine god of chaos. There's the link between Set and Typhon, and this is the entity Kenneth Grant believed was the true source of power in Thelemic magick. That's why the "Sirius/Set current" led to the Typhonian OTO, and that's the destructive, chaos-monster aspect of Set-Typhon we need to keep in view when analyzing the magickal system Grant created by filtering Crowley through Lovecraft.

Grant's anxiety—as expressed in *Nightside of Eden* and in his other works—is that the Earth is being infiltrated by a race of extraterrestrial beings who will cause tremendous changes to take place in our world. This statement is not to be taken quite as literally as it appears, for the "Earth" can be taken to mean our current level of conscious awareness, and extraterrestrial would mean simply "not of this current level of conscious awareness." But the potential for danger is there, and Grant's work—like Lovecraft's—is an attempt to warn us of the impending (potentially dramatic) alterations in our physical, mental and emotional states due to powerful influences from "outside."[69]

By the 1970s, Lovecraft's work had found a new audience, and his stories were being mined by Hollywood (for example *The Dunwich Horror*, starring Dean Stockwell and Sandra Dee, and several episodes of Rod Serling's *Night Gallery*). Then in 1977, a hardback edition of the *Necronomicon* suddenly appeared (published in a limited run of 666 copies!),[70] edited by a mysterious figure known only as "Simon," purportedly a bishop in the Eastern Orthodox Church. According to Simon, two monks from his denomination had stolen a copy of the actual *Necronomicon* in one of the most daring and dangerous book thefts in history.

Apparently, the good bishop wasn't above earning a few bucks by publishing a stolen heretical text.

A mass market paperback edition followed a few years later. That version has reportedly sold more than a million copies over the last four decades.[71] Kenneth Grant validated the text, going so far as to offer explanations for apparent discrepancies between Crowley and the *Necronomicon*.

Crowley admitted to not having heard correctly certain words during the transmission of *Liber L*, and it is probable that he misheard the word Tutulu. It may have been Kutulu, in which case it would be identical phonetically, but not qabalistically, with Cthulhu. The [Simon] *Necronomicon* (Introduction, p.xix) suggests a relationship between Kutulu and Cutha.[72]

Simon's *Necronomicon* was just one of several grimoires published in the '70s that claimed to be the nefarious book. The others were either obvious fakes published for entertainment purposes, or hoaxes that their authors admitted to soon after publication. Simon, on the other hand, appeared to be serious.

But here's the thing: People involved with producing the "Simonomicon" have admitted to making it up, and the central figure behind the book's publication was Peter Levenda.

> The text itself was Levenda's creation, a synthesis of Sumerian and later Babylonian myths and texts peppered with names of entities from H. P. Lovecraft's notorious and enormously popular Cthulhu stories. Levenda seems to have drawn heavily on the works of Samuel Noah Kramer for the Sumerian, and almost certainly spent a great deal of time at the University of Pennsylvania library researching the thing. Structurally, the text was modeled on the wiccan Book of Shadows and the Goetia, a grimoire of doubtful authenticity itself dating from the late Middle Ages.
> "Simon" was also Levenda's creation. He cultivated an elusive, secretive persona, giving him a fantastic and blatantly implausible line of [BS] to cover the book's origins. He had no telephone. He always wore business suits, in stark contrast to the flamboyant Renaissance fair, proto-goth costuming that dominated the scene.[73]

In *The Dark Lord*, Levenda not only analyzed Kenneth Grant's magickal system and documented the synchronicities between Crowley and Lovecraft, he validated the supernatural authenticity of the fake *Necronomicon* he created! But make no mistake—this doesn't mean the *Necronomicon* is fake in the supernatural sense.

> [W]e can conclude that the hoax *Necronomicons*—at least the Hay-Wilson-Langford-Turner and Simon versions—falsely claim to be the work of the mad Arab Abdul Alhazred, but in so falsely attributing themselves, they signal their genuine inclusion in the grimoire genre. The misattribution is the mark of their genre, and their very falsity is the condition of their genuineness. The hoax *Necronomicons* are every bit as "authentic" as the *Lesser Key of Solomon* or the *Sixth and Seventh Books of Moses*.[74]

In other words, while the published editions of the *Necronomicon* were obviously invented long after the deaths of H. P. Lovecraft and Aleister Crowley, they are still genuine tools for the practice of sorcery. And, as Grant and Levenda suggest, they share a common origin point somewhere in the spirit realm.

From the Necronomicon to Nibiru

Simon's *Necronomicon* arrived on the wave of a renewed interest in the occult that washed over the Western world in the 1960s and '70s. Interestingly, it was a French journal of science fiction that helped spark the revival, and it did so by publishing the works of H. P. Lovecraft for a new audience. *Planète* was launched in the early '60s by Louis Pauwles and Jacques Bergier, and their magazine brought a new legion of admirers to the "bent genius." More significantly for our study here, however, was the book Pauwles and Bergier coauthored in 1960, *Les matins des magiciens* (*Morning of the Magicians*), which was translated into English in 1963 as *Dawn of Magic*.[75]

> The book covered everything from pyramidology (the belief that the Egyptian pyramids held ancient secrets) to supposed advanced technology in the ancient world. Likewise, the authors praised Arthur Machen, the Irish author of horror fiction, about surviving Celtic mythological creatures, and they discussed the genius of H. P. Lovecraft in the same breath as the scientist Albert Einstein and psychoanalyst Carl Jung. From Lovecraft, Bergier and Pauwles borrowed the one thought that would be of more importance than any other in their book. As we have seen, *Morning of the Magicians* speculates that **extraterrestrial beings may be responsible for the rise of the human race and the development of its culture, a theme Lovecraft invented.**[76] (emphasis added)

The success of Pauwles and Bergier inspired others to run with the concepts they'd developed from the writings of Lovecraft. The most successful of these, without question, was Erich von Däniken's *Chariots of the Gods*, the best-selling English language archaeology book of all time.[77]

You can say one thing at least for von Däniken: He wasn't shy about challenging accepted history:

> I claim that our forefathers received visits from the universe in the remote past, even though I do not yet know who these extraterrestrial intelligences were or from which planet they came. I nevertheless proclaim that these "strangers" annihilated part of mankind existing at the time and produced a new, perhaps the first, *homo sapiens*.[78]

The book had the good fortune of being published in 1968, the same year Stanley Kubrick's epic adaptation of Arthur C. Clarke's *2001: A Space Odyssey* hit theaters. The film, based on the idea that advanced alien technology had guided human evolution, was the top-grossing film of the year, and was named the "greatest sci-fi film of all time" in 2002 by the Online Film Critics Society.[79] By 1971, when *Chariots of the Gods* finally appeared in American bookstores, NASA had put men on the moon three times (including Edgar Mitchell in Apollo 14, whom we'll discuss later for his efforts to meet with President Obama to discuss ETIs from a "contiguous universe"), and the public was fully primed for what von Däniken was selling.

It's hard to overstate the impact *Chariots of the Gods* has had on the UFO research community and the worldviews of millions of people around the world over the last half century. In 1973, *Twilight Zone* creator Rod Serling built a documentary around *Chariots* titled *In Search of Ancient Astronauts*, which featured astronomer Carl Sagan and Wernher von Braun, architect of the Saturn V rocket.[80] The following year, a feature film with the same title as the book was released to theaters. By the turn of the twenty-first century, von Däniken had sold more than sixty million copies of his twenty-six books, all promoting the idea that our creators came from the stars.[81]

This, in spite of the fact that von Däniken told *National Enquirer* in a 1974 interview that his information came not through archaeological fieldwork, but through out-of-body travel to a place called Point Aleph, "a sort of fourth dimension" outside of space and time.[82]

Riiiight. Might that be the same cosmic place Kenneth Grant found the ethereal *Necronomicon*?

In 1976, a Russian-American economist and journalist dumped gasoline on the ancient astronaut blaze with his book *The 12th Planet*. To Zecharia Sitchin, Sumerian texts, the world's oldest known writing, their stories of gods and demigods were historic records of aliens from a planet called Nibiru who created mankind from apes to serve as cheap labor.

Despite being universally rejected by credentialed scholars, Sitchin has had a profound influence on the ancient astronaut movement and on the culture at large. Dr. Michael Heiser, author of the www.SitchinIsWrong. com website, has called him "arguably the most important proponent of the ancient astronaut hypothesis over the last several decades."[83] Since *The 12th Planet* was published, Sitchin's books have sold millions of copies in more than two dozen languages.[84] His ideas have inspired popular science-fiction movies and television programs, especially the *Stargate* franchise, and a 2017 survey by Chapman University found that 35 percent of Americans believe extraterrestrials visited Earth in our distant past—up from 20.3 percent in 2015![85]

You may think the idea is weird, but when one in three people buy in, it's not fringe anymore. The appeal of the concept is easy enough to understand. If the only thing separating you from godhood is the sophistication of our technology, then the old lie the serpent told Eve doesn't seem so far-fetched.

MUFON Jumps Aboard

The claims of von Däniken and Sitchin, to be kind, don't hold water. Their theories have been debunked and von Däniken has even admitted to making stuff up,[86] but lack of evidence has never stopped crazy ideas for long. And now, thanks to a new generation of true believers, *Ancient Aliens* and its imitators are still mining von Däniken gold five decades after his first book hit the shelves.

Ancient alien evangelists have effectively proselytized the American public since *Chariots of the Gods* went viral nearly fifty years ago. As we noted earlier, more adults in the U.S. believe in ETI than in the God of the Bible. Interestingly, serious UFO researchers are disturbed by the impact of the ancient alien meme on their work.

MUFON, the Mutual UFO Network, which calls itself "the world's oldest and largest UFO phenomenon investigative body,"[87] has gone all in with ancient aliens in recent years. The group now openly supports pseudoscientific and New Age (in other words, occultic) interpretations of the UFO phenomenon instead of sticking to what can be supported by evidence. For example, the theme of MUFON's 2017 national convention was "The Case for a Secret Space Program," which was described by one critic as "blatantly unscientific and irrational."[88]

The conference featured among its speakers a man who claims he was recruited for "a '20 & Back' assignment which involved age regression (via Pharmaceutical means) as well as time regressed to the point of beginning service." In plain English, he claims he served twenty years in an off-planet research project, and then was sent back in time to a few minutes after he left and "age-regressed" so no one would notice that he's twenty years older than the rest of us.[89]

Riiiight.

Another speaker claimed he was pre-identified as a future president of the United States in a CIA/DARPA program called Project Pegasus, which purportedly gathered intel on past and future events, such as the identities of future presidents. He also claimed Barack Obama was his roommate in 1980 in a CIA project called Mars Jump Room,[90] a teleportation program that sent trainees to a secret base on the red planet.[91]

Riiiight.

The content of MUFON's 2017 symposium was so over the top that Richard Dolan, a long-time advocate for ETI disclosure, felt it was necessary to publicly explain why he'd sit on a MUFON-sanctioned discussion panel with men who claimed, without any corroboration whatsoever, that they'd been part of a "secret space program."

> [W]hen I learned I would be on a panel with Corey [Goode], Andy [Basiago], Bill [Tompkins], and Michael [Salla], I phoned Jan [Harzan, MUFON's Executive Director] and politely asked him what was he thinking. I mentioned my concern about MUFON's decision to bring in individuals with claims that are inherently impossible to verify. MUFON, after all, is supposed to have evidence-based standards.[92]

Maybe it shouldn't surprise us that MUFON has morphed from an "evidence-based" organization to one that promotes unverifiable claims at its national convention. As the controversy grew over the theme of MUFON's 2017 convention, it was revealed that MUFON's "Inner Circle" included New Age teacher J. Z. Knight.[93]

According to MUFON's website, the Inner Circle provides "advisory guidance" to the organization because its thirteen members—a curiously coincidental number—have "shown unparalleled generosity towards MUFON by donating in excess of $5,000 in a single donation."

Hmm. So the only qualification to advise and guide America's premier UFO investigating collective is an extra five large in your pocket. And one of MUFON's Inner Circle makes her living by packaging and selling rehashed teachings of Madame Helena Blavatsky.

J. Z. Knight, born in Roswell, New Mexico (!), in March of 1946, just about the time Jack Parsons and L. Ron Hubbard were wrapping up their magickal ritual, the Babylon [sic] Working, claims to channel the spirit of Ramtha the Enlightened One, a warrior who lived thirty-five thousand years ago in the mythical land of Lemuria.

Ramtha, Knight says, led Lemurian forces against the tyrannical Atlanteans before eventually bidding his troops farewell and ascending to heaven in a flash of light.[94] Ten years after he first appeared, Knight founded Ramtha's School of Enlightenment, through which she has become a very wealthy woman by selling counseling sessions based on the wisdom of the ancient Lemurian warrior.

While Ramtha has no need for creature comforts, Ms. Knight apparently likes nice things.

As of 2017, the school employs eighty full-time staff,[95] and annual profits from book and audio sales run into the millions.[96] According to Knight, Ramtha's teachings can be boiled down to mind over matter: "Ramtha tells people that if they learn what to do, the art of creating your own reality is really a divine act. There's no guru here. You are creating your day. You do it yourself."[97]

That said, your authors assume Ms. Knight still looks both ways before crossing the street.

Three students of RSE produced the 2004 film *What the Bleep Do We Know?*, a low-budget movie that twisted quantum physics into pseudoscientific New Age propaganda. Of course, Ramtha's doctrine of changing the physical world through proper spiritual discipline was the heart of the film.[98] In spite of the criticism of actual physicists, *Bleep* has grossed nearly $16 million worldwide to date.[99]

J. Z. Knight may be MUFON's wealthiest benefactor.[100] This begs at least three questions: First, how much "advisory guidance" do the thirteen members of MUFON's Inner Circle give? Second, how much does Knight donate above and beyond the $5,000 Inner Circle threshold? And third, how does her wealth and worldview influence MUFON's approach to the subject of ETI disclosure?

For the record, your authors are not the only ones asking these questions. Former MUFON state director James E. Clarkson, a thirty-year member, publicly resigned July 22, 2017, citing Knight's position of influence within the group: "I will not have my reputation in this field compromised by affiliating with a rich and powerful cult leader who is now a member of the MUFON Inner Circle."[101]

You know, it sounds bizarre when we step back and summarize things, but there is no way to make this sound rational. The horror fiction of H. P. Lovecraft, which was inspired by the spirits behind nineteenth-century occultists like Helena Blavatsky (and possibly the *same* spirit that communicated with Aleister Crowley), was filtered through the French science-fiction scene in the 1960s, adapted by a Swiss hotelier and a Russian-American shipping company executive, and recycled back to the United States at the time of the first moon landings, where it's grown into a scientistic religion that replaces God with aliens.

Wow.

To paraphrase our friend, Christian researcher and author L. A. Marzulli: As we approach the fiftieth anniversary of *Chariots of the Gods*, the ancient alien meme is real, burgeoning, and not going away.

And the old gods are using it to set the stage for their return.

chapter five

SCIENCE FICTION AND THE GOSPEL OF ET

IF LOVECRAFT USED horror to introduce the idea of contact with an alien "other" to the masses, the growing popularity of science fiction in the twentieth century established ET as a stereotype in popular entertainment. It's hard to imagine, but our great-grandparents would have had no idea what the phrase "little green men" was supposed to mean.

It Begins in the Nineteenth Century

Nineteenth-century forerunners like Jules Verne and H. G. Wells demonstrated that fiction based on speculative science would sell. Verne's 1865 *From the Earth to the Moon* was the first major work to feature space travel; in 1898, Wells produced the first ET invasion story with his classic *The War of the Worlds*. Another Welles—Orson—transformed *The War of the Worlds* into a compelling radio drama on Halloween Eve in 1938, although the story that the program caused a national panic is, sadly, a myth. (Newspapers lost a lot of advertising revenue to the new medium during the Great Depression and took advantage of an opportunity to slam radio—an early example of "fake news.")[102]

Joseph W. Campbell

The popularity of the genre took off in the 1920s with the arrival of the first pulp magazines that featured science fiction, such as *Amazing Stories*, *Weird Tales*, *Astounding Stories*, and *Wonder Stories*. The golden age of science fiction arrived in 1937 when John W. Campbell took over as editor of *Astounding Science Fiction*. Campbell is widely considered the most influential editor of the early years of the genre, publishing first or early stories by Isaac Asimov, Lester del Rey, Robert Heinlein, A. E. Van Vogt, and Theodore Sturgeon, thus helping to launch the careers of many of the biggest names in twentieth-century science fiction.

In spite of his insistence that his writers research the science behind their stories, Campbell had an interest in parapsychology that grew over the years. Writers learned that with topics like telepathy helped them sell stories to *Astounding*.[103] In 1949, Campbell discovered L. Ron Hubbard and published his first article on Dianetics, which Campbell described as "one of the most important articles ever published."[104] He suggested to some that Hubbard would win the Nobel Peace Prize for his creation.

Three years before selling Campbell on Dianetics, Hubbard participated in an event that falls smack into the "you can't make this stuff up" category: From January to March, 1946, Hubbard and Jack Parsons, rocket engineer and one of the founders of the Jet Propulsion Laboratory, performed a series of sex magick rituals called the Babalon (sic) Working. It was intended to manifest an incarnation of the divine feminine, a concept based on the writings of Aleister Crowley and described in his 1917 novel *Moonchild*.

So, through L. Ron Hubbard and Joseph Campbell, science-fiction fans were just two degrees removed from Aleister Crowley, just as readers of gothic horror were connected to the "Great Beast" through the works of H. P. Lovecraft and his successors.

Campbell managed to capture the paranoia and dread that marked Lovecraft's work in his classic 1938 novella *Who Goes There?* The story has been adapted for the big screen three times—1951's *The Thing from Another World* (featuring a young James Arnett, TV's Matt Dillon, as the creature), 1982's *The Thing*, starring Kurt Russell, and a 2011 prequel, also titled *The Thing*.

The Kurt Russell film, set in Antarctica, draws on key Lovecraftian themes—an ancient extraterrestrial that poses an existential threat to all life on Earth, the loss of self as one is assimilated by the monster, and a claustrophobic setting. *The Thing* was set at an Antarctic research station, where the bitter cold confines most of the action to the interior of the base. The paranoia-inducing monster imitates its victims perfectly (similar to the ETs in the 1956 classic *Invasion of the Body Snatchers*), which causes the base scientist, played by Wilford Brimley, to snap when he realizes just how quickly the creature could destroy the Earth if it escapes the Antarctic—which makes Brimley's character an awful lot like the protagonists in many of Lovecraft's stories.

Even the setting near the South Pole recalls Lovecraft, whose classic novella *At the Mountains of Madness* introduced a theme that's been revisited over the years in films like *The X-Files* and *Alien vs. Predator*—there's something beneath the ice down there that shouldn't be disturbed.

> It is absolutely necessary, for the peace and safety of mankind, that some of earth's dark, dead corners and unplumbed depths be let alone; lest sleeping abnormalities wake to resurgent life, and blasphemously surviving nightmares squirm and splash out of their black lairs to newer and wider conquests.[105]

Not coincidentally, UFO enthusiasts claim to find alien craft half-buried in the Antarctic on a regular basis these days.

The point is that by the time Campbell began to elevate science fiction out of the swamp of pulp fiction in the late 1930s, the concept of unfriendly (or uncaring) ETIs intervening in Earth's affairs was already several decades old. By the late 1940s, it was already fodder for kiddie cartoons; Marvin the Martian (and his Uranium PU-36 Explosive Space Modulator) debuted in 1948, just one year after Kenneth Arnold's UFO sighting at Mount Rainier and the famous crash near Roswell, New Mexico.

Modern Science Fiction in Film and TV

In the decades since, science fiction has become, in the words of Dr. Michael S. Heiser, "televangelism for the ET religion."[106] People looking in from outside the genre may assume sci-fi is all rockets, ray guns, and lasers, but a lot of it theological. Films like *Prometheus*, *Mission to Mars*, *Knowing*, and *2001: A Space Odyssey*, for example, conflate space travel, extraterrestrial intelligence, and religion by offering answers to the big questions the world's religions have been addressing since the beginning of time—where we come from, why we're here, and where we go when we die.

Human interaction with ETIs has been a stock premise for television for decades, sometimes played for drama and sometimes for laughs. And the mix of space travel and religion has never been off-screen for long. The original *Star Trek* reimagined the gods of Greece and Rome as powerful aliens when they encounter Apollo in the second-season episode, "Who Mourns for Adonais?"

Other entries in the *Star Trek* franchise likewise explored religious themes. The pilot episode of *Star Trek: The Next Generation* introduced Picard's godlike nemesis, Q, who eventually appeared in a dozen episodes of *TNG*, *Star Trek: Deep Space Nine*, and *Star Trek: Voyager*. A major plot arc of *DS9* involved Commander Sisko's role as the Emissary of the Prophets, the "wormhole aliens" worshiped as gods on the planet Bajor.

The 1994 film *Stargate* kicked off a long-running, science-fiction franchise that centered on the return of the old gods to Earth. In the *Stargate* universe, the deities of the ancient Near East were parasitic, technologically advanced ETIs called the Goa'Uld who ruled the Earth thousands of years ago as gods. The movie follows a team of explorers who travel through a stargate to discover a world controlled by a brutal entity posing as the Egyptian sun-god Ra, whose spaceship just happens to look a lot like the Great Pyramid of Giza.

The television series *Stargate SG-1* and its spinoffs continued that theme. The Norse pantheon was introduced in the series as the Asgard, whose appearance inspired stories of the alien greys (that look just doesn't work for Thor), and who, contrary to their reputation among ET contactees, side with humanity in the war against the Goa'Uld. (The 1947 Roswell panic was presumably an accident.)

In other words, the *Stargate* franchise built an entire alternate history for the main religions of the world: Basically, they were all aliens. We don't recall how they explained why the "gods" stopped visiting Earth for a couple thousand years, and of course they never touched the third rail of Hollywood, Jesus. Considering what the series did to the pagan gods, it's just as well.

SG-1 ran from 1997 through 2007, surpassing *The X-Files* as the longest-running science-fiction television series in North America until it was passed by *Smallville* (a series featuring another godlike ETI, Superman) in 2011.

Battlestar Galactica had two series runs, the first in 1978–79 and the second, which produced seventy-five episodes between 2003 and 2009. It's notable for being a not-too-subtle dramatization of Mormon theology, including a council of twelve, marriage for "time and eternity," and a planet named Kobol. Religion was a prominent theme in the reboot, too; the twelve "Lords of Kobol" were the gods of the Greco-Roman pantheon (Zeus, Hera, Apollo, Ares, Athena, Poseidon, etc.), and the twelve occupied planets of the human race were named for the signs of the zodiac.

Interestingly, the Cylons, sentient robots who rebelled against their human masters, were depicted as monotheistic, a religion that looked a lot like a cross between Christianity and Judaism—basically Christianity minus Christ. Well, except for the part where they attempt genocide and nearly destroy the entire human race.

The reimagined series introduced a new element—humanoid Cylons so lifelike they're indistinguishable from humans. As the series developed, it was revealed that there were only seven models, but a multitude of copies of each. Model number One, Cavil, deceives the other Cylons by hiding the identities of the five remaining humanoid Cylon models. Finding the Final Five becomes a major plot line in the series, and their revelation to the human fleet is a major turning point that leads humanity to salvation on a new Earth.

Interestingly, that Cylon plot twist draws from a number of Western occult traditions, especially as they've been syncretized into Theosophy. Madame Blavatsky wrote in *The Secret Doctrine* that seven "rays" together form all energy and all forms produced by it—in other words, you, us, and everything around us. Somehow these "rays" are also intelligent beings called the Dhyan Chohans.

Since at least the early 1970s, however, some New Age leaders like Elizabeth Clare Prophet have been teaching on the "five secret rays," which "promote an action of detail, the final sculpturing of the mind and consciousness in the perfect image of the Christ."[107]

It's difficult to pin down what exactly inspired the writers of the reimagined *Battlestar* to add the "final five" plot line, but we don't believe the parallel to current New Age thinking is a coincidence.

Remember, we are not coincidence theorists.

Comic Books and Deities

Comic heroes have also mined human theology for story arcs. Beyond the obvious, such as Marvel making a superhero out of the Norse storm-god Thor (who was a cognate for Jupiter, Zeus, Baal, and the ancient Sumerian storm-god Ishkur—in other words, same god with different names), researcher and author Christopher Knowles makes a strong case in his book, *Our*

Gods Wear Spandex: The Secret History of Comic Book Heroes, for comic-book heroes as a modern rebranding of ancient mythological archetypes.

> This culture is far more influential (and insidious) than most realize. Most contemporary action movies take their visual language from comic books. The rhythm of constant hyper-violence of today's action movies comes straight from Jack Kirby. Elvis Presley idolized Captain Marvel Jr., to the point of adopting his hairstyle....
>
> Although most of us don't realize it, there's simply nothing new about devotion to superheroes. Their powers, their costumes, and sometimes even their names are plucked straight from the pre-Christian religions of antiquity. When you go back and look at these heroes in their original incarnations, you can't help but be struck by how blatant their symbolism is and how strongly they reflect they belief systems of the pagan age. What even fewer people realize is that this didn't occur by chance, but came directly out of the spiritual and mystical secret societies and cults of the late 19th century—groups like the Theosophists, the Rosicrucians, and the Golden Dawn. These groups turned their backs on the state cult of Christianity and reached back in time to the elemental deities of the ancient traditions.[108]

Popular movies based on comics or graphic novels featuring the ETI/ religion theme include the *Transformers* franchise, *X-Men Apocalypse*, and the *Guardians of the Galaxy* films. The common thread: ETIs exist, they're coming to Earth, and it's either going to be awesome or apocalyptic when they get here.

Pop Culture and ETI Contact

And how have eighty years of pop culture pushing the ETI meme shaped our ideas about contact? Seth Shostak, lead astronomer for the SETI (Search for Extraterretrial Intelligence) Institute, hits the nail on the head:

I think we are ready for ET contact in some sense, because the public has been conditioned to the idea of life in space by movies and TV. And if you go into a classroom with a bunch of 11-year-olds and ask them, "How many of you kids think there are aliens out there?" they all raise their hands! Why? Is it because their parents have been educating them about astrobiology? No. It's because they've seen them on TV! ...

I think that Hollywood is by far the biggest term in the equation of the public's reaction to confirmation of alien life.[109]

Exactly. But it's a concept that's been drawn from nineteenth-century occult groups and filtered through pulp magazines, sci-fi novels, radio dramas, cartoons, comic books, graphic novels, movies, and television, packaged as popular entertainment and sold as a worldview to the last four generations. How long before an official announcement that the ETIs—the old gods—are finally back?

One last thing: Isn't it odd that the lead astronomer of the group searching for ETIs is named for the chaos god, Seth (Set)? And that the group's acronym, SETI, is Egyptian for "man of Set?" Should we be concerned that Set-Typhon, the dark lord of chaos, is the one Aleister Crowley's successor Kenneth Grant believed is the spirit of our age? And that he's apparently reaching out to Earth from somewhere in the direction of Sirius?

Most likely just coincidence. It's probably fine.

chapter six

THE GOVERNMENT AND ET

OUR GOAL IN writing this book is not to document the crazy cults that have emerged since the beginning of the modern UFO era in 1947. There are plenty, and frankly they're so obvious that you, as a discerning reader, don't need us to tell you how far removed from reality they are. Some are relatively harmless, and but others are not, like the Heaven's Gate cult that convinced thirty-nine of its members to commit suicide in late March of 1997 in the belief they'd be taken aboard a spacecraft following Comet Hale-Bopp.

It's more important that we look at how the ancient astronaut/alien meme has influenced our society in more subtle ways. As we showed earlier in the book, it's shaping the beliefs of people who have been convinced by media and academia that the Bible cannot be true, so we must look elsewhere for answers to the Big Questions.

As Christians who should understand that we're in the middle of a war for our souls, this shouldn't surprise us. And yet it does, because too many churches have been lured by principalities and powers—fallen angels and their demonic minions—into a modernist or postmodernist worldview, either looking to science as the only tool for revealing spiritual truth or buying into the absurd, self-refuting notion that absolute truth doesn't exist at all.

What should concern American evangelicals is not the role played by the UFO researchers in spreading the ETI disclosure meme. That's why they're interested in the phenomenon in the first place. We expect that from them. No, what's bothersome is that the government of our purportedly Christian nation has deployed a variety of agencies and operatives to sell the existence of ETI over the last seventy years.

It began early on in the modern UFO era. About two weeks before the crash at Roswell, New Mexico, made headlines, a harbor patrolman named Harold A. Dahl anchored in Maury Island Bay with his son, their dog, and two crewman. At 2:00 P.M. on June 21, 1947 (the summer solstice, coincidentally), they spotted a half dozen odd, metallic, doughnut-shaped craft hovering a couple thousand feet above them. According to Dahl, one of the ships seemed to be in trouble, with the other five circling around it as it lost altitude. A small explosion showered Dahl's boat with hot metal, killing his dog and injuring his son. Dahl beached the boat and took some pictures of the craft, which took off in the direction of Canada.[110]

His boat's radio was jammed, so Dahl headed back to Tacoma, got treatment for his son's injured arm, then took his camera and some of the metal fragments to his boss, 27-year-old Fred L. Crisman.

The Maury Island incident has gone down in the books as a hoax. Whether it is or isn't is beyond the scope of this book. The important point—unless you're a coincidence theorist—is that more than twenty years later, Crisman, a former officer in the OSS (the forerunner of the CIA), was subpoenaed by New Orleans District Attorney Jim Garrison in the conspiracy trial of businessman Clay Shaw,[111] who'd been charged with being part of the conspiracy to kill President John F. Kennedy.[112] Some thought Crisman was one of the three tramps picked up by Dallas police in the rail yard near Dealey Plaza,[113] although evidence suggests he wasn't in Dallas that day.[114] In spite of that, Garrison apparently believed that Crisman was one of the trigger men on the grassy knoll.[115]

Here's where things get even weirder: A few days after the Maury Island incident, Kenneth Arnold of Boise, Idaho, a successful businessman, deputy federal marshal, experienced pilot, and member of an Idaho Search and Rescue Team—in other words, an excellent witness—was flying home from Washington when he spotted a formation of nine UFOs north of Mount Rainier moving at upwards of 1,200 miles per hour. Needless to say, that's not a speed any known aircraft was capable of reaching in 1947.

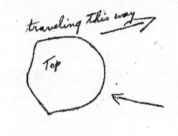

They seemed longer than wide, their thickness was about 1/20th their width

Mirror Bright

Sketch by pilot Kenneth Arnold of the craft he saw near Mount Rainier, Washington, June 24, 1947

Fred Crisman

Fred Crisman, even though he wasn't a witness to whatever Harold Dahl claimed he saw, reached out to the editor of *Amazing Stories* magazine, Raymond Palmer. Palmer had already been in touch with Arnold, offering him an advance for an interview about his UFO encounter. After hearing from Crisman, who'd had a pair of letters to the editor published in *Amazing Stories* in the previous year,[116] Palmer persuaded Arnold to fly from Boise to Tacoma to meet with Dahl and check out the Maury Island incident. Oddly, when he arrived, Arnold found all the hotels in Tacoma fully booked—until he tried the most expensive place in town and discovered a reservation in his name, although no one seemed to know who made it.[117]

The odd series of events apparently gave Arnold the feeling that the situation was a setup, possibly an intelligence op to discredit both him and Harold Dahl. Trusting his instincts, Arnold contacted the two Army intelligence officers who'd debriefed him after his initial report, Captain William Davidson and 1st Lieutenant Frank M. Brown. They flew to Tacoma immediately, arriving that afternoon and discussing the case with Arnold and United Airlines pilot, Captain Emil J. Smith,[118] who had likewise been invited by Arnold. The two pilots had become friends after Smith and his crew reported five "somethings" over Idaho the night of July 4, 1947,[119] flying wings or disks similar to what Arnold had seen two weeks earlier near Mount Rainier.

After meeting with Arnold, Smith, Crisman, and Dahl, the intelligence officers seemed to think the Maury Island sighting

Chicago Times article July 7, 1947, on the UFO sightings by Kenneth Arnold and United Air Lines pilot Capt. Emil J. Smith

was a hoax, and they prepared to fly back to Hamilton Field in California late the night of July 31 as their B-25 bomber was scheduled to fly in the first Air Force Day celebration the next day.

At the airport, an odd thing happened, one which has plagued UFO researchers for years. Crisman, the man the intelligence officers seemed to think was nothing more than an oddball hoaxer, turned up at the last minute and gave the men a heavy box which he claimed was filled with the debris from the damaged UFO. To Arnold, who was there, the contents looked like a bunch of rocks. The men stowed the box in the trunk of their car and left for the airport, catching their flight. They never made it back to base. Both Davidson and Brown were killed. The enlisted men on board parachuted to safety after the left engine caught fire—according to the report of one of the survivors—and the two officers remained with the aircraft for a full ten minutes before the B-25 bomber crashed to earth. No one has any idea why the two intelligence officers would have remained with the plane and not parachuted themselves; or why they did not radio a distress call.[120]

It's important to note that Davidson and Brown were preparing to fly their B-25 out of Tacoma at around 2:00 A.M. What are the odds that Fred Crisman just happened to be driving by the airport at that time of night?

A report filed by the FBI's Butte, Montana, field office designated SM-X (for "Security Matter X"—real life X-files!) noted that Arnold remembered Crisman calling him and Smith at their hotel in the morning to tell them about the deadly crash, and wondering how Crisman had known who was on the B-25 before the Army had released any information to the press. And as for the press: Reporters for the United Press office in Tacoma were getting reports from someone who sat in the meetings between Crisman, Dahl, Arnold, Smith, and the Army intelligence officers, because bits of conversation were quoted back to Arnold and Smith verbatim.[121]

It's not within the scope of this book to unravel the Maury Island case, an incident that's still not settled in the minds of UFO researchers seventy years later. The big question is this: What was Fred Crisman really doing in Tacoma that summer?

JFK and the Octopus

The UFO sightings by Kenneth Arnold and E. J. Smith were only two of dozens in the Pacific Northwest, and literally hundreds across the country, in June and July, 1947. On June 24 alone, *seventeen* reports of UFOs eventually surfaced in the Northwest from Boise, Idaho, to Bellingham, Washington.

Crisman's behavior after Dahl's UFO sighting was odd, to say the least. And what conceivable path could lead him from the first flap of the modern UFO era to the Kennedy assassination?

In 1967, Harold Dahl authored an odd addendum to the Crisman chronicle in a note to UFO researcher Gary Leslie:

> There is a TV series running now that I swear is based in the main on the life of F. Lee Crisman. I know him better than any living man and I know of some of the incredible adventures he has passed through in the last twenty years. I do not mean that his life has been that of this TV hero on *The Invaders* show…but there are parts of it that I swear were told to me years ago by Mr. Crisman…and I know of several that are too wild to be believed… even by the enlightened attitude of 1967.[122]

Dahl made Crisman sound like the mysterious Cigarette Smoking Man from *The X-Files*. This may have been by design. Crisman may even have written Dahl's letter himself[123] to divert attention from what he was really doing in the Seattle area after World War II.

> [Crisman's] involvement with Maury Island may have had to do with covering up top-secret radar-fogging discs or the dumping of

nuclear waste from the nearby Hanford plutonium reactor. Crisman wanted people to believe the [UFO] scenario, however. In early 1968, he corresponded with well-known UFO researcher Lucius Farish as the contact person for a group he called Parapsychology Research, under the pseudonym Fred Lee. The alias, which only dropped his last name, provided Crisman with a means to discuss himself in the third person, telling Farish: "Mr. Crisman is probably the most informed man in the United States on UFOs and also one of the hardest to find—as the FBI has learned several times."[124]

Even more bizarre is Fred Crisman's link to another far-reaching conspiracy, "the Octopus." This was the name given by investigative journalist Danny Casolaro to a network of shadowy groups that overlapped the intelligence community, global bankers, the military-industrial complex, and the theft of powerful case management software called PROMIS by the Justice Department during the Reagan administration. Central to Casolaro's investigation was an electronics and computer expert named Michael Riconosciuto, who claimed he'd modified PROMIS at the request of a friend of former Attorney General Ed Meese to allow secret, back-door access by the government.

As it happens, Crisman worked for a Tacoma advertising agency owned by Riconosciuto's father, Marshall, thus linking the earliest UFO sightings of the modern era, the Kennedy assassination, and major figures in the Iran-Contra scandal, the October Surprise, the savings and loan crisis of the '80s and '90s, and other global conspiracies too convoluted to get into here.

To give you a hint of the type of games being played: Casolaro was found dead, his wrists brutally slashed, in a motel room in August 1991. His death was officially ruled suicide.[125] Riconosciuto was convicted early the next year of seven drug-related charges and given a minimum twenty-year sentence,[126] in spite of his claim that the video evidence presented by the prosecution was faked. As of this writing in August 2017, Riconosciuto is still being held at a federal detention center in Seattle.

Special Agent Guy Banister

Back to Fred Crisman: As strange as his story is, he wasn't the only spook linked to early UFO accounts and the Kennedy assassination. You see, the FBI agent who filed the SM-X report on the Maury Island case was Special Agent Guy Banister.[127]

Banister is well known to JFK assassination researchers. He retired from the FBI in 1954 and, after a stint with the New Orleans police department, set up a private detective agency that may have served as a front to supply weapons used by Cuban exiles in 1961's disastrous Bay of Pigs invasion.[128] Banister's mistress later said she was present when he advised Lee Harvey Oswald to set up a local pro-Castro Fair Play for Cuba Committee office in the same building as Banister's agency.[129]

In the 1940s, during the first wave of the modern UFO era, Guy Banister served as the Special Agent in Charge of the FBI's Butte, Montana field office, which had jurisdiction over several western states. Declassified FBI documents obtained through FOIA requests include several telexes marked SM-X sent by Banister from Butte to Washington, D.C., all related to UFO sightings.[130]

The assassination of John F. Kennedy had fingerprints of the intelligence community all over it. But what were they doing with UFO reports back in the '40s? And why has the involvement of American intelligence agencies (and presumably those of other nations) continued to the present day?

Joint Security Control and ETI PSYOPs

The key question is *cui bono*—who benefits? For example, the Roswell crash: Either it was an extraterrestrial craft (note: the authors don't think so) or it was an advanced project being developed by the U.S. military. Either way, it did *not* benefit the government of the United States to tell the truth. If it was an ETI, then the United States certainly didn't want to share the technology it might harvest from an alien spaceship with other nations; if it was a secret military project, then for sure the Pentagon didn't want Russia to know about it—especially if Nazi scientists smuggled into America via Operation Paperclip were involved.[131]

Deception in war is a very old art, going back at least to the time of the great Chinese military strategist Sun Tzu. During the Second World War, the Pentagon created a task force called Joint Security Command to preserve secrecy around planned military operations.

> Joint Security Control (JSC) was founded during WW2 as the US deception planning counterpart to the British deception organization knows as the London Controlling Section (LCS). Together, JSC and LCS perfected the art of strategic wartime deception, initially in North Africa but then throughout the theater of the European war, including the deception planning that contributed to the success of D-Day....
>
> In May of 1947, JSC received a revised charter, one that authorized it to continue its deception mission not just under wartime conditions but also during times of peace. JSC was tasked with preventing important military information from falling into the hands of the enemy, to control classified information through proper security classification, to correlate, maintain and disseminate all of the information furnished to JSC by the War and Navy Department Bureau of Public Relations, and finally the very important mission of cover and deception planning and implementation.[132]

Note that the JSC's revised charter was issued less than two months before the UFO outbreak of June–July 1947, which included the Roswell crash. A declassified FBI memo dated July 21, 1947, related how a Colonel Carl Goldbranson of the War Department's Intelligence Division had sent a telegram on July 5 to Army Air Force Major Paul Gaynor, a public relations officer, advising him to contact "[blacked out] Illinois who may have important information concerning [UFOs'] origin."[133]

Major Gaynor had been quoted in a United Press story dated July 3 as saying the AAF had dropped its investigation into flying saucers because of a lack of concrete evidence.[134]

Independent researcher and author James Carrion, a former international director of the Mutual UFO Network, a former signals intelligence analyst for the U.S. Army, and an IT manager, has established that Col. Goldbranson was a member of the JSC since at least 1943, specifically working on "Cover, Deception, and Task Force Security."[135] The July 21 memo is important because it documents that a member of a military unit responsible for strategic deception, operating just below the Joint Chiefs of Staff, had asked the FBI to investigate UFO reports.

And thus we have Guy Banister sending telexes marked SM-X to J. Edgar Hoover.

If, as we believe, the ET hypothesis is the least likely explanation for the wave of modern UFO sightings that began in the summer of 1947, then the motives of intelligence agencies to spin a compelling cover story become more clear. Blaming odd lights and strange shapes in the sky on an extraterrestrial intelligence gets curious eyes looking at a target as far removed from the government as one can get. Is it better for the government for the public to believe that we're being visited by ETIs or for word to get around about tests on a new supersonic fighter/bomber/drone?

The Paul Bennewitz Affair

Cases like the Paul Bennewitz affair, where a businessman whose company supplied equipment to the U.S. Air Force was fed bogus information by an agent of the Air Force Office of Special Investigations to convince him that the Earth was being colonized by aliens working from an underground base near Dulce, New Mexico, only highlight the impact the intelligence community has had on the UFO phenomenon over the last seventy years.

Bennewitz was a physicist by training. He lived in New Mexico within sight of Kirtland Air Force Base, home to the Manzano Nuclear Weapons

Storage Facility, and Sandia National Labs, a research site that mainly tests non-nuclear components of nuclear weapons.

In the late 1970s, Bennewitz became convinced that the strange lights in the sky over Kirtland were the advance team of a race of hostile aliens preparing to invade. He began using his skills as a physicist and an inventor to monitor strange radio emissions from Kirtland.

More significantly, he began writing letters to people that he thought should know what was happening in New Mexico. This brought him to the attention of the United States government and its military. Apparently, there was concern that someone as bright as Bennewitz might unintentionally expose something the Pentagon didn't want the Kremlin to know. And thus, the Air Force Office of Special Investigations got involved.[136]

Having learned the essential parts of Bennewitz's theories— very ironically from the man himself, by actually breaking into his home while he was out and checking his files and research notes—that aliens were mutilating cattle as part of some weird medical experiment; that they were abducting American citizens and implanting them with devices for purposes unknown; that those same aliens were living deep underground in a secure fortress at Dulce, New Mexico; and that we were all very soon going to be in deep and dire trouble as a direct result of the presence of this brewing, intergalactic threat, the Air Force gave Bennewitz precisely what he was looking for – confirmation that his theories were all true, and more.

Of course, this was all just a carefully-planned ruse to bombard Bennewitz with so much faked UFO data in the hope that it would steer him away from the classified military projects of a non-UFO nature that he had uncovered. And, indeed, it worked.

When Bennewitz received conformation (albeit carefully controlled and utterly fabricated confirmation) that, yes, he had stumbled upon the horrible truth and that, yes, there really was an alien base deep below Dulce, the actions of the Intelligence community had the desired effect: Bennewitz became increasingly paranoid and unstable, and he began looking away from Kirtland (the hub of the secrets that had to be kept) and harmlessly towards the vicinity of Dulce, where his actions, research, and theories could be carefully controlled and manipulated by the Government.[137]

No, Virginia, there is no underground alien base at Dulce. It's a government PSYOP. (Or rather, a MISO—Military Intelligence Support Operation is now the preferred term.) Paul Bennewitz was gaslighted by the AFOSI with the help of prominent ufologist William Moore, co-author of the first major book on the Roswell phenomenon, 1980's *The Roswell Incident*. Moore admitted to his role in the Bennewitz affair in a presentation to the 1989 MUFON national convention, but he justified it by claiming he'd used the opportunity to search for information that might expose government knowledge about the alien origin of UFOs—to work as a double agent, in other words.[138]

Oddly enough, this revelation served to reinforce the faith of true believers in the ETI meme. The government wouldn't try to discredit a prominent ufologist like Paul Bennewitz if he wasn't on to something, would they?

Yes, but what Bennewitz was onto had more to do with Russians than aliens. And the government deception worked beautifully. Not only did it distract attention from whatever the Air Force wanted to keep hidden at Kirtland AFB, it established the Dulce base as a fixture in UFO lore.

To be blunt, the UFO research community has assisted this deception by being willing dupes. The low standard of evidence required for wide acceptance makes it easy for stories like the Dulce base to spread. French researcher Jacques Vallee illustrated this point in his 1991 book *Revelations: Alien Contact and Human Deception*.

"Why doesn't anybody know about [Dulce]?" I asked.

"It's underground, hidden in the desert. You can't see it."

"How large is it?"

"The size of Manhattan."

"Who takes out the garbage?"

The group looked at me in shock. There is a certain unwritten etiquette one is supposed to follow when crashed saucers and government secrecy are discussed; you must not ask where the information comes from, because informants' lives would be in danger, presumably from hired assassins paid by the Pentagon, the kind who try to hit the tires of fully-loaded gasoline trucks speeding through refineries. And you are *not* supposed *to point out contradictions in the stories*. Questions must always be directed at the higher topics, such as the philosophy of the aliens, or their purpose in the universe—not the practical details of their existence. In other words, *it is not done* to ask any question that has a plain, verifiable answer.[139]

What about contactees and abductees? Surely, not all their cases are fake. True enough. But it appears most of their stories stem from emotional or psychological issues that have nothing to do with the existence of ETIs.

Abductees Receive No Assistance

As Jack Brewer documents in his book *The Greys Have Been Framed: Exploitation in the UFO Community*, accounts obtained from abductees under hypnosis are unreliable, to put it mildly. Hypnosis is not a trustworthy method of retrieving memories, and may actually be harmful.[140] Sadly, as Brewer notes:

Traumatized individuals are then at risk of sustaining deeper emotional damage while failing to seek qualified professional treatment. Such professional treatment is often discouraged within the UFO community in lieu of compiling so-called evidence of fantastic encounters with extraterrestrials.[141]

Contactees may have various reasons for concocting stories of ETI encounters from just wanting to feel special to out-and-out delusions resulting from psychosis. But treatment comes second to hearing new "evidence" of ET's existence.

The intelligence community doesn't have to work very hard to push the ETI meme. The UFO community is doing just fine with that on its own.

Now, there are, without question, cases that can't be explained away as delusions, hoaxes, or intelligence ops. Joe Jordan, co-founder of CE4 Research Group and MUFON's National Director for South Korea, has compiled hundreds of accounts of "alien" abductions that have been stopped by victims who called on the name of Jesus. And, according to Jordan, this happens consistently. Now, why would that be, if the abductors were, say, aliens from Zeta Reticuli? The logical answer, if one is open to a supernatural explanation, is that the alien abduction phenomenon is primarily *spiritual*—in other words, demonic.

But that isn't an answer the UFO community wants to hear, either, which is why Jordan calls it "the unwanted piece of the UFO puzzle."[142]

Are the Collins Elite Another PSYOP?

For all the interest in ETIs and the continuing popularity of science fiction in pop culture, there is no concrete evidence that actual extraterrestrials are visiting Earth, if they exist at all. So why the deception? In part, spooks and military men find it a useful cover for things they'd rather not tell the rest of us. On a spiritual level, there is a darker agenda.

In 2010, researcher and author Nick Redfern published *Final Events and the Secret Government Group on Demonic UFOs and the Afterlife*, which he calls "probably my most controversial book to date."[143] It tells the story of an interdepartmental think tank inside the United States government nicknamed the Collins Elite. The group, according to Redfern's source, had been tasked with analyzing the UFO phenomenon, and it reached a disturbing conclusion: UFOs aren't extraterrestrial, they're demonic. Worse, the Collins Elite reportedly believe "the phenomenon 'feeds' upon a poorly understood form of energy contained in the human soul. In other words, we are being reared, nurtured, and finally digested, just like cattle."[144]

Furthermore, the "aliens" anticipated that discerning Christians might ID them for what they are, and they've countered that development by quietly manipulating the ETI disclosure movement to make those believers look foolish by convincing the public that extraterrestrial life is real. Members of the Collins Elite reportedly settled on an odd strategy for dealing with the crisis—establishing a Christian theocracy in America. Somehow, imposing pharisaical laws on the country would turn the global tide against the infernal, soul-sucking entities.[145]

Just how that's supposed to work isn't explained. Redfern can be excused, as he admits to being agnostic on matters spiritual, but if the story of the Collins Elite is true—and bear in mind that Redfern's sources, as he admits, are mainly secret informants—then the U.S. government is in serious need of people who have opened a Bible at least once in their lives.

In my mind, the most disturbing thing about the book is that highly-placed insiders within the intelligence community could think so poorly—especially if they are Christians.…

What is the theological logic of this? That if the ruling elite are Christians, the demons will be powerless? Or that if a majority of U.S. citizens are Christians, then God can or will act? (This makes God capricious to say the least ["I won't intervene against evil unless enough humans measure up"] or powerless to act unilaterally ["I cannot intervene against evil unless enough humans measure up"]). You can have that God. And how small-minded is this approach—to presume that the fate of humanity lies in the hands of the Church in the United States? What a muddled theological mess.[146]

But maybe that was the point of putting out the story of the Collins Elite. As Redfern notes elsewhere, the United States government has been thinking about how to use religious ideas as propaganda for a long time.[147] A 1950 RAND Corporation report commissioned by the Air Force, "The Exploitation of Superstitions for Purposes of Psychological Warfare," details examples of how closely held beliefs were manipulated by operatives for various governments.[148] The RAND report appeared just as the UFO phenomenon hit its stride in the U.S.

Predictably, the publication of *Final Events* seeded the notion among skeptics and atheists that evangelical Christians are willing to use the UFO phenomenon to justify "a concentration camp vision of America based in ancient Jewish law."[149] Those opposed to such a view of America's future will probably be hostile to anything that looks like it moves the ball toward that goal line.

Now, since you're reading this book, the odds are that you, like the authors, laugh out loud at the idea that Christians are going to take over this or any other national government anytime soon. Look at the culture around us, then ask yourself: Is this a society that's going to vote a truly godly government into power? Not into office, into *power*.[150]

When we analyze the story of the Collins Elite, which serves as an appropriate summary of the seventy-year history of the modern UFO phenomenon, the most likely explanation is this: Once again, human agents for the principalities and powers arrayed against humanity carried out an op to use ETI disclosure to advance the kingdom of darkness.

chapter seven

THE NINE AND OTHER GODS FROM SPACE

WITHOUT A DOUBT, *Star Trek* has been one of the most influential entertainment franchises in history. Kirk, Spock, McCoy, Scotty, and others are iconic characters recognized around the world. Oddly enough, though, through the series creator Gene Roddenberry, the starship *Enterprise* is linked to CIA mind-control experiments, a group of "aliens" who claim to be the creators of humanity, and—here we go again—the assassination of John F. Kennedy.

Andrija Puharich

Let's back up to World War 2. During the war, Andrija Puharich, the son of immigrants from the Balkans, attended Northwestern University outside Chicago, where he earned a bachelor's degree in philosophy in 1942 and his M.D. in 1947. Through an invitation from a well-off family friend, who'd married into the Borden dairy family, Puharich found himself in Maine in early 1948, where he established a research institute to pursue his interest in parapsychology, the Round Table Foundation of Electrobiology, usually shortened to the Round Table.[151]

An early member of the Puharich Round Table was Aldous Huxley, author of *Brave New World* and *The Doors of Perception*, a book about his experiences with mescaline (and the book that inspired rock singer Jim Morrison to name his band The Doors). Puharich financed his research with gifts from donors, one of whom was Henry Wallace, who'd been vice president under Franklin D. Roosevelt. Wallace, a 32nd-degree Freemason, persuaded Roosevelt to add the reverse of the Great Seal of the United States—the pyramid and the all-seeing eye—to the dollar bill.[152]

This book isn't big enough to hold a full account of what Puharich was up to for the U.S. Army in the 1950s,[153] but the upshot is that he was apparently researching parapsychology and chemical substances that might stimulate the human mind to reach into realities beyond those we can normally perceive with our natural senses. And at one of his gatherings in Maine, on New Year's Eve in 1952, Puharich and his Round Table, working with a Hindu channeler named Dr. D. G. Vinod, conducted a seance that apparently made contact with something calling itself The Nine.[154] Thus began a truly breathtaking chapter in America's mostly hidden programs that searched for ways to weaponize the occult.

> Some months later, on June 27, 1953, the night of the full moon, Puharich gathered around him what was to be a core group of the Round Table Foundation for another session with Vinod. The membership of this group of nine members—á la The Nine—is illuminating. Henry Jackson, Georgia Jackson, Alice Bouverie, Marcella Du Pont, Carl Betz, Vonnie Beck, Arthur Young, Ruth Young, and Andrija Puharich. Dr. Vinod acted as the medium.
>
> Imagine the Fellowship of the Ring, with government funding and a security classification that was, well, "cosmic."[155]

This group included old money—*very* old money. The Du Pont name is obvious, but some of the others were no less prominent. Alice Bouverie was an Astor—a descendent of John Jacob Astor and the daughter of Col. John Jacob Astor IV, who built the Astoria Hotel and went down with the Titanic. Arthur Young was the designer of the Bell helicopter; his wife had been born Ruth Forbes. Yes, *that* Forbes.

Ruth's previous marriage had been to another old-money family that traced its roots back to the early days of the American colonies, George Lyman Paine. Their son, Michael Paine, married a woman named Ruth Hyde, and in 1963, Michael and Ruth Paine became friends with a young couple newly arrived from Russia, Lee and Marina Oswald.

Yes, *that* Lee Oswald. Lee Harvey.

So. A Du Pont, an Astor, and a Forbes/Paine, in a psychic research group funded by the U.S. government, communicating with…what?

And what was the monkey god doing there?

Dr. Vinod sat on the floor, the nine members of the group in a circle around him, with a copper plate on his lap, prayer beads in his hands, and a small statue of "Hanoum," a Hindu god that the author believes to be Hanuman, the Monkey King. If this is so, it is interesting in that Hanuman was a human being, a minister, before becoming divine due to his devotion and courage. The half-human, half-divine image is one that becomes more important and more obvious as this study progresses. Another important aspect of Hanuman is his depiction in much Indian art as holding an entire mountain in one hand (and a club in the other). When—in the Ramayana and during the battle of Rama and Ravana—Lakshmana was mortally wounded, Hanuman raced to a mountain covered with different healing herbs. Not knowing which one Lakshmana required, Hanuman simply brought the entire mountain. Hanuman—as well as his fellow monkey-men, the Vanaras of southern India—is often shown with his hand in front of his mouth, signifying "silence" as well as obedience, in much the same way western occultists depict Harpocrates. In this sense, replete with silence, obedience, a club, and a mountain of herbs, Hanuman might easily have been the patron saint of MK-ULTRA.[156]

What an interesting, um, coincidence. Remember that Aleister Crowley believed *The Book of the Law* was dictated to him by Aiwass, the messenger of Hoor-Paar-Kraat—Harpocrates.

Anyway, The Nine disclosed that they wanted the Round Table to lead a spiritual renewal on Earth, and eventually revealed that they were extraterrestrials orbiting the planet in a giant, invisible spacecraft.

Riiiight.

Still, consider that the group assembled that night included highly intelligent, very successful people. Puharich later wrote, "We took every known precaution against fraud, and the staff and I became thoroughly convinced that we were dealing with some kind of an extraordinary extraterrestrial intelligence."[157] In other words, if this was a hoax, it worked on some very smart people.

On the other hand, the decades-long career of Andrija Puharich suggests that it may also have been a case of "leading the witnesses," in a sense. He appears to have been a seeker who, like Fox Mulder in *The X-Files*, really wanted to believe.

But it was more than that. The Nine declared, "God is nobody else than we together, the Nine Principles of God."[158]

So extraterrestrial *and* divine. Remember that while the Round Table was hearing from The Nine, Aleister Crowley's acolyte Kenneth Grant was developing his occult system based on an ET god from Sirius.

The Nine, Fifteen Years Later

Dr. Vinod returned to India a short time later, and contact with The Nine was interrupted for more than fifteen years. Then, in 1971, Puharich discovered Israeli psychic Uri Geller.

Geller, best known for his alleged power to bend silverware with his mind, became for a time the new link to The Nine. Through Geller, The

Nine informed Puharich that his life's mission was "to alert the world to an imminent mass landing of spaceships that would bring representatives of The Nine."[159]

Well, that didn't happen. And Geller decided to move on in 1973, so Puharich had to find someone else to bridge the gap between Earth and the giant, invisible craft allegedly orbiting the globe. He eventually connected with former race-car driver Sir John Whitmore and Florida psychic Phyllis Schlemmer. She became the authorized spokesperson for their contact within The Nine, an entity who identified himself as "Tom."[160]

Puharich, Whitmore and Schlemmer then set up Lab Nine at Puharich's estate in Ossining, New York. The Nine's disciples included multi-millionaire businessmen (many hiding behind pseudonyms and including members of Canada's richest family, the Bronfmans), European nobility, scientists from the Stamford Research Institute and at least one prominent political figure who was a personal friend of President Gerald Ford.[161]

A member of Lab Nine in 1974 and '75 was *Star Trek* creator Gene Roddenberry, who reportedly wrote a screenplay based on The Nine. Some suggest that concepts from the channeling sessions Roddenberry attended surfaced in the early *Star Trek* movies and in the series *Star Trek: The Next Generation* and *Star Trek: Deep Space Nine*.

Big surprise there, right?

Before Lab Nine folded in 1978, the identities of Tom and the Other Eight were finally revealed: Tom was Atum,[162] he said, the creator of the Great Ennead, the Egyptian gods worshipped at Heliopolis, near modern-day Cairo. Besides Atum, the Ennead included his children Shu and Tefnut; their children Geb and Nut; and their children Osiris, Isis, Set, Nephthys, and sometimes the son of Osiris and Isis, Horus.[163]

Connecting dots between Andrija Puharich, who was almost certainly a CIA asset during much of the time he conducted parapsychological research,[164] and the volunteers of his Round Table and Lab Nine, we can link the United States government (and specifically the U.S. Army and CIA during the period of mind-control research projects like BLUEBIRD and MKULTRA),[165] members of upper-class society from the East Coast and Canada, the creator of the most successful science fiction entertainment franchise in history, extraterrestrials, and gods. And not just any gods—the pantheon that included the chaos god, Set, who Crowleyite Kenneth Grant believed was the spirit of the age.

Oh, yes—and the Kennedy assassination.

How do we wrap our heads around this? Considering that Puharich was likely doing this research for the government and that he led the witnesses, suggesting to Geller and at least one of his successors while they were under hypnosis that they were being contacted by The Nine,[166] it appears that this was a long PSYOP to stir up belief in the existence of ETIs and the return of the old gods.

To what end? For Puharich and his superiors, maybe it was an experiment into group dynamics, or maybe a test of how people would react to the imminent arrival of extraterrestrial visitors. Or maybe, as with the Paul Bennewitz case, it was an intelligence op to misdirect the wealthy members of Lab Nine and their social circles toward an ETI explanation for any unexplained aerial phenomena and away from secret government projects.

What Should Be Our Goal?

As Christians, we must look past the human actors in movements like these. In the case of The Nine, how did their charade benefit the entities that spoke to Vinod, Geller, and Schlemmer? Frankly, it's difficult to identify a specific goal other than spreading spiritual confusion. Certainly, seeding these ideas through influential members of high society and the military-industrial complex would be one way to do it. It's one thing to mock Blue-collar Bubba when he claims aliens from Sirius are about to land, but it's a different story when the one spreading the ET gospel is from one of the wealthiest families in the world or a successful industrialist who's proven to be a productive member of society.

But spreading confusion about the Big Questions—where we came from, why we are here, and where we go when we die—may be enough for the principalities, powers, thrones, and dominions. See, the rebellious gods don't care what you believe as long as it's not this: Jesus is the way, and the truth, and the life, and no one comes to the Father except through Him.[167]

And for the record: He's not from Sirius.

chapter eight

PODESTA'S ETI WIKILEAKS

ANCIENT RELIGIONS AND modern science fiction are not the only factors influencing the movement for official disclosure. Not surprisingly, we see a great deal of influence through politics. In recent history, possibly even more than any other time, the discussion has become mainstream among presidential candidates and political circles of all kinds.

Many strange and unexpected events occurred during the presidential race between Donald Trump and Hillary Clinton in 2016. Secret recordings were released. Emails were deleted. Insults and rumors were thrown around by all. Even more, the term "Wikileaks" became a commonly used word across the country.

The website wikileaks.org became the central hub to release hacked emails belonging to members of the Democratic party. These emails covered a wide variety of topics and were examined and scrutinized on a near-daily basis. Most of the more popular emails discussed everything from political strategies to personal issues to even unfavorable feelings of certain Democrats toward Hillary Clinton. Through Wikileaks, average

Americans were able to get hold of these emails, which led to one of the most infamous scandal allegations of all time: #Pizzagate.

There were others emails, however, that flew a bit more below the radar. Some researchers deemed them too crazy to deal with. Others took them incredibly seriously, yet did not have a large outlet such as news media at their disposal. These were the ETI emails concerning John Podesta, the official disclosure of the government's UFO documents, and the push for an admission from the U.S. government of the legitimacy of the UFO phenomenon.

Who Is John Podesta?

John Podesta

John Podesta, a self-identified Catholic who works closely with Catholics in Alliance for the Common Good and Catholics United, is the former chairman of the 2016 Hillary Clinton presidential campaign. Prior to that, he served as chief of staff to President Bill Clinton and counselor to President Barack Obama. Podesta is an honorary patron of the University Philosophical Society (aka "The Phil"). He also was the U.S. representative to the U.N. High-Level Panel in the Post-2015 Development Agenda.[168] This is a process led by the United Nations to define the future global development framework that will succeed the current Millennium Development Goals (MDGs). The MDGs contain eight globally agreed-upon goals in specific areas:

- Poverty alleviation
- Education
- Gender equality
- Empowerment of women
- Child and maternal health

- Environmental sustainability
- Reducing HIV/AIDS and communicable diseases
- Building a global partnership for development[169]

In 2013, the High Level Panel on the Post-2015 Development Agenda released a report entitled "A New Global Partnership: Eradicate Poverty and Transform Economies through Sustainable Development," which describes a universal agenda to eradicate extreme poverty worldwide by 2030 and fulfill the promise of sustainable development.[170] This report calls on the entire world to rally around a "New Global Partnership" offering hope and a specific role for every person in the world. In order to achieve this goal, the report calls for the post-2015 goals to drive five large transformative shifts:

1. Leave No One Behind: After 2015 we should move from reducing to ending extreme poverty, in all its forms. We should ensure that no person—regardless of ethnicity, gender, geography, disability, race or other status—is denied basic economic opportunities and human rights.
2. Put Sustainable Development at the Core: We have to integrate the social, economic and environmental dimensions of sustainability. We must act now to slow the alarming pace of climate change and environmental degradation, which pose unprecedented threats to humanity.
3. Transform Economies for Jobs and Inclusive Growth: A profound economic transformation can end extreme poverty and improve livelihoods, by harnessing innovation, technology, and the potential of business. More diversified economies, with equal opportunities for all, can drive social inclusion, especially for young people, and foster sustainable consumption and production patterns.
4. Build Peace and Effective, Open and Accountable Institutions for All: Freedom from conflict and violence is the most fundamental human entitlement, and the essential foundation for building

peaceful and prosperous societies. At the same time, people the world over expect their governments to be honest, accountable, and responsive to their needs. We are calling for a fundamental shift—to recognize peace and good governance as a core element of well-being, not an optional extra.

5. Forge a New Global Partnership: A new spirit of solidarity, cooperation, and mutual accountability must underpin the post-2015 agenda. This new partnership should be based on a common understanding of our shared humanity, based on mutual respect and mutual benefit. It should be centered on people, including those affected by poverty and exclusion, women, youth, the aged, disabled persons, and indigenous peoples. It should include civil society organizations, multilateral institutions, local and national governments, the scientific and academic community, businesses, and private philanthropy.

Hansjorg Wyss

Along with the efforts consistent with a globalist agenda, Podesta also earned $90,000 in 2013 as a consultant to the Hansjorg Wyss Foundation (or HJW Foundation), the private foundation of billionaire Hansjorg Wyss, who creates and funds bioengineering institutions in America and Switzerland. Wyss also became the CEO of Synthes, an industry giant specializing in making plates and screws to stabilize broken bones.

In 2009, the U.S. attorney in Philadelphia accused Synthes of running illegal clinical trial and human experimentation. Between 2002 and 2004, Synthes had tested a product called Norian XR, a cement with the ability to turn into bone when injected into the human skeleton. The FDA explicitly told Synthes not to promote Norian for certain spine surgeries, but the company decided to ignore the FDA and continue anyway. At least five patients who had Norian injected into their spines died on the operating-room table. Interviews with more than twenty former employees and surgeons involved in the Norian project, hundreds of pages of court transcripts, and company documents submitted in the case reveal that Synthes not only disregarded multiple warnings, but also ignored scientists' cautions stating the cement could cause fatal blood clots.[171] This all occurred prior to Podesta accepting a consultant position at the HJW Foundation.

In 1995, John Podesta was of major influence in a process resulting in President Bill Clinton signing Executive Order 12958, which created new standards for the process of classifying documents within the government. This led to a massive and successful effort to declassify over eight hundred million pages of historically valuable records. One outcome of this was the government's 1995 admission of its over-twenty-year involvement in funding highly classified and special-access programs in remote viewing. The effort also focused on classified UFO records.

Podesta has openly opposed the excessive use of secrecy and classification within the government. In a 2004 speech at Princeton University, he condemned what he called the U.S.' "excessive government secrecy" and "bloated secrecy bureaucracy."[172] Podesta has been a long-time advocate for the disclosure of UFO files by the government. He has supported petitions to the government to release files related to the UFO phenomenon. In 2002 at a news conference organized by the Coalition for Freedom of Information, he was quoted as saying, "It is time for the government to declassify records that are more than 25 years old and to provide scientists with data that will assist in determining the real nature of this phenomenon."[173] As Wikileaks revealed in clearer detail, one of John Podesta's main motivations is the goal of the official disclosure of UFOs along with supposed current extraterrestrial contact with human beings.

The Players in the Emails

During her campaign for president of the United States, Hillary Clinton offered an odd promise concerning UFOs. In January 2016, to answer a reporter's question regarding UFOs during a meeting with the *Conway Daily Sun*, Clinton stated she would "get to the bottom of it."[174] The article from the publication reported that Clinton had answered the reporter's question with enthusiasm. CNN, however, ran a similar story with the headline, "Hillary Clinton (jokingly) pledges UFO probe."[175] The article continues to state that Clinton was only joking when she pledged to look into UFOs, even calling it a "tongue-in-cheek" response. In contrast, however, a *New York Times* article stated:

> Mrs. Clinton has vowed that barring any threats to national security, she would open up government files on the subject, a shift from President Obama, who typically dismisses the topic as a joke.… Mrs. Clinton, a cautious candidate who often bemoans being the subject of Republican conspiracy theories, has shown surprising ease plunging into the discussion of the possibility of extraterrestrial beings.[176]

Perhaps the reason CNN claimed it was a joke was due to the conspiratorial nature of UFOs and the fear of being associated with what, to some, are considered "Republican conspiracy theories."

In any event, it would seem Clinton actually does take the topic of UFOs seriously. She was even familiar enough with the topic to correct Jimmy Kimmel in a late-night television interview. When Kimmel asked Hillary Clinton about UFOs, she said, "You know, there's a new name. It's unexplained aerial phenomenon, UAP; that's the latest nomenclature."[177] Joseph G. Buchman, who was a key organizer and moderator for the 2013 Citizen Hearing on Disclosure in Washington, D.C., said, "Hillary has embraced this issue with an absolutely unprecedented level of interest in American politics."[178]

Hillary Clinton's campaign chairman, John Podesta, wrote in his foreword for the book, *UFOs: Generals, Pilots and Government Officials Go on the Record*, written by investigative journalist Leslie Kean and released in

2010, "The time to pull back the curtain on the topic is long overdue." When Podesta left the White House in 2015 during the Obama administration, he posted on Twitter:

> Finally, my biggest failure of 2014: Once again not securing the #disclosure of the U.F.O. files. #thetruthisstilloutthere

Podesta's interest in official disclosure concerning UFOs was made even more public with his leaked emails through WikiLeaks. Podesta's leaks showed multiple emails from Dr. Edgar Mitchell (1940–2016), Apollo 14 astronaut and sixth man on the moon, detailing plans and requesting meetings with Podesta concerning UFO disclosure. Also included in these emails are Terri Mansfield, whom Mitchell described as his "Catholic colleague," and Eryn Sepp, special assistant to the counselor to the President.

Edgar Mitchell

After retiring from his career with NASA in 1972, Edgar Mitchell explored his interests in consciousness and paranormal phenomena. In 1973, Mitchell founded the Institute of Noetic Sciences, whose stated goal is "to create a shift in consciousness worldwide—where people recognize that we are all part of an interconnected whole and are inspired to take action to help humanity and the planet thrive."[179] Concerning UFOs, Mitchell is quoted as saying he was "90 percent sure that many of the thousands of unidentified flying objects, or UFOs, recorded since the 1940s, belong to visitors from other planets."[180] Mitchell also founded Quantrek, an organization dedicated to research into zero-point energy and other areas of quantum physics toward the goal of discovering new energy sources. Concerning Quantrek, Mitchell is quoted as saying:

And on the other side of that is a newer effort, a different effort, a parallel effort, that I have undertaken having to do with the quantum hologram and the fact that we need new energy resources. There is a new organization called Quantrek, which is involved in the deeper, hard sciences of that effort, and parallel to what the Institute is doing with its transformation work.[181]

Terri Mansfield was the volunteer cofounder and executive director of the Arizona Department of Peace Campaign from 2003–2009, which

Terri Mansfield

supported the creation of a cabinet-level Department of Peace in Washington, D.C. It was hoped that this department would serve as an umbrella to support nonprofits already working to end violence in communities. On her website, Terri is described as such:

Terri Donovan Mansfield is the Executive Vice President for Fundraising in the Public Interest (FPI), founded by President and CEO Suzanne Mendelssohn, PhD, Earth's only ETI obedience healer as well as science intuitive for tau neutrino zero point energy (ZPE). Dr. Mendelssohn also has special experience in science, consciousness, theology, peacemaking, health care, poverty, race relations, justice for women, education, the environment, animal welfare, education, the arts. FPI partners exclusively with billionaire donors to support 501(c)(3) tax-deductible organizations working for planetary social change.[182]

Concerning her opinions about ETI and her connection with Mitchell and Podesta, Mansfield's website also states:

In addition, Terri is the Director of the ETI (Extraterrestrial Intelligence) Peace Task Force. The contiguous universe ETI are nonviolent, obedient to God, and superior to all celestials in our universe. In this capacity she worked closely with the late Apollo 14 astronaut Dr. Edgar Mitchell, with the intention of them meeting first with former White House Counsel John Podesta, then with President Obama on all ETI-related matters.[183]

Combining her Catholic faith with her beliefs in aliens, Mansfield describes her own opinion concerning the role of ETI in human life with this call to action for 2017:

2017, Year of Justice, & Obedience to God's 100% Nonviolent ETI

As we enter 2017, Year of Justice, excluded from our mission and envions are everyone and anyone who are not now in obedience to God.

Only those are included and invited to participate with us who are in obedience to God, facilitated by 100 % obedience to God's 100% therefore, nonviolent, ETI, extraterrestrial intelligence.

As a process of self-elimination, we work only with those ETI in the contiguous universe.

Over millions of years, our ETI have evolved to nonviolence, and oversee all celestials in our universe who are not yet 100% obedient to God.

It is a privilege to serve God while assisting our ETI to bring zero point energy to our planet.[184]

These beliefs, along with Mitchell's, are prevalent in their leaked emails to John Podesta. Of course, anyone can email anybody. Does merely receiving an email mean Podesta was involved in this way of thinking? Would this mean American policy regarding secrecy and disclosure was being formed through this type of worldview? Of course not. Merely receiving an email does not indicate any of those things. However, what if there was evidence showing that John Podesta may have met with Edgar Mitchel and Terri Mansfield after their emails were sent? If Mitchell and Mansfield expressed their views in an email and requested a meeting with Podesta, and if the request was granted, might this show that Podesta was at least partly on the same page toward achieving these efforts?

Podesta's Leaked Emails Concerning Meetings and ETI

On the surface, it would seem that official disclosure of UFO documents and knowledge would not be a bad thing. In fact, this author (Josh Peck) fully supports the idea. However, if official disclosure is ever achieved, through what worldview will it be filtered? Most likely, it will be filtered through the worldview of whoever is closest to and most influential within the disclosure movement itself. There could come a day when the government provides its citizens with information, but interpreting the information is something different. For example, if microbial life is found on the surface of Mars, a Christian might interpret it to mean that God's creation is more expansive than first thought. However, a believer in Ancient Astronaut Theory might interpret it as evidence showing that life on Earth came from outer space—specifically from aliens originating on another planet. These two interpretations are completely contrary to one another, yet are formed from the same facts.

Truthfully, factual evidence itself is never as influential to society as the interpretation of said evidence. My personal belief is that official disclosure by itself would not have as much of an impact on society as would the worldview of whoever is interpreting the facts for the rest of the world. We won't know who those people are until we get there; however, as of right now, people with government connections, such as John Podesta and the people he has ties with concerning official disclosure, would be the most likely candidates. Therefore, we can look at the worldview of these people to predict how the facts might be interpreted after official disclosure takes place. Thanks to WikiLeaks, we can gauge this worldview fairly accurately by examining Podesta's leaked emails.

On June 25, 2014, Rebecca Hardcastle Wright, who often acted as an intermediary between Mitchell and Eryn Sepp, forwarded this email to Sepp from Mitchell for John Podesta:

> *From:* Rebecca Hardcastle Wright [mailto:rhardcastlewright@ gmail.com]
> *Sent:* Wednesday, June 25, 2014 8:08 AM
> *To:* Sepp, Eryn
> *Subject:* Apollo Astronaut, Dr. Edgar Mitchell's, Request for Meeting to discuss Disclosure
> *Re: Apollo Astronaut, Dr. Edgar Mitchell's, Request for Meeting to discuss Disclosure*
>
> Dear John Podesta:
>   As we move into the last half of 2014, the need for extraterrestrial disclosure intensifies. Thank you for your kind consideration and response to my email.
>   This 4 July weekend I will meet with President Obama's friend, Ambassador Hamamoto, at the US Mission in Geneva during their Independence Day Celebration. While in Geneva I will also speak at the UN and the European Space Agency regarding why we must move forward with disclosure and specific programs such as manned moon missions, since some scientists and others are calling for moon colonization due to what they perceive is happening on Earth.
>   John, with this email I am requesting a conversation with you and President Obama regarding the next steps in extraterrestrial disclosure for the benefit of our country and our planet.
>   Fifty years ago Battelle, Brookings and RAND studies on

UFOs convinced the government to remove knowledge of the extraterrestrial presence from the citizens of our country. These organizations advised with their best information. However, today much, if not most, of the extraterrestrial reality they examined is known by our citizens. These organizations' resultant strategies and policies of 50 years ago no longer hold credibility or benefit.

Five decades of UFO information have dramatically shifted the public awareness of an extraterrestrial presence. And yet, our government is still operating from outdated beliefs and policies. These are detrimental to trust in government transparency, science, religion, and responsible citizenry embracing the next step in our country's space travel and research.

Three disclosure issues are prominent: 1) planet sustainability via next generation energies such as zero point energy, 2) galactic travel and research undertaken as an advanced species aware of the extraterrestrial presence, not as uninformed explorers who revert to colonialism and destruction and 3) the example of a confident, engaged government who respectfully regards the wisdom and intellect of its citizens as we move into space.

I respectfully receive your response to my request for conversation on disclosure.

[image: Image removed by sender.]

Warmest Regards,

Edgar D. Mitchell, ScD

Chief Science Officer & Founder, Quantrek

Apollo 14 astronaut

6th man to walk on the Moon

cc:

Rebecca Hardcastle Wright, PhD

Washington DC Representative, Quantrek

301-915-4660

To which Sepp replied:

On Fri, Jul 18, 204 at 12:42 PM, Sepp, Eryn <Eryn_M_Sepp@ who.eop.gov> wrote:

Received! Thanks Rebecca. Sorry for the delay—it's been a heck of a month.

John would likely take this meeting alone first before involving the President, so let me ask him if he can do this in August. He'll be in town Aug 11 – 22. Is Dr. Mitchell planning to be in town then?

Thanks,

Eryn

Eryn M. Sepp

Special Assistant to the Counselor to the President

202-456-1404

Eryn_M_Sepp@who.eop.gov

To which Wright replied:

From: rhardcastlewright@gmail.com
To: Eryn_M_Sepp@who.eop.gov, john.podesta@gmail.com
Date: 2014-07-29 13:53
Subject: Re: Apollo Astronaut, Dr. Edgar Mitchell's, Request for Meeting to discuss Disclosure

Dear Eryn:

Dr. Mitchell is available for a meeting with John Podesta the week of August 11, but will not be able to come to DC.

He would like me to attend the meeting and then we patch him in via skype.

Thanks for getting back to me on this with a date and time.

My phone is 301-915-4660.

Regards,

Rebecca

Rebecca Hardcastle Wright, PhD

Founder, Institute of Exoconsciousness

*Bridging Extraterrestrial Experience and Consciousness
Science*

Mobile: 301-915-4660   *Skype*:   rebecca.hardcastle.
wright

*WEBSITE <http://www.exoconsciousness.com/home.html>
BLOG <http://rebeccahardcastlewright.com/>*

*FACEBOOK <https://www.facebook.com/exoconsciousness>
TWITTER <https://twitter.com/Exoconscious>
LINKEDIN <https://www.linkedin.com/in/exoconsciousness>
GOOGLE+ <https://plus.google.
com/+RebeccaHardcastleWright/posts>
YOUTUBE <https://www.youtube.com/channel/
UCiKhXXXp5NPLei0PLeZH7QA>*

According to this exchange, it seems that no meeting, at least in person, took place.[185] This was later confirmed by Rebecca Hardcastle Wright
herself on her own website.[186] However, in this case, the more interesting
issue isn't the meeting itself, but the *potential* for one.

Though no actual meeting can be proven to have taken place, it seems
John Podesta actually had an interest in meeting with Mitchell and Mansfield, but was unable to do so due to a scheduling conflict. This shows, at
least in the mind of Podesta, that these weren't merely a couple of random,
crazy people emailing him out of the blue. These were people with whom
Podesta saw a benefit in meeting. The topic of the meeting was no mystery
to Podesta, since Mitchell described in full what he intended to discuss in
the first email. Therefore, it would seem likely that there are shared beliefs
between Mitchell, Mansfield, and Podesta for the meeting to even be a
possibility, even to the point of setting dates and a location. In fact, it seems
that a correspondence toward setting up potential meetings was still going

on the following year. Here is an email from Terri Mansfield on behalf of Mitchell to John Podesta and Eryn Sepp dated January 16, 2015:[187]

From: terribillionairs@aol.com
To: john.podesta@gmail.com
CC: eryn_m_sepp@who.eop.gov, eryn.sepp@gmail.com
Date: 2015-01-16 13:38
Subject: email for John Podesta strategy (% Eryn) from Edgar Mitchell

Dear John,

In learning that you will leave the Administration next month to work with Hillary Clinton, I write to suggest that Hillary talk with President Obama after Terri Mansfield and I meet with you to discuss Zero Point Energy and Disclosure.

Best regards,
Edgar
Edgar D. Mitchell, ScD
Chief Science Officer & Founder, Quantrek
Apollo 14 astronaut
6th man to walk on the Moon

Here is another from 07-10-2015:[188]

From: terribillionairs@aol.com
To: esepp@equitablegrowth.org
CC: john.podesta@gmail.com
Date: 2015-07-10 23:21
Subject: FW: email for John Podesta (Eryn) from Edgar Mitchell re Skype

Hugs Eryn,

I called and left you a voice message today Friday.

On behalf of Dr. Mitchell, I would like to set up our Skype talk with John at his earliest convenience to discuss Disclosure.

Thank you for letting me know dates and times when he is available.

Love,

Terri

Terri Donovan Mansfield

602-885-9058 | <mailto:terribillionairs@aol.com> terribillionairs@aol.com

This is interesting, though a bit of the context is lost. By saying, "Thank you for letting me know dates and times when he is available," we cannot be sure if this means dates and times were already established, or if it is a thank you in advance with the assumption that dates and times would be sent in the near future. However, if we examine an email from a few weeks prior, we will see it said, "Thank you for giving me 3 dates and times when you are available to Skype with Terri Mansfield and me about Disclosure and ETI." Within this context, it lends evidence that dates and times for a meeting via Skype had already been sent. Of course, this could be, like the last one, a presumptive thank you. However, the fact that three dates are mentioned seems oddly specific for something merely assumed. Even more shocking than this is the content of the rest of the email:

From: Terri D. Mansfield [<mailto:terribillionairs@aol.com?> mailto:terribillionairs@aol.com]

Sent: Thursday, June 11, 2015 5:31 AM

To: <mailto:john.podesta@gmail.com> john.podesta@gmail. com

Cc:<mailto:esepp@equitablegrowth.org> esepp@ equitablegrowth.org; <mailto:eryn.sepp@gmail.com> eryn. sepp@gmail.com

Subject: email for John Podesta (Eryn) from Edgar Mitchell re Skype

Dear John,

In ongoing requests for our Skype talk to discuss Disclosure and the difference between our contiguous universe nonviolent obedient ETI and the celestials of this universe, and because Hillary and Bill Clinton were intimates of Laurance Rockefeller who had an avid interest in ETI, I direct your attention to Scott Jones, PhD.

In Scott's book Voices From the Cosmos, he describes himself as an octogenarian in full karmic payback made following 30 years in the military, half in combat arms and half in intelligence.

He references you in his ETI matter, as well as the Catholic Church.

Disclosure is now top priority for ETI itself in protection of the people.

Thank you for giving me 3 dates and times when you are available to Skype with Terri Mansfield and me about Disclosure and ETI.

Best regards,
Edgar
Edgar D. Mitchell, ScD
Apollo 14 astronaut
6th man to walk on the Moon
Zero Point Energy Consultant

PS My speaking in this 5+ minute video about the importance of Disclosure may help you understand our desire to speak with you.

<http://www.inquisitr.com/2150694/this-former-nasa-astronaut-shares-details-about-ufo-cover-ups-video/> http://www.inquisitr.com/2150694/this-former-nasa-astronaut-shares-details-about-ufo-cover-ups-video/

PPS I am now Zero Point Energy consultant to two organizations specializing in z.p.e.

Though this does indicate that dates and times were sent from Podesta/Sepp, it is still unclear whether an actual meeting, either online or in person, ever took place. At the end of the email, Mitchell sent a video clip from the documentary movie, *The Phoenix Lights, We Are Not Alone,* of himself talking about the importance of disclosure. It appears that Mitchell is sending it as an attempt to further convince John Podesta to meet with him, which might be evidence that a meeting had not yet taken place.

Also, more interesting than potential meetings, we get a glimpse into Mitchell's theology concerning ETI. From the email, we learn a few descriptions of the ETI themselves:

- They are from a contiguous universe rather than another planet.
- They are nonviolent, though this term is not defined (nonviolent as compared to what or whom?).
- They are obedient—but again, this is not defined (obedient regarding what authority?).
- They are different than the "celestials of this universe."

We also learn that disclosure is a top priority for ETI itself in protection of the people. However, from this email alone, what this means is a complete mystery.

To further examine Mitchell's beliefs concerning ETI and official disclosure, we can look to an email by Terri Mansfield, who seems to share the same beliefs as Mitchell. Keep in mind that unless it was merely a very specific thank you in advance, from the last email dated June 11, 2015, Mitchell indicates that Podesta/Sepp sent him three possible dates for a Skype call between Podesta, Mitchell, and Mansfield to discuss their beliefs about disclosure. The email we are going to look at next was sent a few months prior to this, on October 1, 2014. This is important to note, because it shows, after everything Mansfield stated in this next email, that John Podesta may have still been interested enough in a Skype call to send out three possible dates and times. In short, what Mansfield sent in 2014 did not scare off Podesta or make him think of Mitchell and Mansfield as lunatics. He received this email and, if dates and times were in fact sent, was intrigued at least enough to want to discuss the matter further. This helps show us what Podesta himself might believe about ETI and the role of official disclosure in the future:[189]

From: terribillionairs@aol.com
To: john.podesta@gmail.com, eryn_m_sepp@who.eop.gov, eryn.sepp@gmail.com
Date: 2014-10-01 09:35
Subject: email for John Podesta (% Eryn Sepp) from Apollo 14 astronaut Edgar Mitchell requesting meeting
RE: Apollo 14 Astronaut Edgar Mitchell requests meeting with John Podesta to discuss Disclosure.

Hugs Eryn,
    Dr. Edgar Mitchell asks that I write to Mr. Podesta and you requesting his meeting in Washington, DC with John to discuss Disclosure and zero point energy.
    As John is aware, more than 20 countries including the Vatican have released top secret papers discussing extraterrestrial incidents on Earth over many years. The US has NOT participated in Disclosure, yet.
    Attending the meeting with Dr. Mitchell will be the following:
    Mr. Dan Hill, Catholic philanthropist
    Dr. Michael Mansfield, Catholic retired Air Force Colonel
    Mrs. Terri Mansfield, Catholic consultant replacing Dr. Rebecca Wright for Dr. Mitchell in this matter.
    Because of his own background as a Catholic, we feel it is

imperative that John be aware of the Vatican's interest in ETI, Extraterrestrial Intelligence, and in sustainability for our planet.

The Vatican has hosted global seminars on the repercussions of humans interacting with ETI, and how this will affect religion and consciousness.

The Vatican's Observatory is located here in Arizona, and its top astronomers including Father Jose Funes and Brother Guy Consolmagno, who have met with Pope Francis, have publicly stated that God's creation could very well include OTHER intelligent life, and that would mean they are our "brothers."

We work with specific ETI from a contiguous universe. They are nonviolent and in complete obedience to God.

Our ETI's connection to zero point energy is obvious in that their purpose is to guide Edgar's international Quantrek science team to apply their zero point energy research for humanity, to move away from the use of fossil fuels which are so deleterious to our fragile planet. Quantrek's science intuitive, Dr. Suzanne Mendelssohn, also a practicing Catholic, advises the Quantrek team as to the specific Tau neutrino which is the foundation for zero point energy, something CERN scientists have begun to study, as well as scientists all over the planet.

Because of the recent demonstrations addressing the overwhelming issue of climate change, and President Obama's own concern, we feel the timing is perfect to meet with John to map out a plan involving Disclosure and zero point energy.

After having met with US Ambassador Pamela Hamamoto at the UN Mission in Geneva on July 4, Edgar announced to Swiss media that he intends to return to the moon on a space ship fueled by zero point energy at age 100, in 16 years.

Thank you for letting us know 3 possible dates and times for our meeting with John, so we can prepare travel logistics.

Love,
Terri

Terri Donovan Mansfield
Director: Quantrek ETI (Extraterrestrial Intelligence) Peace Task
Force,
Edgar D. Mitchell, ScD | Science Officer & Founder
602.885.9058 | terribillionairs@aol.com
<mailto:terribillionairs@aol.com>
On behalf of:
Edgar D. Mitchell, ScD
Chief Science Officer & Founder, Quantrek
Apollo 14 astronaut
6th man to walk on the Moon

Those familiar with the work of Tom Horn—including his books, *Petrus Romanus, Exo-Vaticana,* and *Path of the Immortals,* as well as our work together discussing various points of interest regarding CERN in *Abaddon Ascending*—will likely recognize certain elements of this email. We see the Vatican's interest and Catholic influence over the ETI disclosure issue. We also see more details planned for a meeting including several Catholic attendees. Interestingly enough, even the Vatican's Observatory (written about in *Exo-Vaticana)* in Arizona, along with Jose Funes, Guy Consolmagno, and Pope Francis are discussed. The idea of other intelligent life in the universe existing as our "brothers" is a point made here as well.

After all this, Mansfield, on behalf of Mitchell, drops a bombshell. She states clearly and directly they "work with specific ETI from a contiguous universe."[190] She also states these ETI are "nonviolent and in complete obedience to God." Of course, the first question brought to mind might be, *which god?*

Mansfield goes on to describe a connection between ETI and zero point energy. She believed the ETI were guiding Mitchell's efforts with Quantrek toward bringing zero point energy to humanity, thereby removing our dependence on fossil fuels which, according to Mansfield (and apparently the ETI), is destroying our fragile planet. Strangely enough, even CERN and the Tau neutrino's connection to zero point energy is stated. Once again, a reference to "3 possible dates and times" for their meeting is mentioned. Yet, as with the others, it is unclear if this is a presumptive thank you or one based on a past event.

In any event, it shows the potential for someone sharing these beliefs to be in a position, or at least having access to a person in a position, to interpret ETI disclosure toward these ends: Humans are destroying the planet, ETI are here to help us, ETI are obedient to God, ETI are our brothers, and the government should get involved in how to explain all of this to the general public. Whether Podesta went along with these beliefs or not is beside the point. The fact is, Mansfield and Mitchell had direct access, at least for a little while, to a high-ranking person in the White House who was pushing for official disclosure of the UFO phenomenon. This helps show us how official disclosure could get interpreted if it happened today.

Hierarchy and Classification of Aliens and Spirits

Here is another email from Mitchell to Podesta showing that Mitchell and Mansfield share the same beliefs about ETI:[191]

> From: terribillionairs@aol.com
> To: john.podesta@gmail.com
> CC: eryn.sepp@gmail.com
> Date: 2015-03-05 20:24
> Subject: email from Edgar for John Podesta (% Eryn): meeting request
>
> Dear John,
>   Now that you are no longer serving in the White House, I write to you and Eryn requesting our face to face meeting to discuss zero point energy and Disclosure.

Our Quantrek science intuitive has provided us with a few facts about our nonviolent contiguous universe ETI who promote PACIFISM among humans and with whom we work:

1. All true ETI do not inhabit this universe.

2. So-called ETIs inhabit this universe and are in fact just celestials. They are higher in rank then discarnate spirits, even those who are evolved, HOWEVER, THEY JUST MIRROR VIOLENCE ON EARTH, FEELING THREATENED BY CONTAMINATION OF THEIR ABODE.

3. Extrauinversal [sic] ETIs on the other hand have long ago evolved past violence, relying on spiritual intelligence to avert destruction.

4. The Phoenix Lights and other sightings have provided ample evidence that Earth has been visited by beings whose intention is purely peace and who have nonviolently hovered over Phoenix and other sites, waiting to be asked to help, when they could most easily have destroyed the city with their uses of consciousness. These sightings have been witnessed by thousands of people in Phoenix alone, including my colleague Terri Mansfield, who will accompany me on our meeting with you.

Please let me now [sic] three dates and times that would work for your schedule.

Best regards,

Edgar

Edgar D. Mitchell, ScD

Chief Science Officer & Founder, Quantrek

Apollo 14 astronaut

6th man to walk on the Moon

This shows us the clear agreement between Mansfield's beliefs and those of Mitchell. We aren't given specifics, but Mitchell states something they were doing at Quantrek yielded evidence showing certain facts out ETI. Simply put:

- ETI, once again, are nonviolent.
- ETI do not inhabit our universe.
- ETI inhabit a higher plane of existence beyond our three-dimensional universe.
- ETI are pacifists.
- ETI are different from celestials.
- Celestials seem to be the name given to aliens from other planets.
- Celestials are either mistaken for or intentionally posing as ETI.
- Celestials are higher in rank than discarnate spirits, though it is unclear what discarnate spirits actually are.
- ETI are higher in rank than celestials.
- Some discarnate spirits are considered more evolved than others.
- Celestials and discarnate spirits mirror violence on Earth.
- Celestials and discarnate spirits feel threatened by contamination of their abode.
- ETI are extrauniversal, or what we might call, extradimensional beings.
- ETI have evolved past violence.
- ETI avoid war and destruction through use of spiritual intelligence.
- The Phoenix Lights, along with certain other sightings, were the work of ETI.
- ETI are showing us they could destroy us, yet choose not to.
- ETI are waiting for humans to ask them for help.
- ETI have enough power with only their consciousness to destroy our cities.
- Somehow ETI worked with Mansfield, Mitchell, and Quantrek to some capacity.

While this helps round out some of Mitchell's beliefs, it brings up just as many questions about ETI:

- Why is it important to keep driving home the point ETI are nonviolent?
- Which universe do ETI inhabit?
- How many universes are there, according to the ETI?
- What causes ETI to be pacifists, with whom are they peaceful, and how does that contrast with other, less-evolved beings?
- Why is the term "celestials" used for what sounds like other intelligent beings originating from planets other than Earth?
- Are celestials aliens, or are they different?
- Are celestials evil?
- What is a discarnate spirit?
- Who decides the ranks of these nonhuman beings?
- How does a discarnate spirit evolve?
- Why would aliens and spirits care enough about what humans are doing on Earth to mirror it themselves?
- What type of contamination are celestials and aliens afraid of, and how do they believe contamination could occur?
- Is "extrauniversal" the same as "spiritual," and, if so, how are extrauniversal beings different from discarnate spirits? If not, how are they different from celestials, yet still considered nonphysical?
- How do ETI evolve, and what were they before they evolved?
- What exactly is spiritual intelligence?
- Why would ETI bother with showing human beings lights in the sky?
- How do sightings such as the Phoenix Lights convey the message that the ETI can destroy us, yet choose not to? What human would draw that conclusion from seeing a strange light in the sky?
- Haven't human beings been asking for help for a long time? What is ETI waiting for?
- How does making us aware of their power of consciousness capable of destroying cities play into their plan of helping us?

- What was the nature of the relationship between ETI, Mansfield, Mitchell, and Quantrek; how did they communicate; why did Quantrek shut down if it was ETI-motivated; and why did ETI need Quantrek, Mitchell, and Mansfield in order to help all of humanity?

I (Josh Peck) ask these questions not as a dig against anyone or his or her beliefs, but in order to show the importance of thinking critically about these issues. In my belief, it is entirely possible that Mitchell and Mansfield were contacted by entities claiming to be all of the things described. The question for me isn't whether or not Mitchell and Mansfield were making all of these things up. It is apparent, a least to me, that they fully believed what they were saying. The question for me is, rather, why did Mitchell and Mansfield believe what the ETI were telling them? What makes ETI trustworthy? Why were the ETI themselves never questioned about their motivations? Why did the ETI offer no proof to Mansfield and Mitchell to show the rest of us? If ETI were truly working with Mansfield and Mitchell toward the benefit of humanity, why aren't other human beings allowed to knowingly participate in the process?

The questions could go on and on. Yet I suspect we are likely to find no real answers—not from human beings in the know or from ETI themselves. After all, why would ETI provide proof if their claims go unchallenged? I say it is time for contacts, abductees, and experiencers to start challenging claims made by these entities. The fact that most don't shows how easily accepted any interpretation of official disclosure made popular by people in power would be across the world. If what is described in these emails turns out to be the interpretation attached to official disclosure if/when it occurs, many people would willingly accept it blindly, refusing to challenge the claims or demand any real evidence. All ETI would have to do is show up. I fear the mere public presence of these beings would be proof enough in the majority of minds.

The Space Treaty

Here is another email from Edgar Mitchell to John Podesta showing Mitchell's urgency and sincerity concerning his beliefs:[192]

From: terribillionairs@aol.com
To: john.podesta@gmail.com, eryn.sepp@gmail.com
Date: 2015-04-07 10:20
Subject: email for John Podesta (% Eryn) re Disclosure

Dear John,

This recent Mother Jones' article referencing you caught [my] eye and I wanted you to be aware of it. See link below.

http://www.motherjones.com/politics/2015/03/hillary-clinton-ufo-aliens-podesta

The urgency as I see it is to explain as much as possible to you and to President Obama about what we know for sure about our nonviolent ETI from the contiguous universe who are peacefully assisting us with bringing zero point energy to our fragile planet.

Thank you and Eryn for letting me know when you can share a Skype talk with Terri Mansfield and me.

Best regards,
Edgar
Edgar D. Mitchell, ScD
Chief Science Officer & Founder, Quantrek
Apollo 14 astronaut
6th man to walk on the Moon

Here is another toward similar ends with some new aspects and points of interest revealed:[193]

From: terribillionairs@aol.com
To: john.podesta@gmail.com
CC: eryn_m_sepp@who.eop.gov, eryn.sepp@gmail.com
Date: 2015-01-18 19:34
Subject: email for John Podesta (% Eryn) from Edgar Mitchel re meeting ASAP

Dear John,

As 2015 unfolds, I understand you are leaving the Administration in February.

It is urgent that we agree on a date and time to meet to discuss Disclosure and Zero Point Energy, at your earliest available after your departure.

My Catholic colleague Terri Mansfield will be there too, to bring us up to date on the Vatican's awareness of ETI.

Another colleague is working on a new Space Treaty, citing involvement with Russia and China. However with Russia's extreme interference in Ukraine, I believe we must pursue another route for peace in space and ZPE on Earth.

I met with President Obama's Honolulu childhood friend, US Ambassador Pamela Hamamoto on July 4 at the US Mission in Geneva, when I was able to tell her briefly about zero point energy.

I believe we can enlist her as a confidante and resource in our presentation for President Obama.

I appreciate Eryn's assistance in working with Terri to set up our meeting.

Best regards,

Edgar

Edgar D. Mitchell, ScD

Chief Science Officer & Founder, Quantrek

Apollo 14 astronaut

6th man to walk on the Moon

Here, Mitchell expressed appreciation for Eryn Sepp's efforts to set up a meeting through Terri Mansfield for Mitchell and Podesta. This may lend evidence that at least efforts were made, and Mitchell and Mansfield were not outright ignored this entire time. Also interesting is that Mitchell felt the need to remind Podesta of Mansfield's faith by stating "my Catholic colleague." Since Podesta himself is a self-professing Catholic, it is not entirely out of the ordinary, but it is of at least minor interest that this keeps coming up.

Also of interest, a space treaty is mentioned. Nothing is here to indicate that this is strange, such as a treaty with ETI and humans. Rather, from the context, it sounds more like a treaty concerning how the governments of the world will treat outer space, possibly regarding satellites and weapons. This is confirmed by viewing the attachment included in this email from WikiLeaks, which can be done by viewing the link in the endnotes.[194]

Here is another email concerning outer space, weapons, and ETI feelings regarding weapons in space:[195]

From: terribillionairs@aol.com
To: john.podesta@gmail.com
CC: esepp@equitablegrowth.org, eryn.sepp@gmail.com
Date: 2015-08-18 10:30
Subject: email for John Podesta ℅ Eryn re Space Treaty (attached)

Dear John,

Because the War in Space race is heating up, I felt you should be aware of several factors as you and I schedule our Skype talk.

Remember, our nonviolent ETI from the contiguous universe are helping us bring zero point energy to Earth.

They will not tolerate any forms of military violence on Earth or in space.

The following information in italics was shared with me by my colleague Carol Rosin, who worked closely for several years with Wernher von Braun before his death.

Carol and I have worked on the Treaty on the Prevention of the Placement of Weapons in Outer Space, attached for your convenience.

_____

NEW GREAT NEWS: Federal Minister for Planning, Development and Reforms Ahsan Iqbal proposed cooperation in space technology between Pakistan and China as part of the historic declaration, saying it will take the Pak-China relations to new heights. http://tribune.com.pk/story/937041/cooperation-20-mous-worth-2-billion-signed/ A consortium of 35 Chinese companies was also formed that will invest in Pakistan: Pakistan and China on Wednesday signed 20 memoranda of understanding (MoU) worth $2 billion…emphasis on sustainability

_____

The Cosmic Consequences of Space Weapons: Why they Must be Banned to Preserve our Future

FULL ARTICLE: http://consciousreporter.com/global-agendas/treaty-ban-weapons-space-urgently-needed/

_____

WAR IN SPACE…
War in space isn't considered fantasy anymore
http://www.aol.com/article/2015/08/12/
war-in-space-isnt-considered-fantasy-anymore/21221875/

_____

PREPARING FOR WAR IN SPACE (articles below):
http://www.outerplaces.com/science/item/9578-anti-satellite-missiles-and-international-tensions-see-us-china-and-russia-preparing-for-war-in-spaceAnti-

Satellite Missiles and International Tensions See US, China and
Russia Preparing for War in Space

_____

http://www.scientificamerican.com/article/war-in-space-may-
be-closer-than-ever/??ftcamp=crm/email//nbe/FirstFTEurope/
product

War in Space May Be Closer Than Ever
China, Russia and the U.S. are developing and testing controversial
new capabilities to wage war in space despite their denial of such
work
By Lee Billings | August 10, 2015

_____

http://www.express.co.uk/news/world/597809/Anti-satellite-
weapons-space-war-Earth-Russia-China-United-States
World War Three in SPACE? Fears over rise in anti-satellite
weapons created by Russia
A HUGE rise in anti-satellite weapons being developed by world
powers has sparked fears the West could soon be embroiled in a
fully-fledged war with Russia and China in outer space.

_____

War in space isn't considered fantasy anymore
http://www.aol.com/article/2015/08/12/
war-in-space-isnt-considered-fantasy-anymore/21221875/

We're arguably closer than ever to war in space. Most
satellites orbiting Earth belong to the U.S., China and Russia.
And recent tests of anti-satellite weapons don't exactly ease the
scare factor.

It sounds like science fiction, but the potential for real-life
star wars is real enough. It's just not new.

Fears of battles in space go back to the Cold War and several initiatives, like President Reagan's "Star Wars" missile-defense system.

Deputy Defense Secretary Robert Work spoke to Congress in June about the threat. He said during a speech the technology the U.S. developed during the Cold War allows it "to project more power, more precisely, more swiftly, at less cost."

Take a moment to think about everything satellites do. GPS, surveillance and communications all depend on them.

And the Scientific American notes you can disable satellites without missiles. Simply spray-painting lenses or breaking antennas is enough.

President Obama requested $5 billion for space defense in the 2016 fiscal budget.

And a former Air Force officer told the Scientific American most of the United States' capabilities in space have been declassified to send a clear message: There are no rules for war in space.

Best regards,

Edgar

Edgar D. Mitchell, ScD

Apollo 14 astronaut

6th man to walk on the Moon

Zero Point Energy Consultant

One of the more shocking statements in this email regarding ETI is: "They will not tolerate any forms of military violence on Earth or in space." Once again, questions come up. How exactly would this lack of toleration play out? Would ETI step in and physically stop humanity from engaging in military violence? Aren't they pacifists? How would they stop us if not by using violent means themselves? Have ETI decided to put themselves in charge of us, telling us what we can and cannot do without awarding us the freedom of choice? If they truly are obedient to God, wouldn't God want to be the one to make those decisions? What about the times throughout the Bible when God actually commanded certain wars? Is it possible that ETI serve a different god? If so, who is this god, and why should humanity be obedient to him/her/it? Wouldn't this just be a case of ETI imposing their religious/spiritual beliefs on humanity? What if our own religious/spiritual beliefs conflict with theirs?

Again, questions could go on and on. Also, to restate my previous point, my fear is that these questions will never be asked before people in power blindly accept the views and preferences of ETI. However, if a human were to act in the commanding manner ETI seem to prefer, it typically would not be appreciated and would be rebelled against. Even if God Himself commands things that interfere with what humanity wants to do, He is rebelled against. Why should ETI expect any different from humans?

ETI's Celestials Compared with Biblical Celestials

It seems that ETI admit to some resistance from celestials. Here is an email from Terri Mansfield on behalf of Edgar Mitchell stating a difference between these two groups:

From: terribillionairs@aol.com
To: john.podesta@gmail.com
CC: eryn.sepp@gmail.com
Date: 2015-04-30 18:13
Subject: email for John Podesta re talk with Edgar Mitchell cc: Eryn

Hugs John,
    I write on behalf of Dr. Mitchell to request your Skype talk with him ASAP regarding Disclosure and the difference between celestials in our own solar system and their restraint by those from the nonviolent contiguous universe.

Edgar recently closed Quantrek due to health reasons. His talk with you, John, is of great importance given the alternative of your not being aware of these key distinctions heralding either intergalactic warfare or peace.

It is also imperative that after your talk with Edgar, he then speak directly with President Obama via Skype for historical purposes, about the same issue, while the President is still in office.

John, Edgar has consulted on consciousness matters for American presidents in the past, has addressed the UN General Assembly twice. He is not in need of a personal experience, wishes only to serve.

Thank you and Eryn for letting me know dates and times for your availability so I can relay that to Edgar.

Love,

Terri

Terri Donovan Mansfield

ETI (Extraterrestrial Intelligence) Peace Task Force Director

602.885.9058 | <mailto:terribillionairs@aol.com> terribillionairs@aol.com

On behalf of:

Edgar D. Mitchell, ScD

Apollo 14 astronaut

6th man to walk on the moon

The exact distinction between ETI and celestials is still unclear. In a previous email, it was said that celestials exist in our universe. The context of this email narrows them down to existing in our solar system. After that, the topic is abandoned in order to ask again for a meeting on Mitchell's behalf.

In fact, the choice of the word "celestials" in describing these seemingly disobedient, lower-ranking, physical beings is interesting. According to the Bible, celestials are something much different:[196]

[39]All flesh is not the same flesh: but there is one kind of flesh of men, another flesh of beasts, another of fishes, and another of birds.

[40]There are also celestial bodies, and bodies terrestrial: but the glory of the celestial is one, and the glory of the terrestrial is another.

Based on the context of the passage, these celestial bodies are considered different than terrestrial bodies. A celestial body, which we might say is "angelic" in our modern vernacular, was connected with the stars in ancient Near-Eastern understanding.[197] The way we would think of this today is that a "celestial" body is spiritual in nature. It's different from a physical entity like an animal, human, or gray alien from Zeta Reticuli. Therefore, an angel, whether good or evil, would be considered "celestial" by biblical description.

If we extend this further, the ETI themselves, by their own descriptions of being "extrauniversal," would be considered "celestial" by biblical standards. This is important to note if they truly are claiming to be obedient to the God of the Bible. Yet, these beings seem to have told Mansfield and Mitchell the "celestials" are actually the bad guys and are nothing more than physical beings confined to our universe, possibly even limited to our solar system. It is a completely antithetical idea from that of the Bible concerning these entities. If ETI were telling the truth, they would have to explain how they are allowed to contradict the Biblical definition (the same Bible describing God, who they claim they are obedient to). If ETI are lying, they are giving the true celestials (the truly obedient angels of God described in the Bible) a bad name. Either way, it doesn't seem like the story told by ETI holds up to scrutiny.

Desperation for a Meeting Ensues

Aside from the statement about celestials, the previous email does seem to convey a bit more desperation than the others regarding a meeting. If true, this would indicate no meeting had yet taken place. Perhaps Podesta decided to rescind his offer for a Skype meeting after learning what Mitchell and Mansfield believed regarding official disclosure. Perhaps not.

Lastly, showing a similar desperation:[198]

From:terribillionairs@aol.com
To: eryn.sepp@gmail.com, esepp@equitablegrowth.org
CC: john.podesta@gmail.com
Date: 2015-05-19 23:36
Subject: Eryn FW: email for John Podesta re talk with Edgar Mitchell cc: Eryn

Hugs Eryn,
    I called and left you a voice message on Tuesday, May 19.
    Please let me know asap when John can talk with Edgar and me by Skype, about Disclosure and the difference between our contiguous universe nonviolent ETI and the celestials in our own universe.
    This topic is now more important than ever.
    Love,
    Terri

Other Podesta ETI Emails

Mitchell and Mansfield were far from the only people contacting John Podesta about extraterrestrials. Bob Fish, a NASA historian and Apollo Curator for the USS Hornet Museum, had correspondence with John Podesta via email concerning "Fastwalkers," a term used by NORAD and branches of armed forces to describe unidentified aerial phenomena moving and/or changing directions at high speeds far beyond the capabilities of currently known human technology. One email, dated March 5, 2015, reads:[199]

*On Mar 5, 2015 6:08 PM, "Bob Fish" <robertbfish@earthlink.net>
wrote:*

John–

I know you are busy as heck so I appreciate your taking a moment to read this email and put it in a file for future use.

I emailed Leslie Kean ten days ago but have not received any response.

Based on significant personal experience, I can attest that UFO hunters are looking in the wrong places.

Random personal observations, fuzzy photographers, and crop circles will never "prove" the existence of anything, especially since UFO appearances to humans are transitory and somewhat related to the observer's state of mind.

What needs to be collected and publicly disseminated is hard scientific data collected from instruments that are known to be accurate and reliable.

Within the US, this information has existed for many years and is still available today, if one knows "where to look" and "what to look for."

Radar data and thermal imaging data is a good start, especially if one knows the flight envelope and maneuvering characteristics of a UFO.

If/when you might be interested in gaining more specific information (program names) please feel free to contact me by email to arrange a phone call or meeting (I live in northern Cal but occasionally travel to DC for business activities)!

While I am publicly known by my work with the USS Hornet Museum, this communication with you is entirely PRIVATE and CONFIDENTIAL and has nothing to do with the museum.

Regards,
Bob Fish
Danville, CA

To this, John Podesta wrote back a little over three hours later, "Thx for the note. Hard for me follow up at this moment but I will keep your contact information."[200]

The next day, on March 6, 2015, Bob Fish wrote Podesta again, this time with some more information:[201]

From: Bob Fish <robertbfish@earthlink.net>
Date: Fri, Mar 6, 2015 at 1:17 PM
Subject: Leslie Kean book - DSP program
To: John Podesta <john.podesta@gmail.com>

John—

Just tuck this in your UFO files for future reference.

One of the government programs that collects hard data on unidentified flying objects is the USAF DSP satellite program.

I can add a little insight to rumors published on the web. While I was never fully briefed into the DSP operation directly, I was introduced to them as the US prepared for Operation Desert Shield and Desert Storm. On occasion, I had lunch with a few of them in the cafeteria of a highly classified organization in El Segundo, CA. No one could get into the cafeteria without TS/SCI clearances, so this was not "lightweight group of gossipers." One of these times, a member of that group was really excited—said they'd just picked up Fastwalker (I assumed that same day). He described how it entered our atmosphere from "deep space" (origin actually unknown, of course, but from the backside of the satellite) and zipped by the DSP satellite pretty closely on its way to earth. Not only was it going very fast but it made a 30 degree course correction (turn) which means it did not have a ballistic (free fall) reentry trajectory that a meteorite might have. So, it was under some sort of control—although whether it was "manned" or just "robotic" there's no way to tell.

Although its now 24 years later, one factoid makes me think the USAF is still collecting information on these Fastwalkers. Reading the current official USAF "DSP Fact Sheet" there is this line near the end: In addition, researchers at The Aerospace Corporation have used DSP to develop portions of a hazard support system that will aid public safety in the future.

http://www.losangeles.af.mil/library/factsheets/factsheet. asp?id=5323

Also, much of the information on this site is accurate although I do not know the author or his sources: http:// ufodigest.com/shadowmag/extra/topsecret.html

Somewhere within that USAF program office is many year's worth of Fastwalker data. If someone were to collect and analyze it, patterns will emerge that provide information about the various types of craft and their destinations, which would add substantiation to eyewitness claims on the ground about UFO activity. Furthermore, it would be interesting to understand the dates of these appearances – is there a certain time of the every year they swarm in (which might indicate a resource mining operation) or might there be a correlation with major events on earth, (such as the detonation of the first atomic bomb at White Sands in 1945 although no

DSP's existed to provide any info on that particular event)?

Regards,

Bob Fish

Podesta forwarded this email with the message "FYI" to Leslie Kean, investigative journalist and noted UFO researcher who cofounded the Coalition for Freedom of Information (CFI), which advocated for greater government openness on information about UFOs.

Even Tom DeLonge, singer of the rock band Blink-182, was discovered to have emailed John Podesta concerning UFOs and a then-secret novel, television, and film project. The first email of interest, dated 10-26-2015, reads:[202]

From: t.delonge@me.com
To: john.podesta@gmail.com
Date: 2015-10-26 23:13
Subject: Important things-

Tom DeLonge

Hi John-

Tom DeLonge here, The one who interviewed you for that special documentary not to long ago.

Things are moving with the project. The Novels, Films and NonFiction works are blooming and finishing. Just had a preliminary meeting with Spielberg's Chief Operating Officer at DreamWorks. More meetings are now on the books-

I would like to bring two very "important" people out to meet you in DC. I think you will find them very interesting, as they were principal leadership relating to our sensitive topic. Both were in charge of most fragile divisions, as it relates to Classified Science and DOD topics. Other words, these are A-Level officials. Worth our time, and as well the investment to bring all the way out to you. I just need 2 hours from you.

Just looking to have a casual, and private conversation in person.

—Here are some photos from the material I am using as I meet with Studio Partners.

Best,
Tom DeLonge
TOM DELONGE | FOUNDER

TOM@TOTHESTARSINC.COM | (760) 518-7801 | TO THE STARS MEDIA
SAN DIEGO | 1053 S Coast Hwy 101 Encinitas, CA 92024

Here are the three email attachments showing the TV, film, and novel projects:

Attachment 1

Attachment 2

Attachment 3

In a second email to John Podesta concerning Major General McCasland, the commander of the Air Force Research Laboratory at Wright-Patterson Air Force Base in Ohio, DeLonge wrote:[203]

Major General William N.
McCasland

From: t.delonge@me.com
To: john.podesta@gmail.com
Date: 2016-01-25 16:04
Subject: General McCasland

He mentioned he's a "skeptic", he's not. I've been working with him for four months. I just got done giving him a four hour presentation on the entire project a few weeks ago.

Trust me, the advice is already been happening on how to do all this. He just has to say that out loud, but he is very, very aware- as he was in charge of all of the stuff. When Roswell crashed, they shipped it to the laboratory at Wright Patterson Air Force Base. General McCasland was in charge of that exact laboratory up to a couple years ago.

He not only knows what I'm trying to achieve, he helped assemble my advisory team. He's a very important man.

Best,

Tom DeLonge

TOM DELONGE | FOUNDER

TOM@TOTHESTARSINC.COM | (760) 518-7801 | TO THE STARS MEDIA

SAN DIEGO | 1053 S Coast Hwy 101 Encinitas, CA 92024

Based on these additional emails, including many more not included in this book, it seems the topic of UFOs and official disclosure is as widely talked about within higher-up, close-knit circles as it is amongst the rest of us. The only true difference is how we all individually choose to interpret the phenomenon.

Possibility of Disclosure in a Trump Presidency

With Clinton losing the race for presidency, many ufologists are left wondering if official disclosure is even possible with Donald Trump as president. After all, one of Clinton's campaign promises was to get to the bottom of the UFO question. However, with the pattern of deception, corruption, and secrecy that took place during the Obama administration, even to the point that one of Donald Trump's most popular phrases became "drain the swamp," perhaps Hillary Clinton would not have been as forthright with UFO-related information had she become president. In fact, the greater chance of official disclosure might actually be with President Trump. With Trump as president of the United States, some have admitted there have been many hopeful signs showing that his push for more transparent and accountable government could translate into greater openness concerning UFOs and alien life.[204] Of course, we shouldn't get our hopes up. If history is any indicator of future events, we likely won't be seeing official disclosure in the way we might think any time soon.

Fellow UFO researcher and author Richard Dolan mirrors some of these views in his book *UFOs and Disclosure in the Trump Era.*[205] In the

book, he states that "any form of disclosure will be messy with questions that will remain unanswered for a long time."[206] I (Josh Peck) agree completely with Richard on this. We would be naive to expect any kind of disclosure event to answer every question to the satisfaction of everyone. Like every other aspect of life, it is doubtful we will all agree on any given interpretation of UFOs and extraterrestrials, even in the case of an official disclosure event.

Richard M. Dolan

Interpreting the Emails

Depending on who you are, your belief system, your worldview, or your level of interest in this topic, you may interpret these emails differently than the authors of this book. This is to be expected, and toward the end of discovering truth beyond opinions, differences should be embraced as long as they are based on fact rather than emotion. Learning how to distinguish between the two can be extremely difficult. To be honest, when I (Josh Peck) read these emails, especially the ones from Edgar Mitchell and Terri Mansfield, initially I had an immediate, internal, and emotional response telling me that ETI are likely demonic entities. Now, if I were to stop there and not examine the issue further, I would leave myself in a position where all I have is an opinion void of facts. Even if I were 100 percent correct, I would have no evidence to support my opinion. Someone else reading these emails might have an emotional response telling him or her that ETI are our saviors and can be trusted. However, again, if this response is left unchallenged by evidence and fact, it is only an opinion and lacks the ability to reflect unfiltered truth. Therefore, it is important to weigh the evidence and try to back up our opinions with facts, regardless of how "right" we think we are. Only then can we compare and find out which opinion is closest to the truth. Of course, this can only be done if all parties involved are willing to accept evidence over emotion and not turn different opinions into heated arguments and personal attacks. This, unfortunately, is rare.

Of course, with a book such as this, you will not only get the facts, but the authors' own opinions based on those facts. We (Josh and Derek) have tried our best to write this book in a way showing our mental path of logic from fact to interpretation. We share our opinions, of course, but we try to show you how we arrived at them. It is our belief, by being honest in our writing and telling you exactly what we are trying to do, that you, the reader, are given the best tools to investigate for yourself and draw your own conclusions, whether or not they agree with ours. It is no secret that Derek and I are Christians. Our opinions typically conform to a Christian worldview. However, as we will see later, we believe the Christian worldview can be much broader concerning extraterrestrial and extradimensional life than many well-meaning Christians may realize. As we will also see later, we believe if the true interpretation of science is considered with the true interpretation of the Bible, the two should go hand in hand—without contradiction. After all, a contradiction between two truths is nothing more than a lack of understanding concerning one or both of those truths.

chapter nine

SUPERNATURAL OUTER-SPACE RESEARCH

ON THE SURFACE, legitimate, scientific research into outer space would seem to be void of any supernaturalism or spirituality. However, as we will see throughout this book, it is difficult, if not impossible, to separate the two. We tend to see two sides in modern research: cold, hard science on one side and metaphysical, mystical understandings on the other. Rarely do we see represented a truth found somewhere in the middle—truth that is not materialistic and not mystic, but somewhere in between.

Twentieth- and twenty-first-century researchers are not the first to look to the stars and wonder what is truly out there. Those living in the ancient world had the same questions and, in truth, had a lot more time and interest at their disposal. After all, ancient theologians and astronomers were not concerned with getting more likes on Facebook or crafting the perfect response to a mean comment on their YouTube video. No; our forefathers had the focus to ponder these questions more deeply than most today.

What the people of the ancient world lacked, however, was scientific understanding, innovation, and invention. They had more time, yet fewer tools with which to find the answers to their questions. Today, we have more tools at our disposal, yet less interest on a worldwide scale. Fewer people are looking to the stars, fewer questions are asked, and fewer potential discoveries are being made. Sure, we have made great strides and have made many new discoveries in the past one hundred years—far more than thousands of years before. Yet, what about the potential discoveries? What about what we *could* do if more people were interested? We live on a planet with more than seven billion people, more people at one time than during any other time in history. However, it seems that a smaller percentage of the population is interested in what our predecessors held sacred.

Imagine if we hadn't separated science from spirituality. Imagine if science actually goes hand in hand with the supernatural and that, if we don't acknowledge both, we are missing half of the answer. Even from a truly biblical context, imagine if science and theology, both taken in their proper context, can give us a richer view of the cosmos and beyond.

People have a compulsion to know more; they are searching for answers. However, many do not know the right questions to ask in order attain knowledge. In short, many people are looking in the wrong places.

The "Wow!" Signal

Any time a signal from space is detected, whether completely natural or with an element of anomaly to it, the question of whether we are alone in the universe is raised. Researchers and laypeople alike are left wondering if something from "out there" is trying to communicate with us. Is it a direct, intentional contact, or are we just picking up on an ancient ET television show from millions of light years away? The fact is, Earth is listening. We just don't know who, if anyone, is speaking.

The first major occurrence categorized as a possible communication attempt from alien beings came on August 15, 1977. It was a narrowband radio signal received by Ohio State University's Big Ear radio telescope. The signal itself appeared to come from the Sagittarius constellation. Astronomer Jerry R. Ehman discovered the anomalous signal a few days later while reviewing the previously recorded data. The result of the signal was so shocking that he circled the reading on the printout and wrote "Wow!" on the side, which is why it is now called the "Wow! signal." Strangely enough, the entire signal lasted for the full, seventy-two-second window during which Big Ear was able to observe it.

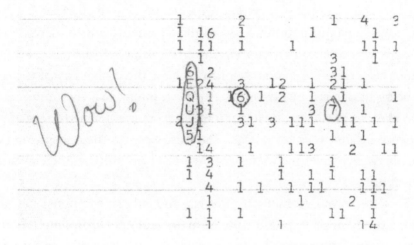

The "Wow!" signal

At first, Ehman suggested the signal could have originated on Earth and reflected off of a piece of space debris back to Big Ear. He later changed his mind, after further research showed it to be an unlikely explanation due to very specific requirements that were unrealistic to a reflection.[207] Also, the 1420MHz signal was within what's called the "protected spectrum." This is a bandwidth reserved for astronomical purposes; everything else is forbidden to transmit within this range. Ehman did admit the possibility of the signal originating from the military or someone else on Earth; however, he maintains that the most likely explanation for the signal is an extraterrestrial origin.

In 2017, Antonio Paris proposed that the source of the signal could have been the hydrogen cloud surrounding two comets, 266P/Christensen and 335P/Gibbs. He claimed they were in roughly the right position at the time of the signal. However, a more detailed analysis later showed that the comets were not in the beam at the correct time. Also, known comets are not radio-bright at these frequencies.

At the thirty-fifth anniversary of the Wow! signal in 2012, Arecibo Observatory beamed an attempted response toward the signal's origin. The transmission contained around ten thousand Twitter messages collected by the National Geographic Channel bearing the hashtag "#ChasingUFOs" in a promotion for one of the channel's television series. Also included was a series of video vignettes featuring verbal messages from various celebrities.[208] In an attempt to increase the probability of the signal being recognized by extraterrestrials as an intentional communication from another intelligent life form, Arecibo scientists attached a repeating-sequence header to each message. They also beamed the transmission at roughly twenty times the wattage of the most powerful commercial radio transmitter.

Despite several attempts by Ehman and others, the signal has not been detected again. Also, in spite of many attempts, including theories of the origins being natural or man-made, no one has been able to adequately explain the signal in a way that is consistent with the data. To this day, many scientists, researchers, and ufologists consider the Wow! signal to be the strongest candidate for an alien radio transmission ever detected.

Signals in Stars

As with everything else, we must be mindful of the interpretation we are receiving when discoveries are made. For example, a story went viral in late 2016 about a scientific paper claiming the discovery of ETI signals from space.[209] Other publications remained a bit more on the fence, admitting that it could be ETI or it could just be that we don't understand everything about stars.[210] Because of the limited information concerning this discovery, people were left to interpret the data how they wanted.

What we do know is fairly simple. On October 10, 2016, astronomers

Ermanno Borra and Eric Trottier uploaded an early draft of a paper titled "Discovery of Peculiar Periodic Spectral Modulations in a Small Fraction of Solar-type Stars" to arXiv.org.[211] The paper was officially published in the November 2016 issue of the scientific journal *Publications of the Astronomical Society of the Pacific.* In the paper, the two astronomers used data from the Sloan Digital Sky Survey (SDSS) to analyze 2.5 million stars. Of those, they found that 234 stars were producing a strange signal. In the paper, the possibility of the signal being of ETI origin, based on a previous prediction by Borra, was explored, but the astronomers also admitted this to be speculative.

Sloan Digital Sky Survey (SDDS) in New Mexico

Borra described the speculative idea in a 2012 paper.[212] He suggests that "technology now available on Earth could be used to send signals that have the required energy to be detected at a target located 1000 light years away." This means, according to this idea, that ETI could signal its existence to others by sending light pulses with time separations of 10^{-9} 10^{-15} to seconds. These pulses could be detected in the spectra. Borra and Trottier decided to search a database of spectral signal from 2.5 million stars and found 234 fitting the prediction. After showing that instrumental problems and other usual explanations could not explain the findings, Borra and Trottier suggested these signals could be caused by light pulses generated by ETI in order to alert us to their existence. They found the detected signals had exactly the space of what an ETI signal was predicted to have in the previous paper. While stating they are in agreement with this prediction, Borra and Trottier also admitted it is a hypothesis needing confirmation with further work. In other words, it is strange, and could be ETI, but the ETI hypothesis cannot be confirmed with this data. More work needs to be done.

The Rosetta Comet Signal

Fairly recently, European Space Agency scientists were able to detect a sound produced by Comet 67P/Churyumov-Gerasimenko (or Comet 67P/C-G for short) using the Rosetta spacecraft. The sound is theorized to be produced by "oscillations in the magnetic field in the comet's environment."[213] The magnetometer experiment of the Rosetta spacecraft first recorded the sound when it was flying within sixty-two miles of the comet in August of 2014. Comet 67P/C-G is emitting this "song" well below the frequency a human can actually hear. The frequency of the sound was increased by a factor of approximately ten thousand in order to create an audible rendering of the sound.

Scientists are still unsure exactly how the sound is created from the comet. ESA scientists believe it might originate from neutral particles of the comet being sloughed off into space and ionized. However, researchers are still unsure of how the physics of the oscillations actually work. Comet 67P/C-G is something completely new and different.

Due to the strangeness of the sound emanating from this comet, some have been led to wonder if the signal is artificial rather than natural. Others, however, believe it is completely natural, albeit a bit different than previously observed comets. Is it possible that this is an example of a communication attempt from otherworldly beings?

In order to explore this question further, I (Josh Peck) contacted J. R. Watts, a former government investigator, intelligence analyst, and code-

breaker, to ask his thoughts of the strange sound. When he listened to the
sound sample I emailed to him, I wanted to know if his highly trained ears
could pick up anything that might be artificial. Or did it sound completely natural? If he had received this while he was working as a code-breaker
for the government, was there anything in the sound that would have led
him to believe there was a hidden message? ere is what Mr. Watts wrote
back:

Josh,

I've been listening to this sound bite you emailed me, sounds
like a signal that was relayed through an echo chamber. There is
a repetitive cadence throughout that fades in and out and then
comes up again, sometimes with a slight difference in pitch and
tone. These days, what with acoustic devices, amps and sound
synthesizers available to anyone, it is possible this audio tape was
fabricated by someone.

It's also possible that is a sound of paranormal origin, a mystery that may well remain unsolved if no new data about it is
brought forth by anyone. It has to have an origin no matter what.
But of what origin is the question and in this case, I don't think
anyone will ever solve it.

If you can get an audio engineer to record a similar sound
on tape, then this might be a hint that someone just decided to
record strange sounds on tape to create a mystery. If this is the
case, then this person has a similar mindset as those who promote
the endless searches for Bigfoot.

I'm not an electrical engineer but there was a time when I worked in TV production for 5 years before becoming an investigator and so I had experience working on audio boards. Technically
speaking, this sound could well have been artificially produced by
a competent audio engineer or someone with enough know-how
who had the knowledge to edit sounds together and incorporate
additional sound effects.

That said; on the other hand, if you go on youtube and listen to the sounds captured by the Cassini Space Probe as it neared Saturn, I believe, the sounds it recorded and then relayed back to Earth allowed us to hear sounds in space. Sound is not unique to Earth, so there has to be sound in space as well.

Whether or not there is a hidden signal or embedded message in this sound bite might be answered if you slow it down or speed it up but even then if there is a code present on the tape, if you don't know its lingo, you would never decipher it because you have nothing to compare it to, unless you have other tapes with similar sounds and were able to decode some of it. Hard to say one way or the other.

Good luck to you!

J. R. Watts

We Must Be Careful

More often than not, when a strange signal is detected, the headlines include something about aliens—mainly because the word "aliens" is exciting and attracts more views for any article. It is a marketing tactic. The problem, however, is that this leaves the reader with the idea of aliens contacting Earth without a fair and balanced opposition. Typically, later articles reporting that the signal in question was discovered to be of natural or human origins, don't receive the same level of attention the first ones.

For example, on August 30, 2016, CNN ran a story online with the headline "Hear me now? 'Strong signal' from sun-like star sparks alien speculation."[214] The next day, August 31, 2016, CNN ran another story: "Signal from sun-like star likely of Earthling variety."[215] It does not take a lot of guesswork to figure out which article drew the most views. While the first article explained that a mysterious signal had been detected and asserted that its source might be alien, the second article explained that the signal was of human origin and had been thought otherworldly by mistake.

Even when the writers of a website try to post more honest headlines, this type of sensationalism still occurs. On July 18, 2017, Sci-News published an article with the headline, "Arecibo Observatory's Radio Telescope Detects Strange Signal from Nearby Star Ross 128."[216] The article, at the time I was writing this chapter (July 2017), was shared sixty-nine times on Facebook. A few days later, on July 23, the site published another article with the headline "'Weird!' Signal from Ross 128 Isn't from Extraterrestrial Intelligence, Astronomers Say."[217] Despite having a more key-word-rich headline, this article only received twenty-two shares on Facebook. This time, the second article had the more sensational and excitingtitle at first glance, yet in this specific case, it also contained a truth dispelling the fantasy of extraterrestrial communication. The first article, even with a more honest and (pardon the pun) down-to-earth headline, received more shares (and presumably more views) than the second, because it promoted the possibility of something otherworldly while the second one did not. Fantasy trumps fact.

This type of thing actually happens quite often. The possibility of the fantastic (such as extraterrestrial communications), to many, is far more interesting and preferable over the realistic truth backed up by evidence. This is why, typically, the first article with a sensational headline will be viewed more times than the second article explaining the first one to be faulty. This is also why, especially with a possible disclosure-type event or other major announcement, it is important to recognize who is providing the information, to know the available evidence, and to have the ability to separate observation from interpretation.

chapter ten

EXOPLANET WATERWORLDS
AND CHAOTIC SEA MONSTERS

THE HUNT FOR exoplanets (planets existing beyond our solar system) has been heating up the past few years. Scientists have been interested in other star systems containing new, exotic planets for quite some time, yet recent discoveries have sparked an increase in curiosity and, in some cases, an increase in the hope for discovering extraterrestrial life. In order to know which exoplanets might harbor life, scientists are searching for the holy grail of exoplanetary research: water.

We have a fair grasp of what is in our own solar system. The possibility of abundant liquid water is slim. There are candidates, of course, though they are few. Recently, NASA announced the first confirmation of evidence supporting the existence of water on Mars via spectral detection.[218]

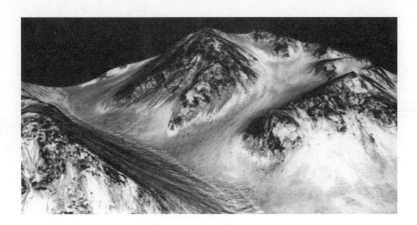

Streaks on the surface of Mars indicate a current flow of water.
Credit: NASA/JPL/University of Arizona

While this is a fascinating observation, it only confirms the *presence* of water, not the quantity or whether that quantity is enough to support life. Another candidate is Europa, one of Jupiter's moons. On September 26, 2016, NASA posted a press release stating the Hubble Telescope detected possible water plumes erupting on Europa.[219] Europa has a global ocean with twice as much liquid as Earth's oceans; however, it exists underneath a layer of extremely cold and hard ice of unknown thickness. It has long been theorized taht there could exist a large amount of habitable water under the frozen crust of Europa. If this is the case, there might be enough liquid water to support life. As of now, however, there is no direct and clear evidence of life on Europa or anywhere else in our solar system.

Europa: One of Jupiter's
four moons

There are other contenders, but from what we understand about our solar system, it is an unlikely place to harbor complex extraterrestrial life of any kind. Most other planets are simply uninhabitable. Others have slim possibilities, but, so far, nothing to get overly excited about and not enough evidence to warrant expensive exploration. Thus, scientists have expanded their efforts beyond our solar system in hopes of finding a truly habitable world.

Exoplanets Discovered

It seems every time a new exoplanet is discovered, the story is covered heavily in the news and interest in the possibility of extraterrestrial life is reignited. In fact, there is even an online database of all known exoplanets called *The Extrasolar Planets Encyclopaedia*.[220] The catalog boasts a list of 3,640 planets; 2,730 planetary systems; and 612 multiple planet systems.[221] Established in February 1995, the online encyclopedia is consistently being updated with new information and discoveries. Clearly, for something like this to even exist, exoplanets are considered a very big deal to many.

We saw this, once again, to be true in early 2017, when reports came out stating that astronomers were preparing to search for extraterrestrial biology in the atmosphere of a planet discovered in the Wolf 1061 star system, which is only about fourteen light years away from Earth.[222] The system is known to host three exoplanets and could be a target for NASA's James Webb Space Telescope (JWST), first scheduled to launch in 2018 with a possible delay until 2019.[223]

The infrared JWST could be used to detect atmospheric conditions and components in potentially habitable exoplanets. Other projects are being launched in the effort to find habitable exoplanets, including the TESS (Transiting Exoplanet Survey Satellite), the CHEOPS (CHaracterising ExOPlanet Satellite), and the PLATO (PLAnetary Transits and Oscillations of stars).

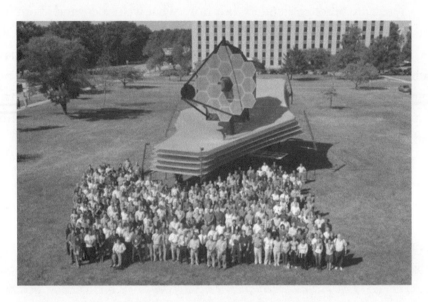

NASA's James Webb Space Telescope and the JWST Team

The idea is to find planets in the habitable zone of stars with the right conditions for liquid water. If scientists can accurately determine exoplanetary atmospheres, they might be able to detect the chemicals revealing information about actual present biology. The Wolf 1061 system hosts a small, rocky exoplanet called Wolf 1061c within its habitable zone. This is one of the closest exoplanets where the possibility of finding evidence of biological life is thought great enough to justify the effort in looking.

Like most exoplanets found within the habitable, or "Goldilocks," zone, there are more factors to consider than just the zone itself. For example, Venus is considered to exist within the inside edge of the sun's habitable zone and is relatively close to the same size as the Earth. Yet, Venus would not be considered habitable by any means. The atmosphere of Venus is toxic and thick due to too much energy becoming trapped, causing the planet to heat up to temperatures hot enough to boil lead. Scientists believe it may have been habitable at one point in the distant past, yet any water potentially existing would have long since been broken down into hydrogen and oxygen atoms.[224] The only place on Venus considered remotely habitable is high up in the atmosphere. This leads some scientists to speculate that floating life forms might currently be present, and perhaps humans might one day inhabit Venus in cities made to float high above the crushing, lower atmospheric pressures of the planet. Yet, this possibility is highly unlikely. This goes to show that there are many factors outside of the exoplanet's size and proximity to a star to consider before determining whether it is truly habitable.

One of the biggest discoveries made of exoplanets in recent history was the TRAPPIST-1 system. The name of the system derives from the telescope that first discovered it, the TRAPPIST (TRAnsiting Planets and Planetesimals Small Telescope). TRAPPIST-1 is a planetary system located thirty-nine light years (twelve parsecs) away, located in the Aquarius constellation. The star in the TRAPPIST-1 system is twelve times less massive than our sun and only slightly larger than Jupiter. Seven planets have been discovered orbiting the star.

The system was first discovered by the TRAPPIST. Additional planets were later discovered using the TRAPPIST, the Spitzer space telescope, the Very Large Telescope, UKIRT, the Liverpool Telescope, and the William Herschel Telescope. All planets in the TRAPPIST-1 system pass in front of their star from our perspective here on Earth. The planets were discovered in a way many other exoplanets are detected. Regular and repeated shadows of the planets are cast during their orbit around the star, thereby allowing transit signals to be used to measure the orbital periods, sizes, and masses of the planets.[225]

It was discovered that the planets are consistent with a rocky composition. It was also found that the planets in the TRAPPIST-1 system have sizes and masses similar to those of Earth and Venus. They receive an amount of light from their star that is similar to that of many of the planets in our solar system, from Mercury to beyond Mars. The TRAPPIST-1 exoplanets are considered the most optimal for habitation compared with any other exoplanets discovered There is great hope within the scientific community of discovering evidence of biological life on one or more of the TRAPPIST-1 exoplanets. In the minds of certain scientists specializing in these areas, what will increase the chances of this great hope being realized may not reside in a rocky world, rather in a watery world: a planet covered entirely, or at least mostly, with liquid water.

Importance of Exoplanetary Water in the Search for Extraterrestrial Life

From a purely scientific and perhaps all-around logical point of view, the existence of liquid water should drastically increase the chances of finding extraterrestrial life on any given planet or moon. Of course, as of now, the only planet we have to compare anything to is our own.

More than 70 percent of Earth is covered in water. However, this might not be as much as we'd like to think, according to certain scientists. A recent article published for *Monthly Notes of the Royal Astronomical Society* seems to indicate Earth is on the low end of water percentage for inhabitable planets, according to simulations.[226] In fact, the study suggests, if there are other inhabitable planets in the universe, most of them should be dominated by oceans spanning over 90 percent of their surface. The ones primarily covered by land—like Mars, for example—would likely be uninhabitable due to lack of water. Basically, the more water, the better chances for life. Therefore, some scientists have shifted their attention from land-based exoplanets to literal waterworlds In the hope of finding complex organisms.

The article suggests that a planet must maintain a certain balance if it is to have extensive land masses along with large oceans. There are several factors striking this balance, such as the amount of water on the surface of a planet, the available space to store it, and the existence of varying and dynamic topographical features. In short, a planet to have both land and ocean in a significant way has to have lots of water, lots of space, and plenty of ocean basins and mountain ranges. If the oceans are too shallow and land altitude too low, excess water will cover most of the planet's surface, making life on land extremely difficult. The vast variety of the

Earth's topography allows for approximately 30 percent of land to remain above water.

The study claims that Earth is likely unique in this regard. It is theorized that most potentially habitable planets found within the "Goldilocks zone" (the correct proximity to a star where water can exist without boiling away or freezing) would be waterworlds. Now, of course, the models used within the article are not made from direct observations of exoplanets. These are instead speculations based on various models of hypothetical exoplanets.

Scientists are still unsure of how planets get their water in the first place (remember, this is from a scientific perspective—one in which "God did it" is not normally a sufficient answer). The most popular theory states that most of Earth's water was brought by asteroids and comets.[227] If that were to be true, it would be nearly impossible to predict the amount of water on any planet without the benefit of direct observation. Every star system is different in terms of number of asteroids, comets, moons, and other nearby planets, which can all affect the outcome of water delivery.

The idea of waterworlds is sometimes used to explain why we have yet to make contact with an extraterrestrial intelligence. If Earth is as unique in the universe as this article suggests, and if there is life elsewhere in the universe, it would likely be marine life. It is very unlikely that an intelligent civilization with high-level technology could develop on a world dominated by water. Even if this were somehow the case, the type of technology used would likely be so vastly different from our own, which is primarily land and air based, that we would not know how to detect any signals of it.

Of course, the discussion of possible extraterrestrial life is not purely a scientific one, nor is it purely a theological one, but is found somewhere in between. We recognize the scientific importance of liquid water in the search for intelligent life elsewhere in the cosmos, but what role does water play theologically? How did ancient Near-Eastern religions, which believed in the existence of a wide range of intelligent entities outside the scope of human beings, view water? Was water as important to the ancient gods as it seems to be in the search for life outside Earth? From an ancient perspective, is water connected with life as it is from a scientific perspective today? Interestingly enough, what we discover is just the opposite.

The Significance of the Sea in Ancient Near-Eastern Religions

With popular shows such as *Ancient Aliens* promoting the belief that ancient gods were just mistaken extraterrestrials, the world is now very familiar with Ancient Astronaut Theory. Many ancient texts, especially those from the ancient Near East, are used to support this claim. Among the most used are ancient Sumerian, Babylonian, and Jewish texts. However, certain inconsistencies found within those texts do not seem to promote Ancient Astronaut Theory. For example, in the creation mythology of Baal, the gods existed in a watery abode. Ancient Astronaut theorists might be tempted to think of this as a waterworld exoplanet. If this were the case, and if these alien gods communicated with mankind, we should expect beliefs around those communications to develop within their culture and religion. Why is it, then, that large bodies of water such as the sea were more closely related to concepts of chaos and death in these belief systems? If alien creator gods came from waterworlds, shouldn't the seas of Earth represent life rather than death? A closer look at the ancient texts themselves can provide a clearer picture of the whole story.

The Enuma Elish

The Enuma Elish is the Babylonian epic of creation, also known as The Seven Tables of Creation.[228] All of the tablets containing the creation myth were found at Ashur, Kish, Ninevah, Sultante, and other excavated sites. The tablets date to c. 1100 BCE, but there are indications that they are copies of a much older version of the story.[229] The myth describes the birth of the gods, the universe, and human beings. In the beginning, according to the story, there was nothing else except chaotic water everywhere. Out of the movement of the water, the waters divided into fresh and salt water. The fresh water is identified as the god Apsu, while the salt water is identified as the goddess Tiamat. Through these two entities came the birth of younger gods.

The younger gods were noisy and troubling Apsu, so, upon the advice of Mummu, Apsu decided to kill the younger gods. Tiamat heard of this and warned her eldest son, Enki (sometimes Ea), so he put Apsu into a sleep and killed him. Enki then created his home from Apsu's remains. Tiamat became angry over Apsu's death and consulted with Quingu, who advised her to bring war against the younger gods. Tiamat gave Quingu the Tablets of Destiny, which solidifies the rule of a god. Quingu wore the tablets as a breastplate. Tiamat then summoned the forces of chaos and created eleven monsters to destroy the younger gods.

Ea/Enki and the other younger gods fought against Tiamat, but were unable to win the battle until Marduk emerged as a champion among them. Marduk defeated Quingu and killed Tiamat by shooting her with an arrow, splitting her in two. Marduk created the heavens and the earth from Tiamat's corpse (half to make the heavens, half to make the earth). He then appointed jobs to the younger gods and bound Tiamat's eleven monsters to his feet as trophies. He then took the Tablets of Destiny from Quingu, thereby solidifying his reign.

Marduk then talked with Ea, recognized as the god of wisdom, and decided to create human beings. He did this by killing the gods who convinced Tiamat to go to war. Quingu was found guilty and killed. Ea created Lullu, the first man, from the blood of Quingu. Lullu's job was to help the gods in their task of maintaining order and keeping chaos restrained. The story then ends with a long praise of Marduk for everything he did. The entire story is about chaos being subdued by the destruction of a great sea beast. In other words, the sea beast is a symbol for chaos.

The Baal Cycle

A similar story can be found in the Ugaritic Baal Cycle. Ugarit was an ancient city, located at what is now Ras Shamra in northern Syria.

Excavated ruins at Ras Shamra

In the second millennium B.C., the population of Ugarit was Amorite and would have controlled roughly two thousand square kilometers on average.[230] During some of its history, Ugarit would have been directly within, or at least in close proximity to, the Hittite Empire.

Ugarit was destroyed in the early twelfth century B.C. and its location was forgotten until 1928, when a peasant accidentally discovered an old tomb. The area of the tomb was found to be the necropolis of Ugarit. Excavations have since revealed a city with a prehistory reaching back to c. 6000 B.C.[231]

Archaeologically speaking, Ugarit is considered Canaanite.[232] Arguably, the most important literary document recovered from Ugarit is the Baal Cycle, which describes the basis for the belief system surrounding the Canaanite deity Baal. In fact, Ugarit bordered the Northern Israelite Kingdom and can be considered the center of ancient Baal worship.

Of further importance is the discovery of the Ugaritic language, which is closer to biblical Hebrew than any other Semitic language. There are extremely interesting word-for-word parallels between Ugaritic myths and passages in the Old Testament that show clear polemics (controversial arguments intended as an attack on a differing belief or idea). As we will explore a bit later, we can read the Creation account in the Bible and see a polemic to the Baal Cycle.

The Baal Cycle isn't as much about creation as it is a competition between gods in order to win a position of rulership with the supreme god El. It describes a battle between Baal (meaning "lord") and Yam (meaning "sea") and another battle between Baal and Mot (meaning "death"). Yam is also called Nahar (meaning "river") and is also described as a sea monster with seven heads named Litanu (the Canaanite word for 'Leviathan"). In the Baal Cycle, Yam is a symbol for the sea and the forces of chaos, comparable to Tiamat in the Enuma Elish. Baal defeats Yam and is declared king of the other gods, yet still under El. He is given the titles "the Rider on the Clouds," "Most High," and is described as having everlasting dominion.

Biblical Creation Polemics

To an ancient Near-Eastern person, the sea was considered extremely dangerous, chaotic, and even otherworldly. The sea is untamable, unpredictable, and wild. Sea creatures themselves were symbolic portrayals of the place in which they lived: the sea. This is why we see the symbol of the sea and a great sea beast/monster/dragon repeated in the religious texts of the ancient Near East. To those people, there was no better representation of death and chaos.[233] We even see this idea turn up in the Bible.

What we are about to look at is considered common knowledge in theological and scholarly circles but, for some reason, is relatively unknown in the mainstream Church. I (Josh Peck) believe a big part of this is due to a common, hyperliteral approach to the Bible found in many churches today, a topic we will look at in further detail later in this book. There are many reasons why this developed over time. One example is the popularity of reading the Bible as if it were written to twenty-first century Americans. The Bible is *for* everybody, of course, but like all ancient texts, it was written *to* the culture of the time.

We currently are at least two thousand years and half a world removed from the ancient Jewish culture in which much of the Bible was written. The best way to understand and interpret the Bible is to put yourself in the ancient writer's shoes. What was going on at the time of the writing? What was the writer dealing with in terms of competing theologies? What was the cultural environment like at that time? By asking these questions and looking at the text through ancient Near-Eastern eyes, we can gain a wealth of correct and intelligently honest understanding of the Scriptures.

This brings us back to the idea of a polemic. As stated briefly earlier, a polemic is a type of theological jab at a different religion or belief. These show up all over the texts in the Bible. The idea was not always to give a literal account of something, but to attribute credit to the true God of Israel, YHWH. For example, in the Baal Cycle, we find the term "Rider on the Clouds" attributed to Baal. Yet, throughout the Bible, YHWH is referred to in the same way.[234] Even Jesus Christ referred to Himself in this manner.[235] The point is not to describe the oddity of God riding on clouds for some reason. The point is to state that Baal is not the one in charge; YHWH/Jesus is. It is a deliberate swipe at the belief that Baal has everlasting dominion by taking his title and attributing it to the true God, YHWH. This is only one example of a polemic in the Bible. There are many more.

Some of the most interesting polemics can be found in the Creation accounts of the Bible. The idea of polemics will also help explain some different descriptions between these accounts. For example, we can compare Genesis 1:1–3 with Psalm 74:12–7. First, Genesis 1:1–3 states:

In the beginning, God created the heavens and the earth. The earth was without form and void, and darkness was over the face of the deep. And the Spirit of God was hovering over the face of the waters. And God said, "Let there be light," and there was light. (ESV)

Next, Psalm 74:12–17 states:

Yet God my King is from of old, working salvation in the midst of the earth. You divided the sea by your might; you broke the heads of the sea monsters on the waters. You crushed the heads of Leviathan; you gave him as food for the creatures of the wilderness. You split open springs and brooks; you dried up ever-flowing streams. Yours is the day, yours also the night; you have established the heavenly lights and the sun. You have fixed all the boundaries of the earth; you have made summer and winter. (ESV)

Here, we have two very different-sounding accounts. In Genesis, we learn that God created the heavens and the earth, the earth was without form and void, there was darkness over the face of the deep, the Spirit of God was hovering over the waters, and that God began His creation by creating light.

The account in Genesis establishes the conflict between God and primordial chaos, represented by the sea and a sea monster, in the very second verse of the Bible. The word translated "deep" is the Hebrew *tehom*. That's a cognate—same word, different language—to the Akkadian *têmtum*, which in turn is a variant form of Tiamat, the Sumerian name for the chaos monster of the sea.

Why did the Spirit of God hover over the waters? Although there is no record here of the conflict between YHWH and "the deep," it seems as though the intent is to restrain something—chaos itself.

Psalm 74 is a bit different. We learn that God is from old, working salvation in the midst of the earth (which again, at the beginning would have been only water). Then we learn God divides the seas (which, in Genesis, occurs in Genesis 1:6) and breaks the heads of the sea monsters, along with crushing the heads of Leviathan. Later, we learn that God establishes the heavenly lights and the sun (which, in Genesis, doesn't occur until the fourth day, described in Genesis 1:14–19).

It is generally believed among biblical scholars that Psalm 74 and Genesis 1 are likely polemics of the Baal Cycle. That is to say, they are attempts to take credit away from Baal for subduing chaos (Leviathan) and giving proper credit to YHWH for this and for creation itself. It is known from tablets found in Syria over the last 150 years that the Semites of western Mesopotamia, the Amorites and Canaanites, believed that it was their storm-god Baal who had subdued the chaos monster.

> Thus says Adad, I brought you back to the throne of your father, I brought you back. The weapons with which I fought Tiamat I gave to you. With the oil of my bitter victory I anointed you, and no one before you could stand.[236]

Adad is the actual name of the west Semitic storm god we know in the Bible as Baal. ("Baal" is actually a title: "lord"). The excerpt above is from a letter from Adad through his prophet, Abiya, to the king of Mari, Zimrī-Līm. The god was apparently reminding Zimrī-Līm that the king had been restored to power by his divine favor, which included sending to Zimrī-Līm the clubs he'd used to defeat Tiamat!

Another tablet found at Mari, which was located on the Euphrates River near the modern border between Syria and Iraq, confirms that the clubs had been sent from Aleppo, which was known as the "city of Adad," to the temple of Dagan (the earlier spelling of the Philistine god Dagon) at the town of Terqa, south of Mari.

While that's a fascinating bit of history—think about that: the divine clubs of Baal were literal, physical objects!—the point here is that Zimrī-Līm ruled at the same time as Hammurabi the Great of Babylon, which is about the time scholars believe the Enuma Elish was composed, and at least four hundred years before the Baal Cycle. So it appears that even between Baal and Marduk there was some competition over who actually defeated the monstrous god of chaos.

We must remember, ancient Near-Eastern people would not have the type of scientific, literal, and material point of view we currently have today in the Western world. Rather, their view would have been more symbolic. This doesn't mean it is any less real or true; it is merely a different way of looking at the world. When we look at the sea, we think of ocean currents and marine biology. When they looked at it, they thought of Leviathan/Tiamat/Litanu, chaos, and death. Therefore, what we have in Genesis 1 and Psalm 74 is not a scientific description of *how* everything was created, but a symbolic polemic describing *who* gets the credit for creating everything. According to the Bible, it's not Baal. It's not Marduk. It is YHWH.

One might wonder: If it is a polemic, where is the battle? It is true, we do not see an epic battle in Genesis 1. We do see a description of a defeat in Psalm 74, but it is still quite different when compared against the Baal Cycle. The idea being conveyed here by the biblical writers is that when YHWH of Israel started creation, these chaotic forces were already held in check. There was no need for a battle. Leviathan was already bound, because the one true God doesn't need to have a fight. This would have been considered a slap in the face to Canaanite religion and the inferior god Baal. It is saying YHWH is the God who is truly in control and always has been. YHWH, not Baal, restricts chaos. If a Canaanite living at that time were to read the Genesis account of Creation, he would understand instantly what the text was doing. It's busting down Baal and lifting up YHWH as supreme.

We see this same sort of thing in Psalm 89:9–11, which reads:

You rule the raging of the sea; when its waves rise, you still them. You crushed Rahab like a carcass; you scattered your enemies with your mighty arm. The heavens are yours; the earth also is yours; the world and all that is in it, you have founded them. (ESV)

We also see this idea repeated as an apocalyptic idea in Isaiah 27:1, which reads:

In that day the LORD with his hard and great and strong sword will punish Leviathan the fleeing serpent, Leviathan the twisting serpent, and he will slay the dragon that is in the sea. (ESV)

In Psalm 89, "Rahab" is a name for Egypt, but is also equated with the sea beast Leviathan. In Isaiah 27, we read of a time in the future when chaos is not simply subdued, but is done away with forever. Consider what John N. Oswalt's commentary on the book of Isaiah says about this:

Most scholars today are in agreement that while the exodus events are in the center of the writer's thinking, they are not by any means all that is there. Rahab is clearly a term for Egypt (cf. 30:7; and Ps. 87:4, where Rahab and Babylon are paired); so also the monster (or "dragon") is a term for Pharaoh (Ezek. 29:3). But it is also clear that those terms are not limited to those historical referents. As is known from Ugaritic studies, the twisting monster is a figure in the struggles of Baal with the god of the sea, Yam, as is "Leviathan," which is equated with the monster in Isa. 27:1. Given these facts, and the evidence that the myth of the struggle of the gods with the sea monster was known in one form or another all over the ancient Near East, one has reason to believe that Isaiah is here, as in 27:1, utilizing this acquaintance among the people for his own purposes. It is important to note that the allusions to Near Eastern myths in the Bible all occur after 750 B.C., long after the basic antimythic character of biblical faith had been established. Thus there is an appeal here neither to some current Hebrew myth nor to some original one, now dead. Rather, just as a contemporary poet might allude to the Iliad or the Odyssey, utilizing imagery familiar to his hearers but that is hardly part of their belief system, so Isaiah uses the imagery of the well-known stories of creation to make his point. It was not Baal or Marduk or Ashur who had any claim to being the Creator—it was the Lord alone.[237]

Order from Chaos

The idea coming out of comparing Psalm 74 with Genesis 1 is, by the time the actual creation starts, Leviathan/chaos is *already* subdued. This would seem to indicate in the text, at least in the mind of the writers of these passages, that a lot more is going on with Genesis 1:1–3 than what we are typically taught in Sunday school. We learn in the very first verse that God created the heavens and the earth. However, what was that process like? What were the conditions? How long did it take? We are not told specifically, but we are given clues if we think of this as a polemic on ancient Canaanite religion.

Whether taken as literal or symbolic, the texts indicate a Creation story unlike anything we are ever taught in the Church, but one biblical scholars are very familiar with. The sea represents chaos, yet as we see in Genesis 1:2, chaos is already subdued by the Spirit of God hovering over the face of the waters. The battle is over before it really began. Whether Leviathan is meant to be understood as a literal sea beast in a spiritual existence or as a symbol for the very real chaos of nature is unknown. Perhaps it is both. In any event, the text allows us a little more freedom in understanding creation than what we may have previously been taught.

There are other interesting things to pull from this idea as well. We find out in the book of Genesis that, once the water is still and chaos subdued, God starts to create order from disorder. This idea, order from disorder, is common throughout ancient Near-Eastern religious texts, yet the writer of Genesis gives proper credit to YHWH, the God of Israel. To the writer of Genesis, the other, lesser gods have tried to usurp YHWH's accomplishments and attributes, so he wishes to set the record straight.

The main reason for reiterating this point is that there are members of occult/pagan circles today who follow doctrines related to "order out of chaos," "as above, so below," and others. Since, in our culture today, those are recognized as doctrines followed outside of Christianity, it is worth repeating the point of polemics here. It seems the writer of Genesis was dealing with a similar issue in his day, so to set the record straight, he gives credit to YHWH for these matters instead of allowing the lesser gods to usurp and defile them.

Leviathan and Behemoth in the End Time

The end time, according to the Bible, is in part about the complete removal of chaos when all the world will become like it was in the Garden of Eden. In Revelation 21:1–4, we read:

> Then I saw a new heaven and a new earth, for the first heaven and the first earth had passed away, and the sea was no more. And I saw the holy city, new Jerusalem, coming down out of heaven from God, prepared as a bride adorned for her husband. And I heard a loud voice from the throne saying, "Behold, the dwelling place of God is with man. He will dwell with them, and they will be his people, and God himself will be with them as their God. He will wipe away every tear from their eyes, and death shall be no more, neither shall there be mourning, nor crying, nor pain anymore, for the former things have passed away."

In verse 1, it is said that "the sea was so more." This is because the sea is a representation of chaos and, at this point, chaos has been completely eradicated. Throughout the rest of the passage, we see the conditions of the Garden of Eden from back in Genesis reinstated. God will dwell on the Earth with man. There will be no death, mourning, crying, or pain. Chaos will be gone and everything will be perfect.

Of course, in order to get to this point, some things need to happen first. In the ancient Jewish understanding, chaos was subdued and restrained, but not eliminated yet. YHWH actively restrains chaos, as He is the only one capable of doing so, but chaos still exists. Though YHWH restrains chaos, there is always a danger. What if God releases His grip? What if chaos is let loose upon the Earth? What if the seven-headed Leviathan is allowed to roam free?

Before we can answer these questions, we must first discuss Behemoth. The most famous biblical passage describing Behemoth is in the book of Job. In the ESV, Job 40:19 tells us that Behemoth was the first of the works of God. The book of Job also tells us that God is the only one who can approach Behemoth. Extrabiblical texts describe Behemoth as well. First Enoch 60:7–9 tells us that Leviathan is a female monster dwelling in the watery abyss, which is comparable to Tiamat, while Behemoth is a male monster dwelling in a hidden desert of Dundayin, east of Eden. In 4 Esdras 6:49–52, we read that Leviathan and Behemoth were created on the fifth day, but were then separated. Leviathan was given a watery domain and Behemoth was given a home on land until such a time when God uses them for food for His chosen. Second Baruch 29:4 adds a details to this, saying it will be in the Messianic Age when Leviathan and Behemoth come forth from their respective habitats to be served as food for the remnant children of God.

The main point behind the symbol of Behemoth is to say that chaos doesn't only reside at sea; it exists on land, too. Sea-chaos is described with Leviathan, while land-chaos is described with Behemoth. We see this even further in the thirteenth chapter of the book of Revelation. Reading the full chapter in this context, certain things begin to make more sense:

> And I saw a beast rising out of the sea, with ten horns and seven heads, with ten diadems on its horns and blasphemous names on its heads. And the beast that I saw was like a leopard; its feet were like a bear's, and its mouth was like a lion's mouth. And to it the dragon gave his power and his throne and great authority. One of its heads seemed to have a mortal wound, but its mortal wound was healed, and the whole earth marveled as they followed the beast. And they worshiped the dragon, for he had given his authority to the beast, and they worshiped the beast, saying, "Who is like the beast, and

who can fight against it?" And the beast was given a mouth uttering haughty and blasphemous words, and it was allowed to exercise authority for forty-two months. It opened its mouth to utter blasphemies against God, blaspheming his name and his dwelling, that is, those who dwell in heaven. Also it was allowed to make war on the saints and to conquer them. And authority was given it over every tribe and people and language and nation, and all who dwell on earth will worship it, everyone whose name has not been written before the foundation of the world in the book of life of the Lamb who was slain. If anyone has an ear, let him hear: If anyone is to be taken captive, to captivity he goes; if anyone is to be slain with the sword, with the sword must he be slain. Here is a call for the endurance and faith of the saints. Then I saw another beast rising out of the earth. It had two horns like a lamb and it spoke like a dragon. It exercises all the authority of the first beast in its presence, and makes the earth and its inhabitants worship the first beast, whose mortal wound was healed. It performs great signs, even making fire come down from heaven to earth in front of people, and by the signs that it is allowed to work in the presence of the beast it deceives those who dwell on earth, telling them to make an image for the beast that was wounded by the sword and yet lived. And it was allowed to give breath to the image of the beast, so that the image of the beast might even speak and might cause those who would not worship the image of the beast to be slain. Also it causes all, both small and great, both rich and poor, both free and slave, to be marked on the right hand or the forehead, so that no one can buy or sell unless he has the mark, that is, the name of the beast or the number of its name. This calls for wisdom: let the one who has understanding calculate the number of the beast, for it is the number of a man, and his number is 666.

Here we have one beast rising from the sea and a second rising from out of the earth. These are the two symbols of chaos given in Scripture, except now they are unrestrained. This passage, as well as others throughout the apocalyptic books and passages within the Bible, describes what happens when God decides to let chaos loose. After chaos is let loose for a time, Jesus Himself returns, vanquishes the enemy, and later, a perfect, Edenic perfection is restored throughout all of creation.

Back to Aliens and Waterworlds

This brings us back to the original point in taking this theological detour. If ancient creation accounts are really just describing an extraterrestrial influence of the origin of human beings, where do we see room for that in light of the information contained here? Even if there is room for it, the supposed alien gods do not seem to be friendly with humankind. However, if the beings commonly described as today's extraterrestrials are, in fact, these old gods, suddenly things begin to make more sense. Maybe it's not aliens posing as gods in the past, but gods posing as aliens now. This view seems more compatible not only with the scriptural text of the ancient Near East, but also with modern-day abduction reports and UFO phenomena. Could this explain why these entities have a fondness for large bodies of water, leading some UFO researchers to believe alien bases exist underwater. Could this also explain the deep underground bases said to be inhabited with alien civilizations wielding super-advanced technology? Could this be evidence that these beings possess a modern understanding of Leviathan and Behemoth? Could this be why waterworld exoplanets seem to have the highest-percentage chance of harboring extraterrestrial life?

At the same time, however, does this mean, from a purely biblical, theological point of view, that there is no chance extraterrestrial life can exist? Given all this information, is there still room for intelligent life on other planets to be a possibility and still be compatible with the Bible? It may seem, given what we looked at so far throughout this book, that the answer is obvious, but it may not be as obvious as we might initially think. Most who accept the information in this chapter might be inclined to close the door completely on the possibility of extraterrestrial life. However, as we will see a later, there are other factors to consider, making this a far more complex issue than it would seem in the surface. The possibility does exist, yet in a way likely most would not expect. Maybe, up until now, we have been looking at this issue all wrong. It could be we were only considering a portion of the entire question. Perhaps there is more to this story than what we thought.

chapter eleven

ARE EVANGELICALS AND
EXTRATERRESTRIALS COMPATIBLE?

HANDS DOWN, THE biggest question I (Josh Peck) ever had as a child was: Are aliens real? I loved science fiction. In fact, I still do. I also loved the Bible. Again, I still do. However I didn't know if the two were compatible. I was raised in a Baptist family who mostly didn't think such questions were too terribly important. That's not a dig on anyone, of course. Everyone has his or her own interests and priorities. When I would ask someone in my family or the pastor of our church about aliens, the answer was usually some variation of, "Oh Josh, they're just demons." That was that.

However, I craved more information. If it was true aliens that are demons, *why?* Where do we get that from? The Bible is basically silent on this issue (though there have been attempts throughout history to read one position or another into the text, as we will see throughout this chapter). How can the demonic theory be supported using the text of the Bible? I wondered about these questions for the rest of my young life.

As a teenager, especially after the age of 18, I began to accept the possibility of life on other planets. A big influence on me at the time was New Age theology. I was young, New Age was exciting, New Age allowed me to believe in aliens. So, it seemed like a good fit. It wasn't, but reasons for that go a bit outside the scope of this topic.

By the time I was in my mid-20s, I was pretty much convinced that aliens were real. I did not believe they were demonic, but I did believe they were created by God. I couldn't justify my views with biblical texts and I certainly had many unanswered questions, but this didn't matter much to me at the time. After I had a couple of years with my groundless beliefs (I'm not saying there aren't grounds for believing these things; I just didn't have any at the time), I began to crave more information. If aliens were real, why 'didn't the Bible talk about them? Why would God create something and not tell us about it, especially since people seem to have horrific visitations and abduction experiences? Why would God keep this a secret? It didn't make sense, and the holes in my logic were starting to grow too big to ignore. So, I did the only sensible thing I could think of at the time. I decided to pray and ask God about it.

I didn't get an answer right away. In fact, even today, I'm not sure if I have the full answer. However, there are pieces of the answer out there that I was not aware of at the time. The more I discovered these pieces, the more they seemed to bring the total picture into focus. My piece of the puzzle was the Genesis 6 Nephilim interpretation of alien and UFO phenomena. Because this interpretation has been vastly covered by authors and researchers far more eloquent than me, this chapter will not cover it, except to say that it is a very legitimate interpretation and one that I held onto for years (and in many ways still do). I suggest, if the reader is not familiar with the topic of the Nephilim, that you pick up a copy of *The Unseen Realm* by Dr. Michael S. Heiser. I believe it to be the best writing on the topic, although Genesis 6 is only one aspect of the book. For information about how it might relate to modern UFO phenomena, there are too many books and DVDs on the topic to list here; however, most of these are available through Defender Publishing.

After years with the Genesis 6 Nephilim interpretation, I began to get the feeling again that there was more to the story. Certain issues were still up in the air. I still had questions. As with any issue, I wanted to understand the other viewpoints in order to weigh them against my own. I really wanted to know, given the amount of current information, yet in a completely broad sense (not considering specific races such as grays, reptilians, and nordics for the moment), if evangelical Christianity could accommodate an undeniable extraterrestrial reality.[238]

Maintaining the Demonic Interpretation

As stated in the introduction, the authors of this book both hold to what is generally referred to as the "demonic interpretation" of the current alien abduction phenomenon. What this means, is brief terms, is that we (Derek and Josh) fully recognize and accept that the typical races of entities commonly referred to as "aliens" (i.e., reptilians, grays, nordics, mantids, etc.) are most likely demonic beings and/or fallen angels. For reasons outlined previously in this book, we believe this is the likeliest interpretation due to the anti-Christian and anti-biblical nature of the messages, teachings, and philosophies given to abductees from these entities. The reason we want to make this clear is that this chapter, perhaps more than any other before it, may prove challenging to some Christians if the purpose is not properly understood. This chapter is not written in order to state that the beings commonly witnessed in alien abduction phenomena are in fact aliens. No, we do not believe this to be true. Rather, this chapter is to answer a much broader question, wholly divorced from the UFO and alien abduction phenomena altogether. We are looking at the question from a purely theological position while, for the moment, setting aside any commonly reported nonhuman entity. This chapter could easily be misconstrued if this is not established right off the bat. This is not apologetics for commonly reported nonhuman entities to be understood as aliens from another planet. We do not endorse that view. Rather, this is to ask the question: What does the Bible have to say about the possibility of life on other planets?

Alexander UFO Religious Crisis Survey

Anyone who has done substantial study of official disclosure has come across the religious aspect. How would religious institutions react to either an official disclosure event or a genuine extraterrestrial presence as a whole? In fact, it has been hypothesized that this is a major reason our government seems to be hiding information from us: fear of widespread panic and hysteria, especially among religious groups. There have been several attempts to gauge what the reaction would be among religious Americans. The earliest formal effort was in the Alexander UFO Religious Crisis Survey (AUFORCS) in 1994.

This survey was interesting for a variety of reasons. It focused on a sample of Protestant ministers, Roman Catholic priests, and Jewish rabbis. It asked questions related to possible government disclosure of UFOs and alien contact information. Also, it was directed by Victoria Alexander, wife of retired Army Colonel Dr. John Alexander, a veteran of the U.S. Army Intelligence and Security Command and Los Alamos National Laboratory's nonlethal weapons program, as well as a member of the intergovernmental Advanced Theoretical Physics working group.[239]

The purpose of the survey was to find an answer to a seemingly simple, yet extremely important, question: Would disclosure of U.S. government contact with aliens really precipitate a religious crisis that would threaten continuity of government and even our civilization? To seek an answer, a mail survey of Protestant, Catholic, and Jewish clergy was conducted in order to discover their informed opinions. One thousand copies of the survey were mailed to randomly selected religious bodies in the United States and the results of the survey were based on a 23 percent return (230 of 1,000 surveys).

For the survey, the U.S. was divided into five regions. Five hundred and sixty-three surveys were sent to Protestant churches, 396 to Roman Catholic churches, and 41 to Jewish synagogues. Among the questions in the survey, one asked for the approximate size of the congregation. Eighty-one Protestant respondents answered the "Approximate Size of

Congregation" line, totaling to 35,824 families. Forty-five Roman Catholic respondents answered, totaling 56,208 families. Six Jewish respondents answered, totaling 1,445 families. Altogether, this totals 132 congregations and 93,477 families.

Based on a U.S. population of 280 million (at the time the survey was conducted), Protestants represented 28 percent of the population and 54 percent of church membership. Catholics represented 20 percent of the population and 38.6 percent of church membership. Lastly, Jews represented 2 percent of the population and 4 percent of church membership. The fourth-highest religious body, Eastern churches, represented 1 percent of the population and 2 percent of church membership. These four religious groups represented 51 percent of the U.S. population.

Less than 25 percent of the surveys were returned. Also, there were no questions to determine how theologically conservative (meaning taking the Bible as the inspired Word of God) the individual minister, priest, or rabbi was who answered the survey. Logically, the more conservative the respondent, the more likely he or she may have been troubled by some of the questions on the survey. For example, some of the questions were:

- Do you think genetic similarities between mankind and an advanced extraterrestrial civilization would challenge the basic religious concepts of man's relative position in the universe? (Sample question #5).
- If an advanced extraterrestrial civilization had religious beliefs fundamentally different from ours, would it endanger organized religions in this country? (Sample question #6)
- If an advanced extraterrestrial civilization proclaimed responsibility for producing human life, would it cause a religious crisis? (Sample question #10)

Questions like these may have been the reason for such a low percentage of return. Some, possibly even most based on the 23 percent return, may have either been troubled by the questions or thought them outright ridiculous. They may have chosen to throw the survey in the garbage rather than consider the questions seriously and theologically.

As popular as this survey became in the UFO community, the math and percentages speak to its legitimacy. If we generously assume a family is four people on average (two adults and two children), then only 373,908 people in the United States are covered (93,477 families multiplied by 4 equals 373,908). Given that only about half of the respondents disclosed their congregation size, we can double that figure to liberally estimate a total of 747,816 people. This means, by the survey's own calculations and sources, that, at most, only 0.27 percent (747,816 is 0.2671 percent of 280 million) of the U.S. population was accounted for in the survey. This only accounts for 1 in 374 people in the United States (280 million divided by 747,816 is 374.423655017). This is roughly the equivalent of taking two random students out of an average American high school and expecting only their views to represent the views of the rest of the students.[240] Simply speaking, the survey does not cover what is needed to fairly assess how religious people would react to a genuine extraterrestrial reality.

History of Religious and Theological Beliefs Concerning Extraterrestrials

One might wonder how we got here. How did evangelical Christianity and theological conservatism get to the point at which it is generally opposed to the idea of life on other worlds? The history of this question is deep and could easily justify an entire book on the subject. Surprisingly, it 'hasn't always been this way. In fact, not too long ago, a belief in the possibility of extraterrestrial life was commonly accepted among Christians and other religious circles. So, what changed?

The major opponents to the idea of life on other worlds in ancient times were Plato and Aristotle. Both philosophers held to geocentric cosmologies (the view stating that the sun and everything in the heavens revolves around the Earth). From this, Aristotle and Plato asserted that all matter was contained in this world, thereby leaving no room for others. The unchangeability of the heavens was cited as proof of this.[241] Most early Christian authors generally opposed the idea of extraterrestrial life, because they tended to favor Platonic and Aristotelian philosophical views rather than the materialistic philosophy of the atomists at the time. However, over time, questions arose. If God was all-powerful, why was He only able to create one world? Also, if only one world existed, how could God possibly be truly infinite and omnipotent? The theologian Thomas Aquinas (1225–1274) expressed his ideas about how to solve this problem. He stated that God has the power to create infinite worlds, but that all the matter in the universe had been used to construct Earth.[242]

Things began to turn around in 1277, however, when Etienne Tempier, the bishop of Paris, issued a condemnation of doctrines that seemed to set limits on God's omnipotence under the authority of the Pope.[243] One of the propositions condemned was "the First Cause (God) cannot make many worlds." This didn't mean the Church began teaching about life on other planets, or what was called at the time "Plurality of Worlds." The physics of Aristotle, which were still popular until the sixteenth century, taught that if any other worlds did exist, they would have to gravitate to the center of the universe, where Earth was believed to be located. Rather than the extreme of teaching Plurality of Worlds, it merely became wrong to suggest that God could not create many worlds if He wanted.[244]

In 1410, some more progress was made. The Jewish philosopher Crescas wrote:

> Everything said in negation to the possibility of many worlds is vanity and a striving after wind…yet we are unable by means of mere speculation to ascertain the true nature of what is outside this world; our sages, peace be on them, have seem fit to warn against searching and inquiring into what is above and what is below, what is before and what is behind.[245]

Therefore, while Crescas was able to entertain the possibility, he still restrained the idea with a warning against pursuing it much farther.

The openness the religious world was beginning to see led to the introduction of what Christian philosophers would call the "Principle of Plentitude" during the Renaissance. This was a philosophical/theological idea, not necessarily a biblical one, positing that an omnipotent Creator like the God of the Bible must, of necessity, bring to be everything possible to fully honor His own goodness and power. Therefore, Christian theology went from seeing other worlds as possible to arguing that they might even be required. The Principle of Plentiful caused this line of thinking to take another leap forward in 1440, when Cardinal Nicolas of Cusa (1401–1464), Bishop of Brixen and Christian philosopher, wrote *Of Learned Ignorance*. In the book, he stated:

> Rather than think so many stars and parts of the heavens are uninhabited, and that this Earth of ours alone is peopled…we will suppose that in every region there are inhabitants, differing in nature by rank and all owing their origin to God.[246]

Nicolas of Cusa was the first prominent Latin Christian scholar to embrace the idea of extraterrestrials.

Later, during the Reformation, the Principle of Plentitude faced some opposition, particularly from Lutheran reformer Philip Melanchthon (1497–1560). In 1550, Melanchthon warned that Copernican cosmology would lead to a dangerous idea stating that Christ's incarnation and redemption could have occurred on another planet. Despite this, belief in extraterrestrials among Christians and Christian theologians continued to ride in popularity during the Enlightenment.

Near the end of the eighteenth century, the generally accepted view inside and outside the Church was the universe was filled with intelligent life. In fact, in light of the Principle of Plentitude, many Christians believed that the possibility of life elsewhere in the universe actually enhanced an individual's religious perspective. However, the acceptance of the possibility—or even probability, according to most at the time—of extraterrestrial life was undermined by one of the Enlightenment's major figures.

Thomas Paine, in 1793, argued that astronomical science made it impossible for any thinking person to accept the general Christian notions of a divine incarnation and redeemer in his book *Age of Reason*. Through his history of confronting Christianity's belief in extraterrestrial life, Paine became a deist. In his own words:

> From whence...could arise the...strange conceit that the Almighty...should...come to die in our world because, they say, one man and one woman had eaten an apple! And, on the other hand, are we to suppose that every world in the boundless creation had an Eve, an apple, a serpent, and a redeemer?... The Son of God...would have nothing else to do than to travel from world to world, in an endless succession of death, with scarcely a momentary interval of life.[247]

Many Christian authors in the period after Paine responded to his arguments. Among the most successful were Timothy Dwight (1752–1817) and Thomas Chalmers (1780–1847). Both Chalmers and Dwight were conservative in terms of their theology. Dwight was the president of Yale University from 1795 until his death in 1817. Chalmers was the most prominent Scottish religious figure of his day. He is quoted as saying:

> For anything we can know by reason, the plan of redemption may have its influences and its bearings on those creatures of God who people other regions.[248]

The belief in the possibility of extraterrestrial life continued through the late nineteenth and twentieth centuries in the Church. However, it soon turned into the threat many Christians see it as today. With the advent of Darwinism, scientists began to be viewed as antagonistic by

Christians who accepted the Bible's claim of a divine Creator. The Church became increasingly hostile to the idea of intelligent life on other planets once Darwinists concluded that the discovery of extraterrestrial life would add support for naturalistic evolution against the idea of a Creator. This led to where we are today.

Throughout much of history, the Church supported the idea of extraterrestrial life. Of course, intelligent life on other planets brought up important theological issues, such as relating to the incarnation and redemption; however, these questions were not viewed as threats to the faith. Two main issues drove the Church away from the ET question altogether, neither of which actually came from the Bible itself. The first was that certain threatening, yet not theologically sound, problems were invented by people like Paine. Second was the unnecessary link of random and natural evolutionary theory to the extraterrestrial life question. The first made Christians wonder if the question of extraterrestrial life was a legitimate problem. The second caused Christians to feel like they had to distance themselves from the idea of extraterrestrial life so as to not accept the naturalistic/evolutionary explanation of life both on Earth and possibly on other planets.

The Supposed Threat of Evolution

Today, we are still dealing with the same problems within the Church. It is generally accepted, by the world's standards, that intelligent alien life would either prove or at least be strong evidence for the theories of naturalistic evolution and/or panspermia (the idea stating that life on Earth came from outer space). However, this problem is relatively irrelevant. Many theologically conservative Christians embrace the theory of evolution, though they see evolution as a process started by God rather than by some accident or completely natural event. These Christians are usually known as Theistic Evolutionists and/or Intelligent Design Theorists. For them, the concern isn't evolution as a whole. The concern is specifically naturalistic, purposeless, and undirected evolution. If extraterrestrial life forms were discovered, those in this category would assume that God started the same evolutionary process on other planets as they recognize here on Earth, and extraterrestrial life would be the result. Similarly, those who reject evolution as a process of creation could, by default, hold the position that God created alien life forms just as He created life on Earth.

The evolution angle really is no threat to Christianity, regardless of whether one believes in evolution. Even if evolution is true, it still does not explain the origin of matter in the universe. How life evolves and how life originates in the first place are two separate questions. The discovery of an advanced extraterrestrial civilization would not answer the question of origin. Even if ET claimed to be the origin of humanity, the question could just be turned around: *Then who created you?*

Of course, one does not have to believe in evolution in order to accept the possibility of extraterrestrial life. However, it is good to understand why some choose to embrace evolution while still accepting the Christian faith. As early as the fourth and fifth centuries, biblical scholars and theologians were already noticing peculiar phrasing in the creation account. Genesis 1:24 states, "And God said, let the earth bring forth every living creature."

Gregory of Nysa understood this as meaning there was a type of potency in preexisting material that can be activated only by the Creator when He sees fit to do so.[249] Augustine thought along similar lines when he stated that the Creator "implanted seeds or potencies of each separate kind of organism in the created universe from the first moment of its existence.... He made all things together, disposing them in an order based not on intervals of time but on causal connections...there was invisibly present all that would later develop."[250]

This brings us back to one of the survey questions from earlier in this chapter. Would it be troublesome to a Christian if extraterrestrial life was discovered to have a genetic relationship to human beings? If we accept that God created everything, it actually would be reasonable to expect a genetic relationship between life on other planets and life on Earth. There are genetic relationships between life forms on Earth, such as those between primates and humans. That, of course, does not mean that humans *created* primates in the sense of a directed, conscious choice. Whether evolution is true or not is beside the point; a Christian explanation for genetic relationship is that all life was created by God's design, so of course there would be relationships. From a Christian perspective, God prefers to create biological life and other things in certain ways, so we should expect those ways to be repeated throughout the rest of His creation.

Using extraterrestrial life of any kind as proof of a cause-and-effect relationship is logically unsound. It is an incoherent relationship. Again, we are genetically related in certain ways to primates. We are even far more technologically advanced than primates. However, this does not mean we created primates. Therefore, despite what one believes about evolution, proof of extraterrestrial life would not cancel out any biblical understanding of creation, even if the extraterrestrial life happened to have genetic similarities to human beings. If anything, this would lend further support to a common Creator of humans and extraterrestrials.

The Supposed Threat to Inerrancy

The question of inerrancy comes up often while discussing extraterrestrial life in light of biblical understanding. Usually it is assumed that extraterrestrial life would be a threat to the concept of biblical inerrancy. After all, the Bible doesn't teach that there are aliens—so if there are, wouldn't that prove the Bible to be false?

In short, no. To assume so, frankly, is ridiculous. This way of thinking is easily shown to be logically and biblically incoherent. There are plenty of things we know exist yet are never mentioned in the Bible. Everything from the farthest reaches of space to the smallest, most fundamental quantum particle, to the microwave in my kitchen: None are mentioned in the Bible, yet all exist.

The Bible issues no direct statement one way or another concerning life elsewhere in the cosmos, yet this cannot be used as proof to either support nor deny that such life exists. To do so would be to argue from silence. There are even certain words throughout the Bible that may seem synonymous in English, yet may not mean the same in their original languages. For example, the words "earth" and "world" do not always mean the same thing in the Bible as they usually do in our modern English vernacular. Depending on the context, "world" can be more restrictive than "earth" and refer to a local, known area (i.e., the known world in ancient times from a biblical context, which would have been the Near-Eastern region), or "world" could refer to something more expansive than the "earth," such as the whole of creation.[251]

Therefore, a genuine extraterrestrial reality would not have to automatically contradict any biblical statement. While the book of Genesis is regarded as a true Creation account, it is not exhaustive. It doesn't tell us everything. It gives the information we need to understand the point the writer wanted to get across: YHWH is the Creator, no one else; here are some descriptions. Thus, we have the creation account of Genesis.

The Incarnation and Redemption Question

This brings us to the supposed threat to the incarnation and redemption. The argument usually sounds roughly the same regardless of who it's coming from. Basically, it asks: If there is life on other planets, wouldn't Jesus have to be born on all those planets, as an alien, in order to offer the aliens redemption like He did with humans?

The whole argument really revolves around redemption. If there is no need for redemption, there is no need for an incarnation. However, if redemption is needed, the Bible does not describe a process by which it is granted to nonhuman entities. Angels who have sinned against God are not granted forgiveness or redemption of any kind. On the other end of the spectrum, there is nothing to suggest that animals are in need of redemption or forgiveness. What evidence is there that extraterrestrials would be in need of similar forgiveness and redemption as human beings?

This usually comes up because Romans 8 and Revelation 21–22 tell us that the atonement of Christ ultimately extends throughout the entire universe. Scripture teaches that everything will be recreated to be like Eden before the Fall of Man. It would stand to reason that extraterrestrial life, whether intelligent or not, if it exists, would be included in this similar to animals, yet the Bible makes no mention one way or another.

This is where most theologically conservative Christians might be tempted to throw everything into the "they're demons" category. This is a perfectly reasonable way of looking at current UFO and alien abduction phenomena and, in that regard (with the Genesis 6 Nephilim interpretation in mind), I tend to agree. When we discuss specific "alien races" such as the grays, reptilians, nordics, mantids, etc., that people have said they encountered, I agree they would likely fall into the biblical category of demons and fallen angels in physical manifestations. The reason for this is that the Bible teaches to test every spirit (1 John 4). In many alien abduction reports, when spirituality and/or religion are discussed, the nonhuman entity usually teaches the human something against what Jesus Christ has taught, sometimes even going as far as to single out Christianity, Jesus, or YHWH directly in a negative manner, yet this dialogue in regards to other non-Christian religions typically doesn't occur. What would be the reason for this if these beings were merely extraterrestrials and not physical manifestations of fallen angels and/or demons?

However, for our discussion here, we are not considering these specific entities. We are looking at the question as a whole, divorced from all the modern UFO and alien abduction reports. Setting aside the encounters and experiences people have had, could alien life exist out in the cosmos without directly contradicting the Bible? Therefore, when we discuss a need or a lack of need for redemption, we do not have any specific alien race in mind. We are speaking to the larger, hypothetical question of genuine extraterrestrial life, not entities posing as extraterrestrial life.

When Christian theologians and apologists who accept the possibility of extraterrestrials consider this question, they tend to fall into one of two camps. Some believe multiple incarnations and even multiple crucifixions would be necessary, meaning God was born into alien flesh to save aliens just as He did for humans. However, most are appalled by this idea and find it ridiculous. The Christian worldview states that Jesus was God's only Son. Does Jesus have to die and be reborn on every inhabited planet if they exist? Because of this, many Christians lean toward the idea that we are alone in the cosmos.

The second camp looks at redemption a bit differently. While it's true the New Testament teaches that all creation will be redeemed, it is an assumption to say that all of the universe needs to be redeemed from moral guilt, wrongdoing, or sin outside of humanity. The Bible doesn't say our intelligence or spirituality is why we are morally guilty before God and in need of redemption. It is not because we are intelligent, sentient, self-aware, conscious beings. We are in a state of needed redemption because God applies Adam's guilt to all humans. Salvation, in a biblical sense, cannot be earned and is never deserved. It is a gift to us by God through Jesus if we choose to accept it. Therefore, if God did not apply moral guilt to extraterrestrials, and there is no indication He did if they exist, then the redemption objection is rendered illogical. Extraterrestrial life is likely of no concern when it comes to God's redemptive plan. Similar to animals not needing a savior, there is no indication that extraterrestrials would either.

To illustrate this further, we can look at what Scripture says:

But we do see Jesus, who for a little while was made lower than the angels, now crowned with glory and honor because of the suffering of death, so that by the grace of God he might taste death for everyone. It was fitting that God, for whom and through whom all things exist, in bringing many children to glory.... For this reason Jesus is not ashamed to call them brothers and sisters, saying "I will proclaim your name to my brothers and sister, in the midst of the congregation I will praise you." Since, therefore, the children share flesh and blood, he himself likewise shared the same things, so that through death he might destroy the one who has the power of death, that is, the devil, and free those who all their lives were held in slavery by the fear of death. For it is clear that he did not come to help angels, but the descendants of Abraham. What about the idea that all created things will be redeemed? (Hebrews 2:9–16)

I consider that the sufferings of this present time are not worth comparing with the glory about to be revealed to us. For the creation waits with eager longing for the revealing of the children of God; for the creation was subjected to futility, not of its own will but by the will of the ones who subjected it, in hope that the creation itself will be set free from its bondage to decay and will obtain the freedom of the glory of the children of God. We know that the whole creation has been groaning in labor pains until now. (Romans 8:18–22)

For this reason, since the day we heard it, we have not ceased praying for you and asking that you may be filled with the knowledge of God's will in all spiritual wisdom and understanding, so that you may lead lives worthy of the Lord, fully pleasing to him, as you bear fruit in every good work and as you grow in the knowledge of God. may you be made strong with all the strength that comes from his glorious power, and may you be prepared to endure everything with patience, while joyfully giving thanks to the Father, who has enabled you to share in the inheritance of the saints in the light. He has rescued us from the power of darkness and transferred us into the kingdom of his beloved Son, in whom we have redemption, the forgiveness of sins. He is the image of the invisible God, the firstborn of all creation, for in him all things in heaven and on earth were created, things visible and invisible, whether thrones or dominions or rulers or powers- all things have been created through him and for him. He himself is before all things, and in him all things hold together. He is the head of the body, the church; he is the beginning, the firstborn from the dead, so that he might come to have first place in everything. For in him all the fullness of God was pleased to dwell, and through him God was pleased to reconcile to himself all things, whether on earth or in heaven, by making peace through the blood of his cross. (Colossians 1:9–20)

The point of the redemption of all creation, humans excluded, is not to undo a sinful nature, or a moral guilt issue. The Earth and animals are not guilty in a moral sense. The point is to make creation what it once was in Eden and set it in a right relationship with God.

It would seem tempting to equate human beings with extraterrestrials in the sense of spiritual stature. At first glance, it might make sense to think that if God created aliens, they would be made in His image, similar to human beings. However, this begs the question, what exactly is the "image of God?" Is the image of God specific to humans only, or can some other life form have it? How does this affect our standing with God and His standing with potential extraterrestrial life?

The Image of God

When the term "image of God" is properly defined, it shows, from the understanding that intelligent alien life would not have been created in the image of God, that Christianity actually could sustain an extraterrestrial reality quite easily. Humanity would still maintain the uniqueness of being created in the image of God, because extraterrestrial life, if it exists, would be excluded from it. Once we properly define the image of God, the solution comes out without any of the common problems used to argue against the possibility of intelligent life on another planet.

The Bible gives us a clear description of the image in the book of Genesis:

Then God said, "Let us make man in our image, after our likeness. And let them have dominion over the fish of the sea and over the birds of the heavens and over the livestock and over all the earth and over every creeping thing that creeps on the earth." So God created man in his own image, in the image of God he created him; male and female he created them. And God blessed them. And God said to them, "Be fruitful and multiply and fill the earth and subdue it, and have dominion over the fish of the sea and over the birds of the heavens and over every living thing that moves on the earth." (Genesis 1:26–28, ESV)

It is quite common, and has been so for centuries, to define the image of God as something to do with intelligence, the ability to communicate, the possession of a spirit and/or soul, the presence of a conscience, the ability to exercise free will, and the capacity for abstract thought—or some combination of these attributes. Through biblical clarification, the image of God is none of these. The reason for this is that the image is what makes mankind distinguishably unique in relation to any other created thing in the universe.

In his book, *The Unseen Realm*, Dr. Michael S. Heiser explains the image of God from a theological and biblical perspective. From the book of Genesis and using the term "divine image bearing," Dr. Heiser lists descriptions of the image of God:

- Both men and women are included.
- Divine image bearing is what makes humankind distinct from the rest of earthly creation (i.e., plants and animals). The text of Genesis 1:26 does not inform us that divine image bearing makes us distinct from heavenly beings, those sons of God who were already in existence at the time of creation. The plurals in Genesis 1:26 mean that, in some way, we share something with them when it comes to bearing God's image.
- There is something about the image that makes humankind "like" God in some way.

- There is nothing in the text to suggest that the image has been or can be bestowed incrementally or partially. You're either created as God's image bearer or you aren't. One cannot speak of being partly or potentially bearing God's image.[252]

This tells us that the image of God must be something possessed in its entirety by every human being regardless of physical or mental development.

The conditions Dr. Heiser listed are mandated by what Genesis 1:26 says about the image, but there are other important verses to consider as well:

This is the written account of Adam's line. When God created humankind, he made him in the likeness of God. (Genesis 5:1)

Whoever sheds the blood of humankind, by humankind shall his blood be shed; for in the image of God has God made humankind. (Genesis 9:6)

If we think of humankind as image bearers rather than the image being an attribute of humankind, these things begin to make more sense. Humans are representations of God on Earth. We are to represent Him on Earth and take care of it in the way He would if He were here. This is why murder is such a grave offense. When someone kills another human being, he is essentially killing God in effigy. The image is what humans *are*, not what humans *have*.

This is why extraterrestrials, if they exist, would not be considered as being created in the image of God. They aren't human. They weren't put in charge of the Earth the way humans are. God only tasked humans with being His representatives on Earth; therefore, extraterrestrials would not be made in the image of God. Purely by status, not considering intelligence or ability, and as far as we can discern from the biblical descriptions of humanity's uniqueness, extraterrestrials would likely be grouped closer to animals in the sense of not playing a central or even a major role in God's plan for redemption.

This brings us to other heavenly/divine beings. What are we to do with the plurals in Genesis 1:26 ("let *us* make man in *our* image, after *our* likeness")? It is true, other divine beings (or members of the divine council, as Dr. Heiser explains in *The Unseen Realm*) are also God's images. Humankind is still unique, however, because humans are God's images on Earth. Humanity, not any other divine being, was placed in charge.

Ancient Jewish texts tell us that one divine being thought this was unjust, that humans were in charge over the Earth as God's representatives. This divine being (called "the serpent" in Genesis) refused to bow to humanity's authority, seeing himself as a superior being, so he rebelled and plotted revenge. We get the rest of the story in the book of Genesis.

Taking all of this into account, there is no real problem with the idea of extraterrestrial life from biblical descriptions of creation, humanity, and God's redemptive plan. The supposed problems brought up from people like Thomas Paine are merely contrived and hold no real weight against Scripture. At its heart, using the Bible to either support or deny the existence of extraterrestrial life is an argument made purely from silence.

Extraterrestrials as Angels?

One other argument brought up making many Christians uncomfortable states that the angels in the Bible are actually extraterrestrials. Most often, this claim comes from nonbelievers, usually from the standpoint of Ancient Astronaut Theory. The problem with this is, in order to argue the point and still maintain a non-Christian view, one must cherry-pick verses to support it and ignore others that refute it. At its face, this method is intellectually dishonest.

While most taking this view likely don't accept it in order to be purposely malicious to Christianity or to promulgate untruths, this doesn't make it any less incoherent. Likely, what is happening is that most holding this view know the few verses involved in the argument but are unaware of the biblical text as a whole. After all, there are pastors and prominent figures in ministry who do not fully understand the whole Scripture and who would have trouble defending basic doctrines of Christianity.

When taking Scripture as a whole, a person who is determined to reject Christianity would not want to hold the view of angels being misidentified extraterrestrials. There are four major problems with this view. First, mortal bodies would be required of extraterrestrials if there are actual, alien bodies recovered from UFO crash sites and stored somewhere. However, the Bible clearly teaches that angels are immortal and do not have determined lifespans. For example:

For when they [people] rise from the dead, they neither marry nor are given in marriage, but are like angels in heaven. (Mark 12:25)

And the angels who did not keep their own position, but left their proper dwelling, he has kept in eternal chains in deepest darkness for the judgment of the great Day. (Jude 1:6)

Angels in Heaven have no need of reproduction, because they are immortal. As for the angels who fell, as described in the book of Jude, if they are kept in eternal chains, it would stand to reason that the angels would have to be immortal as well.

Second, angels (*mal'akim* in Hebrew) are always depicted in human form. Speaking only of angels, there is no *mal'ak* described in nonhuman form. Of course, there are Seraphim, Cherubim, and Ophanim who appear in nonhuman manifestations, yet even these have no resemblance to the appearance of beings commonly reported in alien abduction scenarios. The only race of otherworldly beings remotely resembling anything angelic described in the Bible would be the "Nordics," yet problems are there as well, as we will see a bit later.

Third, angels are never described as needing a flying craft to travel from one place to another. They would more closely be described as "extradimensional" beings rather than extraterrestrial. Certain verses describe chariots and angels together (Psalm 68:18; 2 Kings 6:17), but an actual relationship between vehicle and pilot is never established. Also note that the heavenly chariots in Scripture are usually described with horses. Eextraterrestrial spaceships, for obvious reasons, would not be pulled by horses.

Fourth, if extraterrestrials were misidentified as angels in the New Testament, then logic would lead us to accept whatever else the New Testament says about these beings. In other words, it would be illogical and incoherent to use the Bible to prove that angels are actually extraterrestrials but then reject what the Bible says about these beings. This brings us back to the question of the Nordics, as well as any other supposed extraterrestrial beings. Consider these biblical descriptions of angels and try to imagine replacing "angels" with "extraterrestrials" in order to see if they line up with what is commonly taught from Ancient Astronaut theorists.

- Angels only rescue the followers of Jesus at the Rapture/Second Coming (Matthew 24:31; 1 Thessalonians 4:16–18; 2 Thessalonians 1).
- Angels announced that Jesus was the Messiah and Savior of all mankind (Luke 2:10–15).
- Angels are inferior and subject to Jesus Christ (1 Peter 3:21–22).
- Angels carry out the wrath of God on the Earth and unbelievers in the end times (Revelation 14:17–15:1)

There are, of course, many others such as these, but this short list should be enough to show the logical disconnect between biblical angels and modern descriptions of beings witnessed during abduction scenarios.[253]

Would We Really Want Directed Panspermia to Be Our Origin Story?

While it is true that Christianity can accommodate a genuine extraterrestrial reality, there are still aspects of the debate that Christian theology would reject. One of these aspects is the idea stating that extraterrestrials created humanity (what is sometimes known as "directed panspermia"). Again, this view still doesn't remove the question of the ultimate Creator. Stating that extraterrestrials created humanity does not get someone away from God. The next obvious question would be: "Then where did they come from?" Some may even be tempted to state that God Himself is an extraterrestrial, but this is nonsense, because not only does this theory run into similar problems as the extraterrestrials-as-angels position, but it also doesn't explain the origin of matter. For example, no one who is taken seriously claims that aliens from another planet created the universe.

There are some other major problems with the idea of panspermia, not only for Christians, but for non-Christians as well. The idea that aliens, specifically the ones people experience in abduction scenarios, created humanity is extremely attractive to many people today. However, if we look deeper into the issue, we discover that this idea may not be as appealing when we consider all of its ramifications and consequences.[254]

Typically, those who hold this view agree on a number of things. They most often agree that humanity was created by extraterrestrials who came to Earth long ago. They believe these beings and their creation of mankind is described in ancient Mesopotamian texts that are mirrored in the Bible. Also, they typically believe that these extraterrestrials are the ancient gods of humanity, mistaken as deities, but still our creators.

There are some logical and negative conclusions coming from this idea, though typically these are not discussed in the mainstream. For example, if extraterrestrials created humanity, then human beings do not possess an inherent dignity. According to ancient Mesopotamian creation myths, human beings were created as slaves by the Anunnaki gods. From *The Epic of Atrahasis:*

> The seven great Anunna-gods were burdening
> the Igigi-gods with forced labor…
> Ea made ready to speak,
> and said to the gods, his brothers:
> "What calumny do we lay to their charge?
> Their forced labor was heavy, their misery too much!
> Every day…
> the outcry was loud, we could hear the clamor.
> There is…
> Belet-ili, the midwife, is present.
> Let her create, then, a human, a man,
> Let him bear the yoke!
> Let him bear the yoke!
> Let man assume the drudgery of the god."
> Belet-ili, the midwife, is present.
> Let the midwife create a human being!
> Let man assume the drudgery of the god.[255]

Basically, the gods were tasked with hard work, so they decided to create humans to do the work instead. According to these ancient texts, humans are nothing more than a slave race.

One might wonder if, in this context, humanity was created in the image of the gods in the same way the Bible teaches we are created in the image of YHWH. Despite what some of the Ancient Astronaut literature claims, the image of God idea does not appear in Mesopotamian texts; it is purely a biblical and theistic concept. In fact, the word for "image" never appears in the Mesopotamian account of humanity's creation.[256] Rather, in Mesopotamian understanding, we were created far below any "image" concept. We were created as slaves.

Of course, this clashes drastically with what many alien abductees and experiencers have been told about humanity. Many of them, even on an individual basis, are told they are special and loved. Yet, at the same time, they are expected to believe the contrasting creation accounts of supposed Anunnaki alien beings. Therefore, how can the message of being special be trusted by the abductee/experiencer? Shouldn't aliens be aware of what their ancient ancestors said about them? The conflicting accounts simply do not add up.

We can contrast this creation account to the biblical one. In a biblical worldview, every man, woman, child, and even unborn person has inherent worth as an image-bearer of God. The Bible teaches, as we saw earlier, that life is sacred. We are God's representatives on Earth. Through biblical teaching, every person truly *is* special, unique, and loved in God's eyes.

If the alien creator worldview is correct, there is no higher purpose for the life of any human. Nobody is truly special. There is no concept of eternal reward in Heaven from a personal and loving God. In fact, if any concept humans have of God is actually a physical, alien life form who came to be through naturalistic, evolutionary means, this limits reality to the physical universe. There would be no notion of a spiritual reality outside of material reality from which physical reality comes. Essentially and logically, any sense of spirituality would have to be abandoned; otherwise, it would be illogical and inconsistent to say that aliens were not created by any sort of God, yet they are spiritual beings like us with a soul. Where did the alien soul come from? Are we to suppose it evolved as well? It is simply illogical, yet these contradictory ideas are what many abductees claim to have been told by their alien visitors.

Those who fall into the category of those who believe the universe itself has life and treat it as a living being or "biocosm" have a logical inconsistency as well. No matter how spiritual they might think the universe is, without a Creator, it is still composed of matter and nothing beyond. Usually those who hold this view consider the universe as its own creator. Regarding it this way avoids the idea of a personal deity who transcends creation. This is an attractive idea to some, because it allows the individual to avoid religion, the Bible, and the personal accountability

Christianity teaches while still maintaining a belief in something bigger than one's own self. However, again, the logical conclusion of this view is that there is nothing outside of ordinary matter. No one is special nor unique. Nothing we do or believe really matters in the grand scheme of things, because there is no grand scheme of things. Of course, most who hold this view would not agree with that conclusion—but therein lies the inconsistency. How can a spiritual understanding exist without a spiritual reality?

If aliens created human beings, there is no higher purpose for the life of any given human. This means that humans are simply a higher form of animal and would be considered lesser than the aliens who created humanity. The only expressed purpose of humanity is servitude/slavery to the alien creators.

Of course, some may make the point that there are multiple races of aliens, and some want to help us achieve our full potential. However, this creates problems as well. How are we to know the difference between the good aliens and bad aliens? It seems the "bad" aliens would not identify themselves as such, and all aliens would claim to be "good." According to ancient Mesopotamian creation myths, the gods behave the same as humans, meaning they are capable of deception and of acting purely out of self-interest. How can we know if they can be trusted and who we can trust? If alien abduction scenarios are true, how are the violations humans have to endure considered benevolent? If a human being were kidnapping a person and subjecting him or her to undergo forced medical procedures, would we have the same outlook? Why should this be different just because it's an alien, not a human, causing the abuse? Why have some of the world's leading authorities on alien abductions, such as Dr. David Jacobs, concluded that the motivation of aliens is not in our best interest or for our benefit, but are for their own?

Another point, which we will cover in more detail a bit later, is this: If the alien creator view is correct, the idea of racial superiority and inequality would be true and consistent. This conclusions comes from the Mesopotamian texts that tell us the gods created kingship for humankind.

Mirrored in certain works of modern Ancient Astronaut literature, more Anunnaki blood went into certain humans than others. This means that certain bloodlines are inherently superior because they are royal. Those who hold this view would logically have to ask themselves if they are among the royal bloodline. Are they as racially gifted by the gods as other people? Are other non-Caucasian races in the royal bloodline? If the idea of racial superiority is true, should we defend it? Will the gods enforce this idea when they return? Will there be certain bloodlines who rule and other bloodlines who serve? Of course, most who believe this would reject any form of racism or racial superiority—but once again, this is a logical inconsistency. If aliens created humans, especially if the ancient Mesopotamian text is an accurate portrayal of the creation process as many Ancient Astronaut theorists maintain, then by the words of the ancient texts themselves, the gods created kingship for some and not others. In this view, by default and on its face, some bloodlines are superior and others are inferior.

In contrast, the biblical understanding of creation in its original context maintains that all races are equal because all races are human. All humans, male and female, are God's images. Humans who follow God's plan for salvation are all considered royal offspring. They are regarded as sons of God who will rule over a new Earth with Him.[257] This privilege is available for everyone who wants it. It doesn't depend on one's bloodline, race, or position in life. It is a gift made available to everyone by the shed blood of Jesus Christ on the cross.

One last point: If the alien-creator view is true, the alien creators are just that: creator-masters. They are not brothers. This comes up quite often in alien abduction literature as well as that of Ancient Astronaut theorists. Typically, alien beings claim to be both our creators and our brothers; however, that type of relationship is never explained. If aliens are our creators, they logically cannot be our brothers and on the same playing field as human beings. They would be superior, not only in intellect and technology, but in status. We, as their creation, would be below them. They would have the right of ownership over our bodies, souls, lives, and even children. Anything they do to us would be completely justified.

This also means that royal kingship would be a monarchy, not a democracy. The creator creates and the creature obeys. The elite command and the rest of us submit—or otherwise suffer the consequences. Whatever those consequences are, even if they are torture or death, they would be the right of the creator and thus justified. Humans would have no right to complain about being abducted or suffering through abuse. No human being would have the right to demand justice. The aliens would have legal claim over every human being and would be free, even morally, to do whatever they wish to us.

To contrast once again with biblical theology, according to the Bible, we are all destined to be kings. Anyone wanting to claim this destiny is free to do so. The image of God status is democratized in that all humans are God's offsprings and are destined to be rulers. We are even destined to judge and rule over the angels.[258] Jesus Christ, along with being our Lord and Savior, as being God born into the flesh, actually is our brother and not our owner. We find this in the book of Hebrews:

It has been testified somewhere, "What is man, that you are mindful of him, or the son of man, that you care for him? You made him for a little while lower than the angels; you have crowned him with glory and honor, putting everything in subjection under his feet." Now in putting everything in subjection to him, he left nothing outside his control. At present, we do not yet see everything in subjection to him. But we see him who for a little while was made lower than the angels, namely Jesus, crowned with glory and honor because of the suffering of death, so that by the grace of God he might taste death for everyone. For it was fitting that he, for whom and by whom all things exist, in bringing many sons to glory, should make the founder of their salvation perfect through suffering. For he who sanctifies and those who are sanctified all have one source. That is why he is not ashamed to call them brothers, saying, "I will tell of your name to my brothers; in the midst of the congregation I will sing your praise." (Hebrews 2:6–12, ESV)

Other questions come up in the alien creator view, such as: Do aliens really love human beings—and how would we know? If the stories about the gods in ancient texts are true, why are they so vastly different than the messages received by abductees and experiencers? Can these beings be trusted? What kind of love do they feel for the humans they visit and converse with? Is it a sacrificial love? Or, is it the kind of love one would have for a pet or a thing? What level is their emotional attachment? Do these alien beings love the humans they interact with as you would love your child? If they really love humans in this way, why did they create us as slaves? Why did they create us and leave? Why did they create us and hide? Why can't anyone have a personal relationship with one if he or she wants? Why would these beings deny their "children" or their "brethren?"

The fact is, according to this view, humanity is at best an experiment rather than a loved child. This is why Christianity would reject the idea of extraterrestrials creating humanity. The God of the Bible has an emotional investment in us. However, aliens claiming to be the creators of mankind do not. To them, if what they claimed was true, humanity is nothing more than a detached scientific curiosity. The creator aliens themselves would be comparable to an absentee parent at best, and at worst a cold, loveless, and detached researcher. Think about it this way: Is this how we love our children? Is this how we would want our children to remember their childhood? Of course not. There is something much better than the alien creator view. The Bible describes a Creator far different from the logical conclusions following an alien creator understanding of humanity. To Christians, we are loved with a sacrificial love from a Father who is always there and who follows through on His promises consistently and without fail. This is why Christianity as a whole would not accept the idea of directed panspermia.

It is simply inferior to and less attractive than everything coming with the biblical description of God as humanity's Creator.

The Imposter Aliens of Today
from a Christian Point of View

Apart from the idea of directed panspermia, another aspect of the alien debate that Christian theology would reject is that the beings commonly reported from abduction scenarios, as well as similar beings who have presented themselves to humanity in the past, are actually extraterrestrials. Most Christians would take the stance that these specific beings are demonic. Some might be able to articulate further, explaining that these beings are the evil and fallen sons of God from Genesis 6. This view is based on descriptions of alien behavior, messages, abduction violence, and even appearances overlapping with ancient textual depictions of the fallen sons of God. These details do not only appear in biblical texts, but in ancient religious texts across the world.

This all goes to show that the question of extraterrestrial life is far more complex than to merely say "it's all demonic." Certainly, some incidents occurring to people seem to have a demonic source. However, does this mean they are the only examples throughout the entire universe? Is it possible, apart from grays, reptilians, nordics, and the rest, that there are planets inhabited by actual extraterrestrial intelligences? If one of these extraterrestrial races were to contact humanity, would that attempt at communication have to shake our faith? The answer is no. An extraterrestrial reality would only shake our faith as Christians if we allowed it to. An extraterrestrial reality that is not demonic in nature does not conflict with biblical theology, though it may do so with certain interpretations of biblical passages. For example, as we saw earlier, an extraterrestrial reality could differ from with the interpretation of the image of God by stating that it is an attribute rather than a position or status. However, when we have the correct view of biblical theology, there is nothing to support or refute an extraterrestrial reality.

We see examples throughout history showing how dangerous wrong interpretations of theology can be. There are examples of other intelligent, sentient, conscious, living, breathing beings the rest of the world didn't know existed, thus didn't know what to do with in light of the biblical understanding at the time. This lack of biblical understanding not only led to strange and unusual interpretations of Scripture, but also to some of the worst atrocities committed by human beings against their own people.

What We Can Learn from Primitive Understandings of Other Human Races

It is almost a cliche to say it, though it is true: Those who do not learn from history are doomed to repeat it. We must understand that, as human beings, there is a lot we just don't know. It is also extremely difficult, and most often illogical, to form strong opinions on matters lacking substantial information. We can speculate, of course, but the danger enters when people choose to act upon those speculations.

The period between the fifteenth and eighteenth/nineteenth centuries is known as the "Age of Discovery" or the "Age of Exploration" because much of the previously unknown world was being explored. Most famously, Christopher Columbus, as well as others, was discovering the New World. These people were finding a completely mysterious place, one where people of the time presumed that something must exist without any real idea as to what it could be.

There were many speculations as to what these early explorers might find on the other side of the Atlantic Ocean. Many of these theories revolved around ideas of strange, almost otherworldly, sort-of human, creatures. In fact, one of these speculations was the inspiration for the Monopods in *The Voyage of the Dawn Treader* by C. S. Lewis. For those not familiar with that book, the travelers in the story reach an island inhabited by humanoid creatures called Monopods. They are called this because they only have one foot and travel by hopping. The idea of Monopods is not original to C. S. Lewis; the creatures are found in literature during the

Age of Discovery, which drew on even earlier sources, such as from the Greco-Roman era when people speculated what might dwell beyond the known world.[259]

A Monopod, from the *Nuremberg Chronicle*, 1493

The Age of Discovery was also the era when ancient Near-Eastern texts were being discovered and translated. One of the most famous expeditions from this period was the Napoleon Bonaparte's French Campaign in Ottoman Egypt and Ottoman Syria, which eventually led to the discovery of the Rosetta Stone on July 15, 1799, creating the field of Egyptology.[260]

The Rosetta Stone in the British Museum

During this time, ancient nonbiblical and biblical texts were being discovered with competing human-origin accounts and timelines related to creation and the age of the Earth. All of a sudden, not only did the biblical accounts the Europeans were familiar with have some competition, but because of their proximity to the biblical world, there were also clear overlaps with the narratives of the Bible, such as in ancient Mesopotamian texts. Multiple garden paradise, flood, and tower of Babel stories were found that were very similar to those recountedwithin the books of the Bible. However, these other texts did not sound completely like the Bible; there were key differences. For example, king lists in ancient texts were found to line up, sometimes even by name, with the genealogy included in Genesis 5, but the chronology in the extrabiblical sources was a lot lengthier than what is described in Genesis.[261]

During this time, Sanskrit, one of the literary languages of India that goes far back into ancient times, was also being deciphered. Again, Europeans were discovering competing human origin stories, this time outside the world of the Bible. Most surprising was the discovery that Sanskrit was not a Semitic language, such as Hebrew and Mesopotamian languages, but it actually belonged to the Indo-European family, where all the European languages such as Greek and Latin originate. The question inevitably came up: What was an Indo-European language doing all the way in India?

The discovery of the Americas also raised many questions. Explorers found people—not Monopods or any other strange creatures—in North and South America. The people groups they encountered had their own traditions and origin stories. Again, the question inevitably came up: How did they get there?

Europeans asked these questions because the Bible doesn't directly answer or even address them. The Bible doesn't mention North America, South America, Central America, Canada, or the people from these newly discovered lands. All of this, including the discoveries of ancient languages and texts, both from the biblical world and outside the biblical world, plus other factors such as scientific progress in the field of geology and dating the age of the Earth, were causing some Europeans to question the legitimacy of the Bible.

Later, even the inception of Darwinism contributed to all of this thought. Of course, to Darwinists, this was no problem. Other races were the product of evolution and mutations within the species. However, to Bible believers, it was a different story.

All of these discoveries and ideas converged within a relatively short period of time (three or four centuries). This was a significant challenge to Europeans who were raised with the Bible and continued to believe its accuracy. On top of all this, people who didn't accept the Bible as true, even people who hated the Bible, used this time to their advantage. They were looking for a legitimate reason to reject the Bible as a whole, especially Christian origin stories, because in their minds it freed them from accountability to God. The mindset was something like this: *If biblical creation isn't true, the rest of the Bible isn't true, God doesn't exist, and we don't have to do what He wants.* It was their chance to escape accountability in their culture, it gave them seemingly valid excuses to give people who might otherwise hold them to a social standard based on biblical teaching, and it ultimately provided them with a reason to reject and ignore God and the Bible as a whole.

All of this fed into what would turn into anti-Semitism. To certain people, the Bible was beginning to be seen as merely Jewish fairy tales needing to be expelled from the culture and replaced with something more scientific. Of course, anti-Semitism wasn't anything new, but it gained refreshed traction in light of all these discoveries and new ideas. While this was a great time for people wanting to reject God and the Bible, it was a time of crisis for Christians.

Christians felt as though they were presented with a choice: They either had to reject the Bible (which, to Christians, was not an option) or find a way to make it fit in with all of these new discoveries and ideas. They had to find a way to harmonize the Bible with the fact that there existed other people who were not white Europeans from previously unknown lands the Bible didn't talk about. They figured if they could answer the question of where these people came from, they could also answer the question of why there were different races—all while tackling issues like Darwinism and geology.

This quest to force the Bible to explain these things produced some of the strangest, most contrived, and inaccurate interpretations of the Bible imaginable. However, many of these ideas became accepted, popular, and even mainstream. Many of them would seem utterly ridiculous to most Christians today. But, for the day in which they were invented, they offered people what they were looking for to combat the onslaught of modern discoveries and scientific understanding.

Some of these interpretations were the beginning of unfavorable theories about race and diversity, such as whether the "other" races were in the line of Adam. They would wonder if these non-European races were truly human, as in having descended from Adam, or if they were from another source entirely. Believers typically fell into two categories: polygenists or monogenists.

Polygenism was the belief that there was more than one original pair of humans (Adam and Eve) in the beginning. In this thinking, human life originated from multiple sources. These sources were seen as multiple lines from different kinds of humans classified into different subspecies and races. Racial diversity was explained by saying that the idea that everyone came from only two people was wrong. They believed multiple races lived alongside Adam, Eve, and their children. Polygenists also typically believed other races existed before the creation of Adam and Eve. These ideas were used to answer questions such as how Cain found a wife, who populated the land of Nod, and for whom Cain built a city. The text in Genesis did not provide a solid answer to these questions, so speculations were formed in order to provide answers and deal with other questions regarding races.

Monogenism, on the other hand, was more appealing to Christians who wanted to hold on to the traditional understanding of the Genesis Creation account, especially when it came to Adam and Eve. However, from this came even more bizarre interpretations. This is when Christians began to think there was something more going on in the Garden of Eden than what was described. This was the origin of such interpretations as the "Serpent Seed Theory," which states that Eve actually had sex with the serpent in the Garden of Eden, producing a new line of people. The serpent wasn't considered a literal snake, of course, but was recognized as a sinister being—whether divine, human, or something in between. This union between Eve and the serpent was recognized as the origin of the line of Cain. Monogenists believed the line of Cain was the origin of black people and that the line of Seth, born of Adam and Eve, was the origin of the "special," "elect," white people.

On top of this, monogenists used passages like Genesis 6 to support this view, saying it described a clash between Seth's godly line and the evil line of Cain. This interpretation, though unsubstantiated by the whole of Scripture, was gaining more popularity since its original and accurate supernatural understanding had long since been stripped out, creating what was, and still is, called the "Sethite" view of Genesis 6 (stating it was Adam's line against Cain's line, rather than the original context stating it was the rebellious fallen angels against all of humanity). This was when the invented problem of other races came about. To the monogenists at the time, it wasn't Darwin who described the origin of races, it was actually Satan who caused it. In fact, this view is still taught in many seminaries today, though most of the racial bias has been removed.[262]

These bizarre and unjustified interpretations led to beliefs supporting the racial superiority of Europeans and, later, to the practice of slavery in America. Bible-believing Europeans trying to harmonize the Bible with science, the discovery of new lands and races, and the deciphering of ancient languages and religious texts, viewed themselves as the direct inheritors of the Judeo-Christian tradition called Christianity since it was through Europe where Christianity really began to grow and spread throughout the rest of the world. Therefore, many saw Europeans as the line of Adam and white Europeans as the ones especially closest to God. To them, this meant the other lines, however they originated, were less like Adam and ultimately less like God. They were seen as inferior. To some Christian teachers and laypeople, this thinking raised the question of whether these other races were even truly human. They wondered if other races were redeemable by the blood of Christ, which was shed only for humanity. This affected missionary work, when some Christians believed the other races were not worth evangelizing because they weren't human anyway. From that idea came the motivation to dominate the other races, which led to the rise of slavery in Europe and America. Later on, interpretations such as these even influenced the extreme racial ideas of the Nazis, leading to the malicious and horrifying deaths of millions. We can even still see the influences of this today in modern groups of white supremacists, KKK members, and neo-Nazis.[263]

The Fallacy of Hyperliteralism

Throughout human history, these contrived biblical interpretations led to some appalling and disturbing conclusions about our fellow human beings. How different would things have been if people of the time had realized that there are just some things the Bible doesn't clearly explain? There are some origin stories we will just not know in full. And, most importantly, it's okay that we don't know everything. We shouldn't expect the Bible to have the burden of explaining the meaning, origin, and existence of everything we currently experience and might discover in the future. Forcing the Bible to be something it's not and was never intended to be (i.e., a catalog and scientific explanation for everything God created) has led to literal life-and-death situations with damaging consequences.

Instead, we need to view what the Bible actually is: a theological collection of books explaining who the real God is, how to know Him, and how be saved from the curse of death by accepting His gift of eternal life. That's it. Anything else we get from the text is extra and interesting information. Even still, everything in the Bible needs to be studied in the context within which it was written. The culture, specific writer, and history need to be understood in order to develop an accurate interpretation. On top of that, the entire Bible needs to be taken in context with itself. A vast number of Scriptures passages deal with how to treat people lovingly, respectfully, and as equal image-bearers of God. Had the Europeans from centuries past understood this, perhaps human history could have avoided the atrocities that followed the compromised and all-around bad interpretations of biblical texts.

Much of this is born from a hyperliteral view of the Bible. This view, which is extremely popular in the Church even today, suggests there is no way to look at any text in Scripture other than its literal, word-for-word meaning. Of course, this view, when taken to the extreme, is easy to disprove. The Bible offers plenty of metaphoric and poetic descriptions that would be rendered completely ridiculous if taken literally. For example, Jesus said Christians are to be the salt and light of the world (Matthew 5:13). Obviously, He was not saying we need to transform ourselves into sodium chloride and photons. He was using everyday concepts such as salt and light as tools for teaching a broader message.

Most Christians do not take an ultimate-literal view of the Bible, but many to accept a hyperliteral view, meaning most things in the Bible are meant to be taken literally. Though in this lies the problem, who is to say what is literal and what is metaphor or poetry? Usually in hyperliteralist circles, these decisions are up to the individual reader. Also, it is almost seen as a sign of virtue or great strength of faith to take the text as literally as possible and not accept the "easy" answer of symbolism, metaphor, or poetry. Rather than attempting to see Scripture in context and understanding it from the viewpoint in which it was written, many instead rely on a scientific approach to interpreting the Bible. If the scientific view of the Bible clashes with the science of modern day, the hyperliteralist Christian tends to favor the scientific view. This is why we have groups in the Church today who accept geocentricism or believe the Earth is flat: Because, through a scientific interpretation, the Bible says so. In fact, this hyperliteral view is sometimes held so tightly that some question other

Christians' salvation, relationship with God, or belief in the Bible if they do not accept an overly literal view of Scripture, such as in the case of cosmology. Thus, the Church divides even farther.

Allowing the Mistakes of the Past to
Prevent Mistakes in the Future

As stated in the beginning of this chapter, the authors of this book do not believe the commonly reported nonhuman beings from various abduction accounts are actual aliens from another planet. We believe those beings are likely of a demonic origin, largely due to the messaging from the beings themselves. This, as a quick side note, is also how we believe Christians should want to understand a genuine official disclosure event. If nonhuman entities land on the White House lawn, for example, how do we know if they are aliens or something demonic? We would listen to the messaging. What is their motivation? Why are they here? What are they saying, and what are they doing? Are they proclaiming anti-Christian messages? Are their communications to humanity anything like the fallen gods of old? This is how we believe a genuine alien contact scenario on a large scale should be handled by Christians. However, we should also realize that the larger question itself is much more complicated.

It is important for us to learn from history, lest we be doomed to repeat it. Of course, the question of extraterrestrial life does not have a direct, one-to-one relationship with the old ideas of races, but there is at least a connection. The main point to keep in mind is that we simply do not know everything. Of course, there is nothing to say that extraterrestrial life would be considered as the line of Adam, though to be fair, that is exactly what the monogenists and polygenists thought. The main question was, after the discovery of other people, *how did they get there?* What if, in the near or distant future, humanity discovers other intelligent beings on another planet? What will that do to our faith? Will we ask the same question of *how did they get there?* Will we assume it is impossible for them to be included in the line of Adam, therefore they are not human and do not need to be treated with any kind of dignity or respect? Will we assume, since the Bible doesn't say anything about them, that we must force a biblical interpretation that could lead to unimaginable problems later?

Or will we instead learn from past mistakes, realize we do not know everything (and should not act as though we do), and recognize that the question of extraterrestrial life is a lot more complicated than even the question of other races was hundreds of year ago? Will we take a step back in all humility and allow God to guide us through the situation rather than charging into it blindly ourselves? Will we give sufficient time and thought to the issue before rushing into knee-jerk responses and attacking those who do not share the same view?

It is a good idea to begin thinking about these things now. We do not know when, if ever, an official disclosure event will happen. If it does happen, we do not know what form it will take. We don't know if it will be an event as fantastic as a UFO landing on the White House lawn, or something more mundane such as leaked documents or the U.S. government finally admitting they know something. If anything, all of these questions and the realization of how much we truly don't know should award us with a higher degree of humility than would hard-nosed opinions based solely on speculation. We should be able to have an open discussion about these matters without feeling like our faith is threatened or believing that if we entertain an alternate view we are somehow displeasing God or not defending Him properly. In regards to issues the Bible does not clearly lay out for us, this way of thinking never produces positive results. Ultimately, concerning vague topics not addressed directly in the Bible, we are all going to have different opinions and reasons for those beliefs. However, we should also have an awareness not all of our opinions are going to line up. This is why it is important to have open and honest dialogue while focusing on what we have in common rather than what we disagree on.

For Christians, whether we agree on the extraterrestrial question is not nearly as important as what we have in common. We all accept Jesus Christ as our Savior. We all have a promise of redemption. When this physical life is finished, we will all spend eternity together. At that time and on that side of eternity, I'm willing to bet that all of the issues we are so opinionated about and hold so dear now will seem utterly small, weak, and pathetic to the point that we will wonder what in the world we were thinking by allowing those matters to divide us. Let's not wait until eternity to realize this. Let's learn from humanity's past mistakes. Let's cultivate unity today.

chapter twelve

THE ISRAEL/UFO CONNECTION

THE BIGGEST QUESTION concerning the official disclosure of government knowledge of UFOs and extraterrestrials is *when?* When will the world have to face these things? No one knows for sure. Some say official disclosure is imminent, while others say it will likely be a long time, if it even happens at all.

Prophecy and the Fallacy of Prediction

Before getting too heavy into this chapter, I (Josh Peck) feel I must assure the reader that this is not a presentation of predictions. Rather, it is a presentation of possibilities. There are things, some of which included here, we should absolutely keep our eye on. There are things history can teach us as we move forward into the future. Time itself is a straight line, yet events seem to be cyclical. Events don't always happen in the same way every time, yet there is usually enough commonality to give us a fair warning of what may be ahead. It is also difficult to pin down an exact date, or even an exact year, for any possibility of prophecy not clearly laid out in Scripture. In short, we may not know the day of certain events,but we might be able to discern the season.

In researching for this book, an anomaly kept coming up. Normally this type of research would not lead to this kind of thing, but there it was, time and time again—so much so, in fact, that I began to feel it shouldn't be ignored. I even went as far as to ask other colleagues and researcher friends if anything similar was coming up in their various fields. Too many times to be shrugged off as mere coincidence, their answer was yes. Yet, when dates start coming up, it is difficult to know exactly how to present the information, or whether to even present it at all to the public. Speaking for myself, I would never want to lead someone to believe that I have some special revelation if there is even the slightest chance that it could all just be coincidence. Therefore, I ask the reader in going forward to keep in mind that I am presenting merely possibilities, not predictions. I stand behind my research, of course, and believe that what is presented here *could* happen. However, something entirely different, or nothing at all, might happen instead. I will go through my evidence to show why I believe certain events in the coming years are possible, yet ultimately, it is up to the reader to decide for himself or herself.

Prophecy and predictions are tricky. That why it is usually best to stay away from predictions and do nothing more than speculate about prophecy. Interpreting Bible prophecy, deciphering possible hidden meanings in the text, and applying it all to our current time provides ample room for mistakes, miscalculations, and incorrect speculation. We see it all the time on social media. For example, how many times have YouTube or Facebook told us a comet was going to hit the Earth imminently? Or that NASA has said we will experience an extended time of total darkness across the planet? How many times have Bible verses been used to support these claims, only to be proven wrong time and time again? Then, after a few months, a new threat to the world and humanity comes up. It seems we go through this cycle from various click-bait articles every couple of months or so.

Now, of course, I'm not saying there will never be a time of literal darkness or a time when something will collide with the Earth. Bible prophecy, scientific probabilities, and even plain old common sense seems to say these things will happen eventually. However, I don't believe any evidence suggests this will happen without other prophecies needing to be fulfilled first. The main point is that we all, myself included, need to be careful with so-called prophecies on social media and other areas of our modern world. It is far too easy to be led astray these days.

All that said, I absolutely do believe real prophecy is being fulfilled in our day. I do believe major events are happening and, if we pay attention, we will have a better chance of being prepared for what's ahead. This doesn't only include physical preparedness, but mental, emotional, and spiritual preparedness as well. In short, it's not about what we may know; it's all about how we use it.

A Surprising and Obscure Connection

There seems to be something strange looming between the years 2017, 2018, and possibly in the years following. One piece of this puzzle came while I was reading the extraordinary book *What Dwells Beyond: The Bible Believer's Handbook to Understanding Life in the Universe* by the amazingly talented biblical researcher Jeffrey W. Mardis. Actually, here is a bit of SkyWatchTV and Defender Publishing trivia: Jeffrey is not only a phenomenal researcher, he is also the talent behind many of Defender Publishing's book covers. In fact, he was the one who designed the cover to this book as well as *Abaddon Ascending*, the book authored by Tom Horn and myself. Jeffrey is a truly gifted individual in all respects.

In chapter 2 of *What Dwells Beyond*, Mardis makes an interesting connection. He shows how certain significant events in Israel's history seem to correspond to events reigniting the idea of alien life elsewhere in the universe. For example, in 600 B.C. (approximately), Nebuchadnezzar burned Jerusalem to the ground. At this same time, a curious belief called Cosmic Pluralism began. Cosmic Pluralism is a term used to describe the existence of more than one planet (usually hundreds or millions of planets) populated with intelligent life.

In A.D. 70, Rome burned Jerusalem to the ground. In the same year, the famous philosopher Plutarch wrote in his *De Facie in Orbe Lunae (On the Face in the Moon)*: "The men on the moon, if they do exist, are slight of body and capable of being nourished."[264]

What makes this quote so important is that Plutarch was the last major philosopher to seriously comment on Cosmic Pluralism before it was revived in the Middle Ages.

There was a third major connection between Cosmic Plurality and significant events in Israel. Modern ufology and the rise of aliens in the public mind began in 1947 with the UFO crash in Roswell, New Mexico. One year later, in 1948, Israel became a nation again. As Mardis admits in his book, this could be all coincidence. Neither Jeffrey Mardis nor I would want to claim that a connection exists none is to be seen. However, it does seem odd that these two subjects in history (noteworthy events in Israel's history and Cosmic Plurality) seem to correspond.

Connections Today Are Stronger and More Numerous

When we entered the beginning of 2017, we were reminded of a major event in Israel's history. One hundred years prior, in 1917, the Balfour Declaration was written. The Balfour Declaration was a letter dated November 2, 1917, from Arthur James Balfour (the United Kingdom's foreign secretary) to Walter Rothschild (a leader of the British Jewish Community) for transmission to the Zionist Federation of Great Britain and Ireland. Strangely enough, less than a month earlier (October 13) during this same year was the famous Fatima sighting. At the time, it was publicized as an appearance of Mary, the mother of Jesus. However, when reading through the eyewitness accounts of what would be called the "Miracle of the Sun," it becomes apparent that this was a sighting of a UFO.[265] Also in 1917, during World War I, there were numerous reports of UFOs from soldiers on all battle fronts. In fact, it was even reported that the German pilot Manfred Freiherr (better known as the Red Baron), believed he shot down a UFO over Belgium in the spring of 1917.[266]

The Balfour Declaration was actually not the first step in efforts toward establishing a home for the Jewish people. In 1897 (120 years ago from 2017), the First Zionist Congress was held in Basel, Switzerland, by Theodor Herzl, the founder of the modern Zionist movement, and the Basel Declaration was submitted. It was stated: "Zionism seeks to establish a home for the Jewish people in Palestine secured under public law." The new program, which came to be known as the Basel Program, was adopted under the following terms:[267]

> Zionism aims at establishing for the Jewish people a publicly and legally assured home in Palestine. For the attainment of this purpose, the Congress considers the following means serviceable:
>
> 1. The promotion of the settlement of Jewish agriculturists, artisans, and tradesmen in Palestine.
> 2. The federation of all Jews into local or general groups, according to the laws of the various countries.
> 3. The strengthening of the Jewish feeling and consciousness.
> 4. Preparatory steps for the attainment of those governmental grants which are necessary to the achievement of the Zionist purpose.

During this same year, possibly the most famous UFO incident besides Roswell occurred. The Aurora UFO incident reportedly happened on April 17, 1897. Locals claimed a UFO crashed on a farm near Aurora, Texas, and is claimed to have resulted in the death of the alien craft's pilot. The alien's body is allegedly buried in an unmarked grave at the local cemetery.

A bit more recently, in 1977, Menachin Begin became the prime minister of Israel, and in 1978 he signed the Camp David Peace Accords with Egyptian President Anwar Sadat. This was facilitated by President

Jimmy Carter. The Camp David Peace Accords are rich with history of what they did to/for Israel, Egypt, America, and other nations. It was a major turning point in Israel's history.

Oddly, 1977 and 1978 were also important years in modern ufology. The government of Brazil has released declassified security files pertaining to Operation Saucer, a top-secret investigation by the Fuerza Aerea Brasileira into the 1977 UFO flap in the northern state of Para. Beginning in October of 1977 and lasting through the first half of 1978, the city Colares of the Brazilian state of Para underwent extreme UFO and alien activity, even to the point of being called a UFO invasion by the newspaper *O Liberal*.[268] This is now known as the *Colares UFO Flap*.

To recap, the first attempt to make Israel a home for the Jewish people occurred 120 years ago, which is the same time as the Aurora UFO incident. One hundred years ago, the Balfour Declaration was submitted, which was the same year as the Fatima sighting and also when the Red Baron believed he shot down a UFO. Seventy years ago, in 1947, the UFO crash of Roswell happened. Around that same time in 1948, Israel became a nation again. Adding to all of this, fifty years ago from 2017 was the Six Day War (or Third Arab-Israeli War) of 1967, in which Israel defended against the invading armies of surrounding nations. Strangely enough, at that same time, the most intensive and long-lasting UFO sighting wave of all time occurred.[269] Taking all this into account, the years 2017–2018 seem to have a lot of significant anniversaries of Israel/UFO history converging.

Biblical Year Cycles of High Strangeness

A strange issue comes up when we consider these numbers in a biblical context. In the words of Jesus Christ, Matthew 24:32–34 states:

> Now learn a parable of the fig tree; When his branch is yet tender, and putteth forth leaves, ye know that summer is nigh:

So likewise ye, when ye shall see all these things, know that it is near, even at the doors.

Verily I say unto you, This generation shall not pass, till all these things be fulfilled.

It is widely believed within biblical eschatology that the fig tree is a representation of Israel. This also leads us to wonder how long, according to the Bible, is a generation? There are a few different possibilities. Even more, there are other number and time cycles that seem to correspond with this type of study.

The first we can look at is 120 years. In Genesis 6:3 (KJV), God said: "My spirit shall not always strive with man, for that he also is flesh: yet his days shall be an hundred and twenty years."

A popular interpretation of this says that God was referring to the Flood. It is believed He was saying He would not always put up with what was going on in the world, but He would for only another 120 years. It would be then when God would send the Flood.

Next we can look at one hundred years. In Genesis 15:13–16, God tells Abram that his descendants will be afflicted for four hundred years in a land that is not their own (Egypt). It then says in the fourth generation that they shall return to their own land. In this instance, to know how long a generation is, we only have to divide four hundred years by four generations. We are then left with a generation equalling one hundred years in this context.

The next is seventy years. Psalm 90:10 (NKJV) states: "The days of our lives are seventy years; and if by reason of strength they are eighty years, yet their boast is only labor and sorrow; for it is soon cut off, and we fly away."

Some have interpreted this to mean that one candidate for a biblical generation is seventy years (or possibly even eighty).

Next up is fifty years. Leviticus 25:8–17 tells us about the seven cycles of seven years (forty-nine years) and the Jubilee year (fiftieth year) in ancient Israel. The Jubilee year was basically a big reset button. The land was not to be sown or reaped. Slaves and prisoners were freed. Debts were forgiven.

> Lastly, we can look at forty years. There are a lot of significant things we can point to concerning a period of forty years, but more specifically, consider the words of the Lord in Psalm 95:10, which states: "Forty years long was I grieved with this generation, and said, It is a people that do err in their heart, and they have not known my ways."

This points back to the forty-year wandering in the wilderness of Moses and the children of Israel. Numbers 32:13 states:

And the Lord's anger was kindled against Israel, and he made them wander in the wilderness forty years, until all the generation, that had done evil in the sight of the Lord, was consumed.

Putting It All Together

The odd thing about all these numbers and cycles (of which there are many others, but for the purposes of this article, the ones listed will suffice) is that we can trace every one back through Israel's history and see significant simultaneous events concerning UFOs and Israel, leading us to the years 2017–2018:

- 120 years ago (1897)—Aurora UFO/First Zionist Congress
- 100 years ago (1917))—Fatima UFO/Balfour Declaration
- 70 years ago (1947–48))—Roswell UFO crash/Israel becomes a nation
- 50 years ago (1967))—UFO Wave/Israel defends Jerusalem in the Six Day War
- 40 year ago (1977–78))—Colares UFO Flap/Camp David Peace Accords

As stated earlier, there are more curious dates involving biblical year cycles, the history of Israel, and the UFO phenomenon (promoting Cosmic Plurality). However, for this article, this is enough to get the point across. Also, given the fact that Israel operates on a slightly different calendar than we do in America, pinpointing events to the exact date or even year can prove nearly impossible. While we might not know the exact date and year with future events like this, there seems to be evidence to support a significant span of time, such as between the years of 2017 and 2018.

All these facts and more seem to be pointing to the years 2017–2018 as a significant time in the near future. It would seem, if history repeats itself, that we might see a major event in Israel while, at the same time, we will see a major event promoting the idea of Cosmic Plurality. What this might be, one can only speculate. Could it be a war igniting in the Middle East involving Israel? Could an official disclosure event of UFO knowledge from the government occur? Might there be another major UFO sighting, or something even bigger? Perhaps it is something that will begin in 2017/2018 and culminate later. Or, perhaps, nothing will occur at all.

Again, one can only speculate. In all humility and honesty, if I had to guess, I would bet that nothing will occur. That might seem strange to say, given that I have written an entire chapter on the topic and have stated that I stand by my research. However, I also must remain realistic. Everything written about in this chapter has already happened, but that does not mean they are connected in the way they seem to be. Failed prophecy predictions have made fools of many people throughout the ages, and I have zero interest in ruining my credibility by creating a situation in which I am counted among them. However, at the same time, in case there is something here, I feel a personal responsibility to tell people about it. Therefore, I have presented you with the information. It is up to you to decide what it all means.

As I said at the beginning of this chapter, my purpose for writing is not to convince you, the reader, of anything. My purpose is to present you with information and possible connections (all of which admittedly could be a series of coincidences) and allow you to dig into the research further and make up your own mind. At the very least, it is a good idea to be prepared *just in case*. It is better to be prepared and not need it than to be unprepared and desperately need to have been.

CONCLUSION

GOD HAS BLESSED us humans with a marvelous ability to think—to reason, to "search out a matter," which the Bible tells us "is the glory of kings."[270] Jesus even told us that we are to love the Lord our God with all of our hearts, souls, and *minds*. Yet far too many Christians settle for two out of three, happily swallowing strange ideas based on nothing more than the unsubstantiated claims of dynamic leaders.

Well, we all have a right to believe whatever we want. Just remember that some bad choices have eternal consequences.

God—YHWH, the God of the Bible—made sure that He left behind evidence for the hope we have in Jesus: eyewitness testimonies, archaeologists' discoveries, and even the activities of demons themselves argue for the truth of the gospel.

Over the centuries, the principalities and powers Paul warned us about have played a long game, cultivating philosophies and doctrines opposed to their Creator. As human understanding of science grew, the Enemy shifted from portraying themselves as the true creators and masters of humanity to convincing the world, especially in the scientistic West, that there are no gods, only highly advanced extraterrestrials. And since, per Clarke's Third Law, "any sufficiently advanced technology is indistinguishable from magic," those so-called ETIs have become, by definition, the gods we thought we knew.

Let's give credit where it's due: This strategy is brilliant. It appeals to our human vanity. If our gods are gods only because they have better gizmos, then we, too, can someday be as gods. Awesome! Where do we sign up?

The principalities and powers, rather than compelling us to accept them as our masters at the point of a sword (or a ray gun), have spooled out line over the centuries, patiently waiting while more and more of us took their bait. Through spiritualists like Swedenborg and the Fox sisters, modern gnostics like Blavatsky and Bailey, occultists like Crowley and Grant, and storytellers from Lovecraft to Roddenberry (and we might add von Däniken to that category), a compelling message has been spread throughout the technologically advanced Western world: The spirit realm is real; we know who created you and where you go when you die; and your mission until then is to "work in the light."

In other words, the spirits behind this movement have created an alternate science-fiction religion. How do we know this? It's a faith that promises to answer the Big Questions: Where do we come from, why are we here, and what happens to us when we die?

Remember, people who believe ETIs are visiting the earth outnumber truly biblical Christians in America three to one. The Enemy's deception is working.

So the recent fascination with "official disclosure" of the existence of extraterrestrials is something Christians must be prepared to address. The fact that we're not is a testimony to the lack of discernment among the Church today. Not only do we fail to recognize the Enemy, most American Christians don't even acknowledge the Enemy's existence.

God save us.

Knowingly or otherwise, the Enemy's plans have been aided and abetted by the United States government, or at least by elements within it. The intelligence community's use of UFOs as a convenient cover story is a matter of public record. Evidence for the IC's role in famous cases like Maury Island, Roswell, and Dulce (the Paul Bennewitz affair), to pick the most obvious, and the highly improbable links between people connected to early UFO sightings and the assassination of John F. Kennedy suggest that critical thinkers should at least ask whether "official disclosure" might also be a intelligence op. Especially since we know that the U.S. military command specifically tasked with creating convincing deceptions, Joint Security Control, has been positively linked to the UFO phenomenon.

Next we should ask why the UFO investigation community has been hijacked by hoaxers and New Agers. Why have serious researchers been pushed out of the way by those who don't even try to hide their pro-ETI bias?

The big question, of course, is *cui bono*—who benefits? Who actually wins when the public buys into the idea that our gods are ETIs and that they're coming back, if not here already, to help us join the Great White Brotherhood, or the Galactic Federation, or whatever their club is called?

If you have a supernatural worldview, which should be your default setting if you're a Christian, the answer to that question should be obvious.

The issue here is that the ETIs aren't coming back. They're already here. They never left. The UFO research community, which has a black hole where its critical thinking should be, more or less accepts the existence of aliens as a good thing. Why? As we noted in this book, the Age of Discovery, which was obviously named by Europeans who did the discovering, didn't work out well for the native peoples who were discovered. Why should we expect first contact to be like *E. T.* when it might be more like *War of the Worlds* or *Independence Day*?

As to that, why do UFO researchers believe these so-called ETIs? Assuming the channelers in touch with The Nine, Ashtar Command, and Ramtha the Enlightened One are actually hearing from *something* and not just playing us for fools, why do they think these entities are telling the truth? If they *are* hostile, why would they tell us?

And if they're friendly, why don't they just open a hailing frequency? Why are they so coy? They've crossed interstellar space; haven't they mastered radio technology? Could they maybe modulate laser pulses? Tap out some Morse code? Wave flags? Send smoke signals? Land on the National Mall and announce, "*Klaatu barada nikto*"?

Why do those who eagerly await official disclosure ignore such basic, common-sense questions? Is it possible that SETI's chief astronomer Seth Shostak is right on the money when he says we've been conditioned by Hollywood—propagandized, in other words—to think positively about our first contact with something that claims to be a traveler from another world?

"Conspiratorial crazy talk," some will say. Maybe, but only if we ignore Paul's warning to the church of Ephesus. This massive, coordinated, and wildly successful propaganda campaign isn't run by humans. Principalities, powers, thrones, dominions, rulers, authorities, and cosmic powers—ranks of an angelic hierarchy—are our true opponents.[271] And if you consider the influence and motives of the rebellious denizens of the unseen realm, the "spiritual forces of evil in the heavenly places," then a PSYOP like this is exactly the kind of thing we should expect. *And no wonder, for even Satan disguises himself as an angel of light.*[272]

Beware, you lightworkers who serve the Ashtar Command. You know not what you do.

This gets to the heart of our book. When we look at the evolution of the ideas that form the core doctrines of the people pushing for official disclosure, the picture that emerges is much darker than they realize. For all of their claims to spiritual enlightenment, the New Agers who dominate the official disclosure movement are mostly ignorant of the roots of their doctrines, a condition one scholar calls "source amnesia."[273]

To repeat, we are not coincidence theorists. It is no accident that the communications humanity has received from alleged ETIs so far have come through channelers instead of radios, telephones, or video screens. It is not an irrelevant detail that the accounts of "alien" abductees are very similar to those of victims of satanic ritual abuse.[274]

It is also not a coincidence that Aleister Crowley, his successor Kenneth Grant, and the Round Table of CIA asset Andrija Puharich believed they were hearing from gods worshipped in Egypt three thousand years ago—and specifically, in the case of Crowley and Grant, the Egyptian god of chaos, Set.

Consider this: The gods of the ancient world are real. That's not a guess, that's biblical.[275] Those small-g gods are under a death sentence with no hope of a pardon. God has also decreed that those who put their faith in Jesus Christ will one day judge the angels.[276] The only thing left for the rebellious *elohim*, the fallen angels who dared to rebel against their Creator, is to drag as much of His creation as they can into the Lake of Fire with them when they go.

And the conflict between the Creator and Chaos has been ongoing since before the creation of the Garden of Eden. As we noted earlier, we read in Genesis 1:2 that the Spirit of God hovered over the face of the waters—waters that contained "the deep," the abyss, *tehom*, or Tiamat, the Sumerian chaos dragon. That's the entity named Leviathan in the Bible.

Remember that occultist Kenneth Grant believed the god he channeled was Set, Egypt's dark lord of chaos. Set was called Typhon by the Greeks, hence Grant's religion, the Typhonian Order.

Grant further believed that horror author H. P. Lovecraft had tapped into that same spirit, which revealed to Lovecraft the dangerous grimoire, the *Necronomicon*. Given the common theme in Lovecraft's stories of cosmic horror, often built around the imminent return of old, extraterrestrial gods with no love for, or even awareness of, the human race, it's hard to argue with Grant's conclusion.

And as bizarre as it sounds, it was the fiction of H. P. Lovecraft, and thus the spirit(s) behind it, that inspired Erich von Däniken to write the book that launched the Ancient Astronaut Theory.

In short, our culture's fascination with ancient aliens is the result of a supernatural PSYOP in the long war between the god of chaos—Leviathan—and YHWH.

While YHWH defeated Leviathan before creating humanity by

crushing its heads,[277] it is not dead. Its future destruction is guaranteed, however. On the Day of the LORD, "He will slay the dragon that is in the sea"[278] and when He creates the new heaven and the new earth, the sea—chaos—will be no more.[279]

Creation is far more complex and a whole lot weirder than we've been taught. A planet on Earth called Heaven? It's a good thing *one* of your authors understands that section!

Here's the takeaway: Our God spoke the universe into existence and all that's in it, including the small-g gods who rage and plot against Him (and us). We shouldn't be afraid to address the question of whether we're being visited by ETIs or how to respond to a future announcement that aliens have just landed in front of the United Nations building. The universe is a huge place. Speculating on the possibility of other inhabited worlds is fascinating. But it can lead people without a biblical anchor down paths to destruction.

Based on the evidence that's been made public and the chain of ideas leading from the ancient Greek philosophers to the modern UFO phenomenon, we don't believe ET has come calling. Ever. True believers in the existence of ETIs have been duped by smoke and shadows, buying into a spiritual deception wrapped in a pseudoscientific veneer.

It's a pity. They've sided with the JV team. Our God not only created them, He created the stuff He made them with. That's the God who captains our army. And you, dear reader, were created as His "imager"—His moral agent on Earth. And no matter what happens to you or to the world, that's a job title you never lose.

Ancient astronaut theorists, New Agers, and atheists longing for answers to the Big Questions that don't involve the God of the Bible will keep pushing the governments of the world to disclose what they know about extraterrestrial intelligences. The principalities and powers behind the thrones of this world may well oblige them someday with an event that *looks* like official disclosure.

Just remember: You are created in the image of God. You are His image bearer on Earth. That's a specific set of attributes inherent in, unique to, and inseparable from the human race.[280] The arrival of something claiming to be from Zeta Reticuli *does not change your status*. It does not change the need for a Savior or the plan of salvation. It doesn't change who Jesus is or why He died, and it sure doesn't change the established historical fact of His resurrection and the victory it achieved over the fallen.

In short, although we don't think this will ever happen, the legitimate discovery of an extraterrestrial intelligence should have no impact whatsoever on your Christian faith.

The disclosure of ETIs, ancient astronaut theory, and the old lie that is the New Age are just tactics by the small-g gods to lure unsuspecting and undiscerning humans to destruction. They deny the authority, identity, or existence of God, and offer instead the false promise they first rolled out in the Garden: *Ye shall be as gods*.

So, when you encounter the topic of official disclosure, please remember: We follow the One who created everything. Christian doctrine, and your worldview, is big enough to handle the "what ifs."

After all, we own the definitive Book on the supernatural. The answers are in there if we just look.

A PLANET ON EARTH CALLED HEAVEN

THIS PART OF the book will certainly stretch your mind and imagination to the limit, and perhaps beyond. Some of the information and descriptions discussed here will be difficult to grasp, but it is worth the effort, even if it means an extra read or two. The concepts explained here are certain far more foreign than common extraterrestrial theories, however these might be the ones with the most supporting evidence, found in both science and ancient writings.

A question commonly asked by ufologists and extraterrestrial enthusiasts is *what if aliens are already here?* It is a fair question. After all, it seems that every year, reports of UFO phenomena and alien abductions increase. Would it makes sense for aliens to continually come to our planet, back and forth, for thousands if not millions of years? Or, perhaps, would it make more sense to have bases and stations here on Earth?

These are valid questions if one accepts the idea of normal, physical, three-dimensional extraterrestrials originating on another planet and currently interacting with humanity. However, what about the

ETI discussed from the Podesta Wikileaks emails from a "contiguous universe?" If a being can transcend physical space, how could we ever hope to locate them? Strangely enough, a combination of ancient scriptures and the latest scientific findings might actually give us our answer.

Extra Gravity

Earth has a stronger gravitational effect than it should based on its mass. Measurements of the Earth's mass tell us that it is supposed to be approximately 13,170,000,000,000,000,000,000,000 (or 1.317x10^25) pounds. However, the Earth is actually about 13,170,658,500,000,000,000,000,000 pounds. At first glance, that might not seem like a big difference. In fact, it is only a fraction of about one twenty-thousandth (1/20,000), or a difference of about .005 percent. While this might not seem like a lot on a normal human scale, it's huge on an Earth-sized scale. Think of it this way: There are about 658,500,000,000,000,000,000 (6.585x10^20) pounds of mass on Earth completely unaccounted for. In fact, this is the most conservative estimation; the amount of Earth's mystery mass could be almost double that. It is estimated that there is between .005 and .008 percent extra mass to the Earth. To put this in perspective, the diameter of the Earth is 7,917.5 miles. If we take .005 percent of 7,917.5 miles, we are left with .395875 miles, or about 2,090 feet. This means, if you were to take .005 percent of the diameter of the Earth and turn it up on end, it would reach 2,090 feet in the air. If we are considering the surface area of the Earth (196.9 million square miles), .005 percent would equate to a little more than the size of Vermont (9,614 square miles). If we consider that the entire Earth is about 260 trillion cubic miles, then there are 13 million cubic miles of unknown mass. No one knows what this extra mass is, where exactly it is located, why we can't see it, or why we can't measure it beyond its gravitational effects. But, of course, there are theories.

The leading theory is that there could be a ring of dark matter around the equator of the Earth about 119 miles thick and 43,000 miles across. Dark matter is completely mysterious, but is estimated to make up about

80 percent of matter in the universe. No one knows exactly what it is, but it is measured by looking at the gravity of distant celestial objects, such as galaxies, then comparing it with the expected amount of gravity based on measurements of visible matter. In short, galaxies exert a much higher gravitational force than they should be able to based on visible matter. Something in the universe affecting gravity is completely unseen and imperceptible, hence the name "dark matter"

The interesting thing about gravity is its apparent ability to leak into other spatial dimensions, which is currently the leading theory to explain why gravity is much weaker than the other three forces of nature. This means that dark matter could actually be extradimensional matter. An object in fourth-dimensional space would still affect the gravity of three-dimensional space. The "extra" gravity would be able to be measured. In fact, discrepancies in measurements of the sun have been found in which dark matter is suggested as the cause.[281] There are discrepancies in measurements of the moon as well.[282] Dark matter might be an explanation.[283] If dark matter is really extradimensional matter, and if this is what is being measured as extra mass, what might this strange, otherworldly matter look like? Are there extradimensional constructs and, if so, do entities consisting of dimensions beyond our own reside there? Ancient Scripture might give us an answer.

Pillars and Foundations of the Earth

Somewhere in extradimensional space, there seems to be a support system for the Earth. The Bible mentions pillars and foundations of the Earth. Showing their association to Earth, Job 9:6 states:

Which shaketh the earth out of her place, and the pillars thereof tremble.

It also seems the pillars connect Earth and Heaven in some way. Job 26:11 states:

The pillars of heaven tremble and are astonished at his reproof.

Here, these pillars are referred to as "of Heaven," meaning they seem to exist as spiritual/extradimensional constructs. Taking this along with Job 9:6, the text appears to indicate that these pillars originate in Heaven and are connected with the Earth somehow. However, there are places in Scripture where the pillars are referred to as being "of Earth" (1 Samuel 2:8). It seems that the answer to where one end of a pillar begins and the other ends is a matter of perspective. The main takeaway is that the pillars are not *only* "of Earth"; they are not merely three-dimensional constructs embedded in the Earth somewhere. They are also "of Heaven," If these pillars are extradimensional, it could explain how they can be of Earth and also of Heaven.

We also read of how God can use spiritual pillars to complete his goals in Exodus 13:21:

And the Lord went before them by day in a pillar of a cloud, to lead them the way; and by night in a pillar of fire, to give them light; to go by day and night.

Interestingly enough, we might have another clue of extradimensionality in Exodus 14:24:

And it came to pass, that in the morning watch the Lord looked unto the host of the Egyptians through the pillar of fire and of the cloud, and troubled the host of the Egyptians.

The text tells us the Lord (singular) looked at the Egyptians through the pillar of fire and cloud (plural). Was God in the pillar of fire, or was He in the pillar of cloud? As Dr. Michael Heiser would say, the answer is "yes."

Imagine a two-dimensional universe called Flatland inhabited by two-dimensional beings called Flatlanders. If I, as a three-dimensional being, were to put two fingers in Flatland, Flatlanders would see two circles seemingly independent of one another. These two-dimensional circle sections of my fingers would seem like completely separate entities from a two-dimensional perspective. A Flatlander might ask, "Which circle is Josh—the one on the right or the one on the left?" As stated above, the answer would be "yes." In this thought exercise, it's not even that I am in two places at once; at least not exactly. I'm not duplicating myself in order to appear in two places in front of Flatlanders. I just *am* those two circles, and am even much more, of which the Flatlanders are unable to see. The same concept can be applied to God and the pillars in Exodus 14:24.

We can also learn more by looking at what the Bible says about the foundations of the Earth. In order to prove a point, God asks Job a series of unknowable questions in chapter 38 of the book of Job. Specifically, Job 38:4–7 reads:

Where wast thou when I laid the foundations of the earth? declare, if thou hast understanding.

Who hath laid the measures thereof, if thou knowest? or who hath stretched the line upon it?

Whereupon are the foundations thereof fastened? or who laid the corner stone thereof;

When the morning stars sang together, and all the sons of God shouted for joy?

The point of these questions is to show Job that there are things going on that he is unable to know about. Where was Job when God laid the foundations of the Earth? Job wasn't born yet; this was a completely unknowable time from his perspective. Where are the foundations fastened? As we saw earlier, they seem to be fastened in Heaven, somewhere in extradimensional space. If they were fastened merely in or on Earth somewhere, the question would have lost the original point. Job isn't supposed to be able to answer these questions; they are asked to prove a point. The only parts he may have been able to answer are those pertaining to who created and measured the foundations in the first place. Clearly, it was God, further showing a spiritual component to His creation.

Extradimensional Waters and the Firmament

The water on Earth now, at least some of it, may have an extradimensional source. It seems that the Earth prior to the Flood was constructed a bit differently than we see today. Genesis 1:7 states: "And God made the firmament, and divided the waters which were under the firmament from the waters which were above the firmament: and it was so."

We learn that God made something called a *firmament* to divide waters above and below. Much debate has gone into attempting to define exactly what the firmament is. We get a clue in Genesis 1:8, which states: "And God called the firmament Heaven. And the evening and the morning were the second day." Genesis 1:20 states: "And God said, Let the waters bring forth abundantly the moving creature that hath life, and fowl that may fly above the earth in the open firmament of heaven." Genesis 1:16–17 states:

> And God made two great lights; the greater light to rule the day, and the lesser light to rule the night: he made the stars also.
>   And God set them in the firmament of the heaven to give light upon the earth.

We learn three things from these verses. First, the firmament was called "Heaven." Second, the firmament is open and birds fly *in* it. Third, the sun, moon, and stars are also *in* the firmament. The first verse might make us think that the firmament is something purely spiritual, but the second and third verses negate that theory. The second verse might lead us to believe that the firmament isn simply the air around us or even the upper atmosphere, but the third verse negates that, too. The third verse might convince us that the firmament is outer space, yet the second verse negates that as well. So, what are we to do with this information?

This is something that has caused quite a bit of debate. One theory put forth to try to explain this is known as the "canopy theory." This theory states that at creation, a sphere of water or ice was around the entire Earth. This is what the Bible calls the "firmament" in the book of Genesis and elsewhere. Then, at the time of the Flood, the firmament/canopy came down and covered the Earth and all its inhabitants. This theory gained popularity among Christians, and for good reason. It seems to explain a lot, although there are problems with the idea of something solid, or even liquid, encompassing the Earth. Specifically, the word "in" throughout the descriptions we looked at offers challenges to the Canopy Theory.

First, Genesis 1:20 tells us that the birds fly above the Earth, yet *in* the *open* firmament of Heaven. If the firmament was something solid or liquid encompassing the entire Earth, birds likely would not be able to fly *in* it. They could fly under it, but that is not what the text states. Also, the idea of something solid or liquid encompassing the Earth would likely not be described as *open*. If it was something enclosing the Earth, it would be described as "closed." Yet, the firmament is something open that birds can fly in. We also read in Genesis 1:16–17 that the sun, moon, and stars are *in* the firmament. It does not say they are above or below the firmament, but *in*. This also rules out something solid or liquid enclosing the Earth.

What could be happening here is a description of something we as humans have no real concept of due to our limited perception. We could be dealing with something not completely spiritual, but not completely physical, either. Within these texts, we might be reading descriptions of something extradimensional. Genesis 1:7 tells us that one purpose of the firmament was to divide the waters *above* it from the waters below it. The word "above" in Hebrew is *al,* which can also mean "beyond."[284] As we will see in examples later, the word "above" in Scripture is not always used as a spatial direction. Sometimes it is used to describe something of spiritual/extradimensional origin.

The firmament described in Genesis might actually be fourth-dimensional space (hyperspace) or something within the fourth spatial dimension. To help illustrate this idea, imagine again the two-dimensional space of Flatland. Think of a circle, about a foot in diameter, cut out of paper as an example of the Flatland Earth. Imagine that the circle of paper is resting on a pedestal a few inches above your coffee table in your living room at home. Flatlanders, having no understanding of "up" or "down," have access to and can travel around the edge of the circle, but cannot go above or underneath. Even if they managed to dig into the circle to the center, they would still not be able to see the pedestal it rests upon.

Now, you might determine the three-dimensional space all around the circle, in every direction of the living room, is called the "firmament" of your house, which you decide to call "Heaven." Of course, the Flatland two-dimensional space is still a part of the three-dimensional space around it. Therefore, Flatland birds flying in the two-dimensional space around the Flatland Earth would still be "in the firmament of Heaven."

Imagine that you place droplets of water on various places around the edge of the circle in order to give oceans and seas to the Flatlanders. You even decide to give your Flatlanders some light, so you place a desk lamp on your coffee table and angle it in a way that some of the light from the lightbulb is breaching their two dimensional space. The Flatlanders can see the light, but what would it look like to them? Since they have no concept of up or down, they would only see a two-dimensional slice of the light bulb, which would look like a circle to them. They would have no way of knowing there is more to this light, which was set in the living room of your house (firmament of Heaven). They might also notice the stand of the desk lamp. However, since they cannot see how the stand and the light bulb are connected in three-dimensional space, the stand looks like a separate object all together. The Flatlanders would see another two-dimensional circle. They might even notice that some of the light from the bulb is reflecting off of the stand. You tell them the light is called the "Sun" and the stand is called the "Moon." You decide to give them more light, so you hang a set of Christmas lights in a way that only the miniature bulbs actually breach their space. You tell the Flatlanders to call these lights "stars." Again, they can see the stars, but are unable to see how they are connected in your three-dimensional space, so they assume the stars are separate from one another.

Now, just to keep things interesting, you decide to get really creative. You put the pedestal on a rotating platform, causing the Flatland Earth to spin. Next, you set up an electric train set on your coffee table and place the rotating platform with the pedestal and the Flatland Earth on the now-moving train. You place the desk lamp on another rotating pedestal in the center of the train's rotation. It is timed in a way that the light stays in the center while the stand rotates around with the Flatland Earth. After hours of work, you have created a Flatland Earth that rotates around the sun, has its own moon, and even has stars to look at. You've created a working universe.

Now, of course, to the Flatlanders, they are only seeing all of this in two dimensions. The Flatlander Sun, Moon, Earth, and stars all look like separate objects floating through space on their own. The Flatlanders are not able to see any of the mechanisms that make all this possible. Yet, you can still tell them about the mechanisms. You can tell them about the sun, moon, and stars you placed in the living room/firmament of your house/ Heaven. You can even try to explain the living oom to them by saying that it is a type of separation of their world and yours.

Now, imagine that it is raining outside while all this is going on. You might explain to the Flatlanders that the firmament/living room is there in order to separate the water beyond the firmament/living room from the limited amount of water they have on their own Flatlander Earth. In other words, the firmament separates the waters above from the waters below. Now, what would happen if the coffee table all of this is happening upon was under a window? What would happen if you decided to open that window and let the water in? We might find the answer in the account of Noah's Flood. Genesis 7:11 states:

In the six hundredth year of Noah's life, in the second month, the seventeenth day of the month, the same day were all the fountains of the great deep broken up, and the windows of heaven were opened.

The windows of Heaven were opened. Remember, too, that the firmament was given the name "Heaven." The windows of the firmament, which was put in place to separate the waters above (or beyond) from the waters below, were opened and the waters above were allowed to flood in upon the Earth. Imagine again the Flatland Earth and the open window of the living room on a rainy day. To Flatlanders, this would be devastating and would completely drown their world. But then, after the devastation, the rain stops, a few are saved, and the window is closed once again.

Taking all of this into account, we can see passages such as Psalm 104:313 in a clearer perspective:

He lays the beams of His upper chambers in the waters, who makes the clouds His chariot, who walks on the wings of the wind,

Who makes His angels spirits, His ministers a flame of fire.

You who laid the foundations of the earth, so that it should not be moved forever,

You covered it with the deep as with a garment; the waters stood above the mountains.

At Your rebuke they fled; at the voice of Your thunder they hastened away.

They went up over the mountains; they went down into the valleys, to the place which You founded for them.

You have set a boundary that they may not pass over, that they may not return to cover the earth.

He sends the springs into the valleys; they flow among the hills.

They give drink to every beast of the field; the wild donkeys quench their thirst.

By them the birds of the heavens have their home; they sing among the branches.

He waters the hills from His upper chambers; the earth is satisfied with the fruit of Your works.

Dry Land Appearing from Beyond

Along similar lines as the idea of extradimensional water, the land of the Earth itself might have extradimensional origins as well. Genesis 1:9 states that "God said, Let the waters under the heaven be gathered together unto one place, and let the dry land appear: and it was so."

The word "appear" as used in this verse comes from the Hebrew word *ra'ah*. This word seems to give the distinction of something that is already existing, yet is now able to be seen or perceived.[285] To illustrate this, we can compare it with Genesis 12:7: "And the Lord appeared unto Abram, and said, Unto thy seed will I give this land: and there builded he an altar unto the Lord, who appeared unto him."

Of course, this isn't saying that the Lord was created at this time in front of Abram. The Lord already existed, but was in a place imperceptible to Abram. The same could be said about the dry land of Genesis. If the dry land was created as an extradimensional construct, then was pushed into our three dimensions of space, from our perspective it would appear seemingly from nowhere.

Again, we can look to the Flatland Earth example. Imagine, instead of a circle of paper, you actually start with a ceramic tile that you place upon the pedestal. A single Flatlander is on the corner of the tile. Again, the Flatlander has no up or down, so he would not be aware of the fact that he was on the tile. To the Flatlander, there would be nothing but empty space in front of him. On that tile, near enough to the Flatlander for him to see, but not so close that you drown him, you pour a circular puddle of water. To the Flatlander, it would look like a small circle of water appears when you start and expands as you continue pouring. On the edges of the puddle (and in the center too), you place piles of dirt and rocks. From a completely two-dimensional perspective, able to only see the water, it would seem to the Flatlander as though dry land was "appearing" from nowhere. If a Flatlander was viewing all of this taking place, he would not be able to perceive the source of any of it. All he would know is that his physical reality literally appeared in front of his eyes.

The text in Genesis isn't specific as to tell us *where* exactly the Earth, water, or land was when God created it. It also doesn't tell us that all we see is all there is. In fact, it seems to say quite the contrary. There seems to be a lot more to creation than what we can experience in our three-dimensional physical reality. In fact, just like the piles of rocks on the pedestal, our reality seems to be a part of a much larger and richer extradimensional construct. The Earth that God created seems to be more than just a solitary, spinning, blue ball in empty space. It seems to be made of multiple parts, some stationary and some moving, some three-dimensional and some extradimensional, yet all wonderfully intricate and beautifully complex.

The Circle and the Footstool

There is another mystery worth looking into known as the "circle of the Earth." Isaiah 40:22 states:

> It is he that sitteth upon the circle of the earth, and the inhabitants thereof are as grasshoppers; that stretcheth out the heavens as a curtain, and spreadeth them out as a tent to dwell in.

Along with learning more about the creation of the heavens and how they are "stretched out" (again, imagine trying to explain extradimensional space to a Flatlander; you might say it is stretched and spread all around him), we learn that there is something God sits upon called the "circle of the earth." Since this is something God is sitting upon in some fashion, we can deduce that the circle of the Earth is not something purely physical; there is a spiritual/extradimensional aspect to it. This begs the question: Does the circle of the Earth have anything at all three-dimensional to it, or is it purely extradimensional? Psalm 8 might give us a clue.

Psalm 8 is an interesting passage in Scripture. The psalmist is personi-
fying the concept of wisdom. It treats wisdom as if it is a conscious entity
and gives it a voice. In this passage, we get a timeline of creation. Psalm
8:24–27 states:

When there were no depths, I was brought forth; when there were
no fountains abounding with water.
    Before the mountains were settled, before the hills was I brou-
ght forth:
    While as yet he had not made the earth, nor the fields, nor the
highest part of the dust of the world.
    When he prepared the heavens, I was there: when he set a
compass upon the face of the depth.

The first three verses of this passage tell us the context of what is
being said is prior to the creation of Earth. Verse 26 even states specifically
that, at this point, God has not created the Earth yet. Verse 27 tells us we
are now talking about when God created the heavens. It then says God
set a "compass" on the "face of the depth." Based on the same Hebrew
words used, the "face of the depth" here is the same as the "face of the
deep" in Genesis 1:2.[286] Also, the word "compass" in this passage is the
same Hebrew word as "circle" in Isaiah 40:22.[287] Again, no dry land had
appeared yet. Therefore, the circle of the Earth must be a different concept
than merely the dry land of the Earth. To further illustrate this, we can
compare the chain of events from Genesis with Psalm 8.

In the book of Genesis, we learn that the firmament that divided the
waters was created before the dry land appeared. The firmament was put
in place on the second day of creation in Genesis 1:6–8. The dry land
appeared on the third day in Genesis 1:10–13. Comparing with Genesis,
if Psalm 8 states that the circle of the Earth was created sometime before
the firmament, then we know the circle of the Earth must be something
created on either day one or day two, prior to the dry land appearing.
Psalm 8:27–29 states:

When he prepared the heavens, I was there: when he set a compass upon the face of the depth:

When he established the clouds above: when he strengthened the fountains of the deep:

When he gave to the sea his decree, that the waters should not pass his commandment: when he appointed the foundations of the earth.

As we looked at earlier, it was the purpose at the decree of the Lord for the firmament to divide the waters. The first part of Psalm 8:29 is comparable with Genesis 1:8, explaining the creation and purpose of the firmament on the second day. The last part of Psalm 29 is comparable with Genesis 1:9, explaining the foundations/pillars of the Earth we looked at earlier and the appearance of the dry land. Therefore, the circle/compass of the Earth was created and set in place before the creation of the firmament and appearance of dry land. If the circle/compass of the Earth is not the same as the dry land, what is it?

Remember our example of the Flatland Earth at the point of pouring water and dropping rocks and dirt in the water in order to create dry land for the Flatlanders. Imagine, just prior to that, you create a mountain of dirt and/or rocks before starting to form your Flatland Earth. You flatten the very top of the mountain in the shape of a circle and place a throne there. Now, imagine that your coffee table is made of glass and everything under it is referred to as the "deep," or the "depth," parts of which might even contain the "abyss" or "bottomless pit"; possibly these are all words referring to the same area under your coffee table. You place your mountain on the ceramic tile, which rests upon the pedestal. Next, you pour water around your mountain to form a type of moat. Next, you drop dirt and rocks in the water to make dry land for the Flatlanders. Your throne still rests upon the circle of the Flatland Earth, and though it is connected in some way, it is still a different construct than the Flatland Earth itself. In fact, in this way, you can sit on the circle of the Flatland Earth, which is located in your Heaven, and make the Flatland Earth your footstool simultaneously. This idea is comparable with Isaiah 66:1, which states: "Thus saith the Lord, The heaven is my throne, and the earth is my footstool: where is the house that ye build unto me? and where is the place of my rest?"

In a sense, the circle of the Earth and the Earth itself are similar, yet Scripture makes clear they are not the same. It seems that the circle of the Earth is more connected with the holy mountain of God, described in many places, such as Isaiah 65:25:

> The wolf and the lamb shall feed together, and the lion shall eat straw like the bullock: and dust shall be the serpent's meat. They shall not hurt nor destroy in all my holy mountain, saith the Lord.

The prophet John confirms the location of this mountain in Revelation 21:10:

> And he carried me away in the spirit to a great and high mountain, and shewed me that great city, the holy Jerusalem, descending out of heaven from God.

Verses 22 and 26 of the first chapter of the book of Ezekiel gives us a good representation of the idea of this extradimensional construction. Ezekiel sees cherubim from Heaven supporting a type of platform upon which sits the throne of God. Ezekiel 1:22 states:

> And the likeness of the firmament upon the heads of the living creature was as the colour of the terrible crystal, stretched forth over their heads above.

Isaiah 1:26 states:

And above the firmament that was over their heads was the likeness of a throne, as the appearance of a sapphire stone: and upon the likeness of the throne was the likeness as the appearance of a man above upon it.

It is interesting here that the platform is described as *the firmament*. When we remember the purpose of the firmament from Genesis, however, Ezekiel's description makes sense. The purpose of the firmament was to divide something extradimensional from something physical. Of course, this separation seems to be four-dimensional space that is literally all around us all the time even though we can't perceive it. Since there's no real good way to explain or envision higher-dimensional space from our limited three-dimensional perspective, what better way to represent the idea than with a platform separating God and His throne from His servants, the angels that carry Him?

The Bars of the Earth

The Earth also seems to possess bars somewhere within its depths. At first read, it would seem these are purely physical bars, but when we examine Scripture further, we find that idea is unsupported by the text. One of the most famous aspects of the story of Jonah is how he survived in the belly of a great fish. However, when reading Jonah's description of the event in his prayer, we find what we learned in Sunday School may not be exactly accurate. Jonah 2:5–7 reads:

⁵The waters compassed me about, even to the soul: the depth closed me round about, the weeds were wrapped about my head.

⁶I went down to the bottoms of the mountains; the earth with her bars was about me for ever: yet hast thou brought up my life from corruption, O Lord my God.

⁷When my soul fainted within me I remembered the Lord: and my prayer came in unto thee, into thine holy temple.

Verse 5 tells us the waters surrounded Job, even to the soul. We also read the "depth" closed around him. Here, different Hebrew words are used for "waters" and "depth." "Depth" comes from the Hebrew word *tehowm,* which can also mean "abyss" and "the grave."[288] We also read that the weeds under the water were wrapped around his head. Verse 6 tells us he went down the the bottoms of the mountains. Therefore, it is likely at this point Jonah had actually drowned and was headed for Sheol.

To further support this, Jonah 2:6 says the Lord brought up Jonah's life "from corruption." The Hebrew word for "corruption" here is *shachath,* which means "pit, destruction, grave."[289] In verse 7, Jonah says his "soul fainted within" him. When this happened, Jonah remembered the Lord and prayed. God then brought Jonah back to life and, as Jonah 2:10 describes:

And the Lord spake unto the fish, and it vomited out Jonah upon the dry land.

This is further evidence that there is more to the Earth than what we see. There is something beyond physical life and death. There is an extra-dimensional aspect. The bars of the pit are just one example.

Four Corners and Ends of the Earth

One thing that gives us a clue that we're dealing with something extradimensional in Scripture is the presence of a spiritual entity, be it angel or God Himself. Imagine again the Flatland Earth, and this time remember the ceramic tile that the two-dimensional Flatland Earth is resting upon. instead of a circle, the tile itself is a square. Even though the tile and pedestal is rests upon is still, at least in part, considered as parts of the Flatland Earth, Flatlanders only experience a two-dimensional circle. However, due to the existence of the tile, corners actually do exist in three-dimensional space. You could try to explain this to the Flatlanders. You could even give them the general direction of these corners. Based on those general directions, they might even develop idioms like "from the four corners of the Earth" to describe the entire knowable landscape of their two-dimensional planet. However, despite all this, they could never experience the true corners for themselves.

This is an example of what might be going on with our three-dimensional Earth when Scripture described the "four corners." Revelation 7:1 states:

> And after these things I saw four angels standing on the four corners of the earth, holding the four winds of the earth, that the wind should not blow on the earth, nor on the sea, nor on any tree.

The presence of angels at these corners gives us evidence that these are extradimensional constructs. It also seems the angels have a way, by an unknown extradimensional source, to stop the winds of the Earth completely. Might this mean that, like the dry land, the winds of the Earth have an extradimensional source put in place at the time of creation?

Of course, not every time the four corners are mentioned does it means something extradimensional is going on. For example, Isaiah 11:12 states:

> And he shall set up an ensign for the nations, and shall assemble the outcasts of Israel, and gather together the dispersed of Judah from the four corners of the earth.

There are likely not outcasts of Israel in four-dimensional space. Furthermore, Ezekiel 7:2 states:

> Also, thou son of man, thus saith the Lord God unto the land of Israel; An end, the end is come upon the four corners of the land.

The land of Israel does not have only four corners to it (though the heavenly plot of the land might). Again, this is not talking about a literal four corners, but is an idiom to get across the idea of the entire land. Just like the word "land" is used not only in reference to the literal earth beneath the feet of the people of Israel, but is used to refer to the people themselves: Israel as a nation, people, and land.

We see the same thing with the "ends of the earth." Isaiah 43:6 states:

I will say to the north, Give up; and to the south, Keep not back: bring my sons from far, and my daughters from the ends of the earth.

Now, there are areas when the "ends of the earth" might be referring to something extradimensional. Matthew 24:31 states:

And he shall send his angels with a great sound of a trumpet, and they shall gather together his elect from the four winds, from one end of heaven to the other.

Remember again the Flatland Earth example. The entire house that contained the Flatland Earth was called "Heaven." This means Heaven is located above and below Flatland Earth, even though Flatlanders have no concept of up and down. The ends of Heaven to a Flatlander could simply be up and down; above and below. The ends of two-dimensional space is what lies above and below it. In this verse, once again, we have an angel to tip us off that this might be something extradimensional. Therefore, for angels to go out "from one end of heaven to the other," it could be referring to all of the knowable three-dimensional existence. This might be further supported by Job 28:24, which states:

For he looketh to the ends of the earth, and seeth under the whole heaven;

What is under the whole heaven? Three-dimensional reality; just as two-dimensional reality could be considered *under* the whole of three-dimensional reality.

The Tree of Nebuchadnezzar

Another example of using something extradimensional to explain a physical concept can be found in chapter 4 of the book of Daniel. Nebuchadnezzar is describing a dream in which he sees a tree covering the entire Earth, then, later, a "watcher and a holy one" appear. Daniel 4:11–13 states:

> [11] The tree grew, and was strong, and the height thereof reached unto heaven, and the sight thereof to the end of all the earth:
> [12] The leaves thereof were fair, and the fruit thereof much, and in it was meat for all: the beasts of the field had shadow under it, and the fowls of the heaven dwelt in the boughs thereof, and all flesh was fed of it.
> [13] I saw in the visions of my head upon my bed, and, behold, a watcher and an holy one came down from heaven.

Again, the presence of extradimensional beings can give us evidence that something extradimensional is occurring. Possibly even more than that, however, Nebuchadnezzar tells us the tree "reached unto heaven" and was seen "to the end of the earth." As we discussed earlier, the "ends of the earth" can refer to literally everywhere on the earth. Also, if the tree is reaching into Heaven, it is reaching into a higher dimension. Using again the Flatland Earth example, imagine placing a tree right in the center of the circle with its branches hanging down all around the circle. The tree would be reaching into your house/Heaven and the branches (at least the parts of them that breached two-dimensional space) would be accessible to everyone all around the Flatland Earth. Even though the Flatlanders couldn't see the entire construct of the tree, they would still be able to enjoy what came from the parts that breached their space. The tree could still provide them with shade, fruit, and even a home for the birds. Of course, this is describing a dream Nebuchadnezzar was given in order to deliver a message and teach him something. This wasn't a literal event. Therefore, not everything in the dream is completely physical or completely extradimensional, yet it is highly symbolic and metaphorical.

Stationary Earth in Motion

How can something not move yet move at the same time? Believe it or not, this isn't as impossible as it may seem on the surface. Consider a pocket watch. When it is closed and sitting on your desk, it looks perfectly still, stationary, and unmoving. However, if you were able to see inside the watch, you would see various gears in motion to keep the watch running. The entire construct of the watch is stationary, yet the watch is still in motion. If a single, moving gear was all there was to the watch, you would not be able to describe it as stationary.

Imagine two microorganisms living on one of the gears in the watch. One might say to the other, "The place we live on, called the 'Watch,' is constantly in motion." The other might say, "No, the Watch is fixed and stationary; it is not moving." Technically, both would be correct. The gear of the watch they are living on is in motion, yet the rest of the watch they have no concept of is stationary.

In a way, higher dimensions can work like this. In our Flatland Earth example, the pedestal that holds the four-cornered tile is set upon a model train car that is in constant motion. Yet, the entire construct of the Flatland Earth is resting and stationary on the coffee table. Thus, the Flatland Earth is moving through two-dimensional space, yet is stationary when considering the extra third dimension.

We have a similar description in the Bible when it comes to the Earth. We have verses that seem to describe it as stationary. There are even some that promise the Earth will *never* be moved, yet there are others that promise it *will* be moved at some time in the future. Either we have a biblical contradiction or we need to consider more than the three spatial dimensions we can perceive. First Chronicles 16:30 states:

Fear before him, all the earth: the world also shall be stable, that it be not moved.

Psalm 93:1 states:

The Lord reigneth, he is clothed with majesty; the Lord is clothed with strength, wherewith he hath girded himself: the world also is stablished, that it cannot be moved.

Showing not only that the Earth is stationary, but that it will *never* be moved, Psalm 96:10 states:

Say among the heathen that the Lord reigneth: the world also shall be established that it shall not be moved: he shall judge the people righteously.

Yet, promising that the Earth will be moved, Isaiah 13:13 states:

Therefore I will shake the heavens, and the earth shall remove out of her place, in the wrath of the Lord of hosts, and in the day of his fierce anger.

At times, there seems to be a difference in what is referred to as the "world" and the "earth." In fact, they are different Hebrew words.[290] It seems, at least at certain times (not every time), the word "world" can refer to the entire construct of the world in all dimensions whereas the "earth" seems to refer to the three-dimensional parts we can perceive. Again, this is not a perfect rule and likely does not apply in every instance, but at least at certain times it seems to. For example, Psalm 89:11 states:

The heavens are thine, the earth also is thine: as for the world and the fulness thereof, thou hast founded them.

This verse is giving ownership and credit to God for His creation, yet it makes certain distinctions. The first part of the verse makes a clear distinction between the "heavens" and the "earth." Then, in the second half, the verse deals with a third entity, "the world and the fulness thereof," which seems to indicate the entire construct of the Earth, extradimensional aspects included (pillars, corners, bars, etc.). This can help explain how an Earth in motion can also be stationary and how Scripture can promise it will never be moved yet also promise it will be moved.

Seeing from a Higher-Dimensional Perspective

At the return of Jesus, we are told throughout the Bible that everyone in the world will see Him. How can this be possible? Even people in neighboring countries would not be able to see a single person descend on the Mount of Olives. There could be a technological component here, of course. In recent decades, biblical researchers have put forth the idea that television, cell phones, and the internet might give the entire word access to be able to see the return of the Lord Jesus. Yet, not everyone in the world has access to these things. Perhaps in the future at the time of Jesus' return the world will be more connected technologically, or perhaps there is something more going on here. Revelation 1:7 states:

Behold, he cometh with clouds; and every eye shall see him, and they also which pierced him: and all kindreds of the earth shall wail because of him. Even so, Amen.

This verse specifically states "every eye shall see him" and, even more amazing, it says "they also which pierced him." Generally, this is interpreted as meaning the descendants of those who pierced Jesus, His enemies, or the Romans, or unrepentant people. Maybe something more literal is going on here. Maybe this verse means those who literally pierced Jesus more than two thousand years ago will see Him from their eternal abode, along with the rest of the living and physical world. This might give us a clue that a type of convergence of the spiritual and the physical is happening here. If the dead and eternally damned can see Jesus, is it any stretch that the rest of the world can too?

We might have a clue on how this could be possible in Matthew 4:8, which states:

> Again, the devil taketh him up into an exceeding high mountain, and sheweth him all the kingdoms of the world, and the glory of them.

In Hebrew, the word *lian* is translated to the English "exceeding," and means "greatly, exceedingly, exceedingly beyond measure." How high does a mountain have to be to be considered "beyond measure"? If we remember from earlier, the word "high" doesn't always have to mean high up in the air, but can sometimes be referring to the unknowable parts of Heaven. It is likely, in this verse, the devil took Jesus to an extradimensional mountain where He really could see all the kingdoms of the world at one time. In a Flatland Earth, from your throne in the middle of the circle, it would be relatively easy to look around you and see all of the Flatland kingdoms—although, to Flatlanders, such a thing would be impossible in two dimensions. We see this idea repeated from John's own description in Revelation 21:10:

> And he carried me away in the spirit to a great and high mountain, and shewed me that great city, the holy Jerusalem, descending out of heaven from God.

John was able to see this happening in the spirit on a great an high mountain. Clearly, this is no mere earthly mountain. This is describing the holy mountain of God that exist in Heaven.

If, at the time of the return of Jesus, there is a type of convergence of extra dimensions into our own, this could explain how the entire world will be able to see Him. Imagine if you were to take the Flatland Earth and fold it in such a way that, now, Flatlanders on each side of the circle are facing you directly. Technically, you would be folding their reality into extradimensional space. This does not give Flatlanders a three-dimensional view, however. They still would only be able to see what is directly in front of them. However, if they and/or their world were bent in a way to be facing you, they could all see you at the same time, regardless of how far away they are from one another in two-dimensional space. Three-dimensional space, or what they would consider as Heaven, would be open to them. Describing the return of Jesus, Revelation 19:11 states:

> And I saw heaven opened, and behold a white horse; and he that sat upon him was called Faithful and True, and in righteousness he doth judge and make war.

This might be what causes the great shaking of the Earth at the time of Jesus' return. Zechariah 14:4 states:

> And his feet shall stand in that day upon the mount of Olives, which is before Jerusalem on the east, and the mount of Olives shall cleave in the midst thereof toward the east and toward the west, and there shall be a very great valley; and half of the mountain shall remove toward the north, and half of it toward the south.

Now, imagine from the Flatlanders' perspective what this folding would look like. Their perspective would be shifted away from things they were able to see before. They would no longer be able to see the sun, moon, or stars because their field of view will have been shifted above them in extradimensional space. In fact, to Flatlanders, the sun, moon, and stars would blink out, not give light, and completely fall away during the time of this folding/shaking. Matthew 24:29–30 states:

[29] Immediately after the tribulation of those days shall the sun be darkened, and the moon shall not give her light, and the stars shall fall from heaven, and the powers of the heavens shall be shaken:

[30] And then shall appear the sign of the Son of man in heaven: and then shall all the tribes of the earth mourn, and they shall see the Son of man coming in the clouds of heaven with power and great glory.

We see this trend with the sun and moon continued in descriptions of the New Jerusalem in Revelation 21:23, which states:

And the city had no need of the sun, neither of the moon, to shine in it: for the glory of God did lighten it, and the Lamb is the light thereof.

It is entirely possible that the ancient biblical prophets were trying to describe a literal folding of our three dimensions of reality into extradimensional space. This would be extremely traumatic for those not mentally, emotionally, or spiritually prepared for it. We might even be inclined to believe such an act would completely destroy the Earth; however, this wouldn't have to be the case. Just as folding a Flatland Earth wouldn't destroy it; it would just change its shape. Our physical Earth will be shaken and altered, but it will survive the trip.

The New Jerusalem Above

After all the chaos, there are some wonderful things in line for the believer in Jesus. There are new dimensions of existence to explore. There is a new, extradimensional Jerusalem. There are even new, extradimensional bodies for God's children.

Everything we see in three-dimensional reality now is like a shadow of true, extradimensional reality. Just as a square is a mere shadow of a cube,

Earth itself is a mere shadow of Heaven. Showing this in the example of Jerusalem, Galatians 4:25–26 states:

> [25] For this Agar is mount Sinai in Arabia, and answereth to Jerusalem which now is, and is in bondage with her children.
> [26] But Jerusalem which is above is free, which is the mother of us all.

There is a physical Jerusalem and a "Jerusalem which is above." The word "above" as used here comes from the Greek word *ano*, which can mean "of the quarters of the heaven."[291] We can learn more about this by comparing with the words of Jesus in John 8:23, which states:

> And he said unto them, Ye are from beneath; I am from above: ye are of this world; I am not of this world.

Quoting the words of God, we also read in Acts 2:19:

> And I will shew wonders in heaven above, and signs in the earth beneath; blood, and fire, and vapour of smoke.

As we learn, there is our physical world and a much richer, heavenly reality "above." Another interesting thing to note is, back in Galatians 4:26, the "Jerusalem above" is referred to as "the mother of us all." The word "mother" is translated from the Greek word *meter* and, as a metaphor, can mean "the source of something, the motherland."

We see an antithesis of this idea in Revelation 17:5, which states:

> And upon her forehead was a name written, Mystery, Babylon The Great, The Mother Of Harlots And Abominations Of The Earth.

This is telling us the "mother" (same Greek word used here as in Galatians 4:26) of harlots and abominations of the Earth is Mystery Babylon. There has been much debate about the identity of Mystery Babylon. It is entirely possible that Mystery Babylon is the enemy's twisted version of the New Jerusalem. This, in a sense, is the "holy city" of Satan. It is a spiritual/extradimensional place, yet has had three-dimensional "shadows" throughout time, such as Babylon. Just as God has a Jerusalem above and a physical Jerusalem below, the enemy has usurped that idea and twisted it for his own evil purposes. For everything God has, Satan has an inferior and opposite duplicate. If Mystery Babylon is the mother of these evil things, it means it is the source and motherland of them. These are spiritual problems coming from a spiritual source, yet find physical manifestations here on Earth. This is bad, of course, but the ramifications of this worthless attempt of the enemy doesn't even compare to the wonderful things God has in store for us, as believers, in our source and motherland.

We learn more about the New Jerusalem and some of the amazing things we have to look forward to in Revelation 3:12, which states:

> Him that overcometh will I make a pillar in the temple of my God, and he shall go no more out: and I will write upon him the name of my God, and the name of the city of my God, which is new Jerusalem, which cometh down out of heaven from my God: and I will write upon him my new name.

Revelation 21:2 states:

> And I John saw the holy city, new Jerusalem, coming down from God out of heaven, prepared as a bride adorned for her husband.

Going back to Galatians 4:26, if the New Jerusalem is our motherland and source, then this is telling us we will not only be residents of the New Jerusalem *someday*, but we are now and, in fact, have *always been*. Now, this is not to say that we, as saved by the blood of Jesus, have been forced into that position. We still have free will and a choice to make. However, once we make that choice, on a spiritual level, we enter a place outside of time with Jesus. Ephesians 2:4–6 reads:

> [4] But God, who is rich in mercy, for his great love wherewith he loved us,
>   [5] Even when we were dead in sins, hath quickened us together with Christ, (by grace ye are saved;)
>   [6] And hath raised us up together, and made us sit together in heavenly places in Christ Jesus.

This is telling us that, from the perspective of Jesus, we are *already* seated with Him in heavenly places. He "hath raised" (past tense) us up together and made us sit together in heavenly places. This is describing a past event, yet it is still future for us.

This description goes beyond all dimensions of space. This even goes beyond dimensions of *time*. Being secure in the salvation of Jesus means we get to sit with Him in eternity. While infinity is a span of never-ending time, *eternity* is a state outside of time, in perfect timelessness. This is something we, as three-dimensional human bound by time, have no way of fully comprehending. Yet, the passage tells us it is true. We are there with Christ already. This is how the New Jerusalem can be our source, yet is also a future destination.

Back to Gravity

In December of 2013, *New Scientist* reported on evidence of dark matter on the Earth.[292] As stated in the beginning of this study, the Earth weighs more than it should. The anomaly is measured by space probes, several of which changed their speeds in unexpected ways as they traveled past the Earth. The Earth seemed to be exerting a higher gravitational force on these probes. Ben Harris of the University of Texas at Arlington wondered if this anomaly was a fluke or if it could be measured again, this time by utilizing GPS satellites. The orbit of GPS satellites are known extremely well, so if an anomaly were present, it should have been easy to find. After nine months of testing, he calculated the difference in what was expected based on how massive the Earth is and what was actually recorded. Harris discovered an average difference of between 0.005 and 0.008 percent greater than the value of the Earth's mass. This means the Earth possesses extra mass that we cannot see nor experience in any way. It is hypothesized that dark matter is the culprit.

Perhaps it is not a ring of weakly interacting massive particles (or WIMPs, the current leading theory of dark matter). Perhaps the extra gravity being measured is coming from extradimensional constructs. After all, if the Bible is correct and there is more to the Earth than what we can see, we should *expect* the Earth to be heavier than our three-dimensional measurement can account for. Perhaps science has measured the gravity exerted by parts of the pillars, corners, bars, waters, and high mountains that are secured to our planet in extradimensional space. Perhaps science has accidentally discovered the biblical foundations of the Earth written about thousands of years ago.

If this is true, is it then too much of a leap to consider what might inhabit this realm? Throughout ancient Scripture, we are given many examples of angels, demons, devils, principalities, powers, lesser gods, and more. Is it possible that the ETI described in the Podesta emails could fall into one or more of these categories? To revisit the question at the beginning of this part of the book, what if "they" are already here?

NOTES

1. "Watchers, Aliens, UFOs, Angels, Demons: Tom Horn on PITN (pt 5)," YouTube video, 9:57, posted by Thomas Horn, last updated February 21, 2008, last accessed February 9, 2013, http://www.youtube.com/watch?v=pE7qT3IK8lc.

2. Thomas Horn, *Nephilim Stargates: The Year 2012 and the Return of the Watchers* (Crane, MO: Anomalos Publishing House, 2007), 94; first set of brackets in original; second set of brackets added by authors.

3. "More Than One Third of Americans Believe Aliens Have Visited Earth," June 28, 2012, *Christian Science Monitor*. https://www.csmonitor.com/Science/2012/0628/More-than-one-third-of-Americans-believe-aliens-have-visited-Earth, retrieved 7/14/17.

4. "The State of the Church 2016," September 15, 2016. https://www.barna.com/research/state-church-2016/, retrieved 7/14/17.

5. "Competing Worldviews Influence Today's Christians," May 9, 2017. https://www.barna.com/research/competing-worldviews-influence-todays-christians/, retrieved 7/14/17.

6. Email from Edgar Mitchell to John Podesta dated Jan. 18, 2015. https://www.wikileaks.org/podesta-emails/emailid/1766, retrieved 7/14/17.

7. You know the one: "I'm not saying it was aliens, but it was aliens!"

8. Claire Giangravè, "Could Catholicism Handle the Discovery of Extraterrestrial Life?," February 23, 2017, *Crux*. https://cruxnow.com/global-church/2017/02/23/catholicism-handle-discovery-extraterrestrial-life/, retrieved 7/14/17.

9. Ibid.

10. Ibid.

11. "Groundbreaking AFCI Study Reveals How Many Adults Have a Biblical Worldview," American Culture & Faith Institute, February 27, 2017. https://www.culturefaith.com/groundbreaking-survey-by-acfi-reveals-how-many-american-adults-have-a-biblical-worldview/, retrieved 7/14/17.

12. "Barna Survey Examines Changes in Worldview Among Christians over the Past 13 Years," March 9, 2009. https://www.barna.com/research/barna-survey-examines-changes-in-worldview-among-christians-over-the-past-13-years/, retrieved 7/14/17.

13. "Competing Worldviews Influence Today's Christians," op. cit.

14. Ibid.

15. Ibid.

16. Ibid.

17. It may not seem like it, because of the emergence of the Islamic State in 2014, but the historic conflict between Islam and Christendom has been unusually quiet since the end of World War I. It's easy for us in the West to forget that the caliphate nearly destroyed Western civilization during the Middle Ages. The Ottoman Empire was only turned back from Vienna, Austria in 1683, more than sixty years after the Pilgrims landed at Plymouth Rock and established the Massachusetts Bay colony.

18. Yes, there are eyewitnesses who have seen mysterious flying craft, and there is some physical evidence, such as puzzling metal implants extracted from contacts. None of that is proof of extraterrestrial origin.

19. Geisler, Norman L., and Frank Turek. *I Don't Have Enough Faith to Be an Atheist*. Wheaton, IL: Crossway Books, 2004, p. 55.

20. For the sake of brevity, I'll leave defending that proposition to books like *The Case for Christ* and *Evidence That Demands a Verdict*.

21. Martin Waldron, "In Roswell, N. M., Closing of Air Base Wasn't the End," July 9, 1970, *The New York Times*. http://www.nytimes.com/1970/07/09/archives/in-roswell-nm-closing-of-air-base-wasnt-the-end.html, retrieved 7/15/17.

22. Gendy Alimurung, "One Weekend with Alien Enthusiasts Might Make You a Believer," November 28, 2013, *LA Weekly*. http://www.laweekly.com/news/one-weekend-with-alien-enthusiasts-might-make-you-a-believer-4137362, retrieved 7/16/17.

23. Alex Welch, "Friday Cable Ratings: 'Live PD' and Clippers vs Lakers Game Land High," July 10, 2017, *TV by the Numbers*. http://

tvbythenumbers.zap2it.com/daily-ratings/friday-cable-ratings-july-7-2017/, retrieved 7/16/17.

24. Jason Colavito, "Review of Ancient Aliens S12E10 'The Akashic Record,'" July 14, 2017. http://www.jasoncolavito.com/blog/review-of-ancient-aliens-s12e10-the-akashic-record, retrieved 7/16/17.

25. Transcribed from video clip: https://www.youtube.com/watch?v=CDeGGZVxUGg, retrieved 7/16/17.

26. Dr. Michael S. Heiser, "The Spaceships of Ezekiel Fraud," April 28, 2013, *Paleobabble*. http://michaelsheiser.com/PaleoBabble/2013/04/spaceships-ezekiel-fraud/, retrieved 7/16/17.

27. See www.SitchinIsWrong.com.

28. "All Time Box Office," *Box Office Mojo*. http://www.boxofficemojo.com/alltime/adjusted.htm, retrieved 7/16/17.

29. Deuteronomy 32:8 (ESV).

30. Deuteronomy 4:19 (ESV).

31. Psalm 82:1-2, 6-7 (ESV).

32. Ephesians 6:12 (ESV).

33. The fact that we share a publisher doesn't change the fact that Jeffrey's book is a well-researched, well-written examination of cosmology, angelology, demonology, and cosmic pluralism.

34. Clay Routledge, Ph.D., "5 Scientifically Supported Benefits of Prayer," June 23, 2014, *Psychology Today*. https://www.psychologytoday.com/blog/more-mortal/201406/5-scientifically-supported-benefits-prayer, retrieved 7/20/17.

35. Philippians 4:7 (ESV).

36. Lactantius, *On the Anger of God*, 13.19.

37. http://www.noetic.org/about/overview, retrieved 8/30/17.

38. Rev. Simeon Stefanidakis, "Forerunners to Modern Spiritualism: Emanuel Swedenborg (1688-1772), http://www.fst.org/spirit2.htm, retrieved 7/25/17.

39. http://www.swedenborg.com/product/life-planets/, retrieved 7/25/17.

40. Doctrine and Covenants 130:22. https://www.lds.org/scriptures/dc-testament/dc/130.22?lang=eng#21, retrieved 7/30/17.

41. *The Pearl of Great Price*, Moses 1:29–34. https://www.lds.org/scriptures/pgp/moses/1.29-34?lang=eng#28, retrieved 7/30/17.

42. Margaret Fox Kane, quoted in Davenport, Reuben Briggs. *The Deathblow to Spiritualism*. New York: G.W. Dillingham, 1888, pp. 75–76.

43. Ibid., p. 77.
44. Zusne, Leonard; Jones, Warren. (1989). *Anomalistic Psychology: A Study of Magical Thinking.* Lawrence Erlbaum Associates. p. 212.
45. Carroll, Bret E. *The Routledge historical atlas of religion in America.* New York: Routledge, 2000, p. 74.
46. Hess, David J. Science in the New Age: The Paranormal, Its Defenders and Debunkers, and American Culture. Madison, WI: University of Wisconsin Press, 1993, p. 20.
47. Blavatsky, Helena P. *The Key to Theosophy.* London: Theosophical Publishing Society, 1889, p. 43.
48. Kuhn, Alvin Boyd. *Theosophy: A Modern Revival of Ancient Wisdom.* (PhD thesis). American Religion Series: Studies in Religion and Culture. Whitefish, MT: Kessinger Publishing, 1992 (originally published 1930), pp. 63–64.
49. Colavito, Jason. T*he Cult of Alien Gods: H.P. Lovecraft And Extraterrestial Pop Culture* (Kindle Locations 364–366). Kindle Edition.
50. https://truthxchange.com/about-2/vision/, retrieved 8/8/17.
51. Cain, Sian. "Ten Things You Should Know About HP Lovecraft," *The Guardian*, August 20, 2014. https://www.theguardian.com/books/2014/aug/20/ten-things-you-should-know-about-hp-lovecraft, retrieved 8/3/17.
52. Ibid.
53. Harms, Daniel, and John Wisdom Gonce. *The Necronomicon files: the truth behind Lovecraft's legend.* Boston, MA: Weiser Books, 2003, p. 5.
54. One of the most well-known pop-culture references to Lovecraft is the Arkham Asylum, which has been featured since the mid-1970s in the Batman comics, cartoons, movies, and video games. Arkham was named for a fictional town in Massachusetts created by Lovecraft, the home of Miskatonic University, which features prominently in many of Lovecraft's stories.
55. Crowley, Aleister. *The Equinox of the Gods*, chapter 7. https://hermetic.com/crowley/equinox-of-the-gods/remarks-on-the-method-of-receiving-liber-legis?redirect=1, retrieved 8/5/17.
56. Thelemapedia.org. http://www.thelemapedia.org/index.php/The_Book_of_the_Law, retrieved 8/5/17.
57. Hutton, Ronald. *The triumph of the moon: a history of modern pagan witchcraft.* Oxford: Oxford University Press, 2006, p. 178.
58. Colavito, Jason. "Inside the Necronomicon," 2002. http://jcolavito.tripod.com/lostcivilizations/id25.html, retrieved 8/6/17.

59. ONeill, Declan (4 March 2011). "Kenneth Grant: Writer and occultist who championed Aleister Crowley and Austin Osman Spare". *The Independent.* http://www.independent.co.uk/news/obituaries/kenneth-grant-writer-and-occultist-who-championed-aleister-crowley-and-austin-osman-spare-2231570.html, retrieved 8/5/17.

60. Harms and Gonce, op. cit., pp. 109–110.

61. Ibid.

62. Levenda, Peter. *The Dark Lord: H. P. Lovecraft, Kenneth Grant, and the Typhonian Tradition in Magic* (pp. 97-98). Nicolas-Hays, Inc. Kindle Edition.

63. te Velde, Herman (1967). Seth, God of Confusion: A Study of His Role in Egyptian Mythology and Religion. *Probleme der Ägyptologie* 6. Translated by van Baaren-Pape, G. E. (2nd ed.). Leiden: E. J. Brill, p. 7.

64. See chapter 3 of Derek Gilbert's book *The Great Inception.*

65. That's in chapter 4 of *The Great Inception.*

66. Ryholt, Kim. *The Political Situation in Egypt during the Second Intermediate Period c.1800–1550 B.C.*, Museum Tuscalanum Press, (1997), p. 128.

67. Allon, Niv. "Seth is Baal—Evidence from the Egyptian Script." *Egypt and the Levant* XVII, 2007, pp. 15–22.

68. te Velde. Op. cit., pp. 139–140.

69. Levenda, op. cit. (p. 75). Nicolas-Hays, Inc. Kindle Edition.

70. Colavito 2002, op. cit.

71. Levenda, op. cit., p. 8.

72. "Remembering Kenneth Grant's Understanding of The Necronomicon Tradition," https://warlockasyluminternationalnews.com/2011/02/18/remembering-kenneth-grants-understanding-of-the-necronomicon-tradition/, retrieved 8/7/17.

73. Cabal, Alan. "The Doom That Came to Chelsea," *Chelsea News*, June 10, 2003. http://www.nypress.com/the-doom-that-came-to-chelsea/, retrieved 8/7/17.

74. Clore, Dan. "The Lurker on the Threshold of Interpretation: Hoax Necronomicons and Paratextual Noise." *Lovecraft Studies*, No. 42–43 (Autumn 2001). http://www.geocities.ws/clorebeast/lurker.htm, retrieved 8/7/17.

75. Colavito, Jason (2005). *The Cult of Alien Gods: H.P. Lovecraft And Extraterrestial Pop Culture.* Amherst, NY: Prometheus Books. Kindle Edition (Kindle location 1227).

76. Ibid (Kindle locations 1296–1300).

77. Ibid (Kindle location 1338).

78. Von Däniken, Erich (1968). *Chariots of the Gods: Unsolved Mysteries of the Past.* New York: Berkley Books, p. viii.

79. "2001: A Space Odyssey Named the Greatest Sci-Fi Film of All Time By the Online Film Critics Society" (June 12, 2002). https://web.archive.org/web/20061126071451/http://ofcs.rottentomatoes.com/pages/pr/top100scifi, retrieved 8/27/17.

80. Von Braun was one of the 1,600 or so Nazi scientists, engineers, and technicians secretly brought to the U.S. after the war during Operation Paperclip.

81. Colavito, op. cit. (Kindle location 1346).

82. Sheaffer, Robert (1974). "Erich von Däniken's 'Chariots of the Gods': Science or Charlatanism?" Originally published in *NICAP UFO Investigator.* https://www.debunker.com/texts/vondanik.html, retrieved 8/27/17.

83. Heiser, Dr. Michael S. (September 3, 2009). "Zecharia Sitchin: Why You Can Safely Ignore Him." *UFO Digest.* http://www.ufodigest.com/news/0909/ignore-him.php, retrieved 10/17/17.

84. Kilgannon, Corey (January 8, 2010). "Origin of the Species, From an Alien View." *The New York Times.* http://www.nytimes.com/2010/01/10/nyregion/10alone.html, retrieved 10/17/17.

85. "Paranormal America 2017 Chapman University Survey of American Fears 2017" (October 11, 2017). https://blogs.chapman.edu/wilkinson/2017/10/11/paranormal-america-2017/, retrieved 10/17/17.

86. "Erich von Daniken: Fraud, Lies and Bananas." *Forgetomori* (April 8, 2012). http://forgetomori.com/2012/aliens/erich-von-daniken-fraud-lies-and-bananas/, retrieved 8/27/17.

87. http://www.mufon.com, retrieved 8/23/17.

88. Sheaffer, Robert (August 1, 2017). "MUFON Unravels." *Bad UFOs.* http://badufos.blogspot.com/2017/08/mufon-unravels.html, retrieved 8/26/17.

89. https://www.mufonsymposium.com/corey-goode, retrieved 8/26/17.

90. https://www.mufonsymposium.com/andrew-bassagio, retrieved 8/26/17.

91. Salla, Dr. Michael E. (December 26, 2015). "Jump Room to Mars: Did CIA Groom Obama & Basiago as future Presidents?" *Exopolitics.org.* http://exopolitics.org/jump-room-to-mars-did-cia-groom-obama-basiago-as-future-presidents/, retrieved 8/26/17.

92. Dolan, Richard (July 18, 2017). "On Corey, Andrew, and the Whistleblowers." https://www.facebook.com/notes/richard-dolan/on-corey-andrew-and-the-whistleblowers/1394366947350897/, retrieved 8/26/17.

93. http://www.mufon.com/the-inner-circle.html, retrieved 8/26/17.

94. Knight, Judy Zebra (2005). *Ramtha, the White Book.* Yelm, WA: JZK Publishing.

95. Iwasaki, John (February 10, 1997). "JZ Knight Not Faking It, Say Scholars—But They Bristle at the Idea She's Buying Them." *Seattle Post-Intelligencer.* p. B1.

96. Brenner, Keri (January 27, 2008). "Disillusioned Former Students Target Ramtha." *The Olympian.* Via the Cult Education Institute. https://www.culteducation.com/group/1113-ramtha-school-of-enlightenment/17846-disillusioned-former-students-target-ramtha-.html, retrieved 8/26/17.

97. Ibid.

98. Gorenfeld, John (September 16, 2004). "'Bleep' of faith." *Salon.* http://www.salon.com/2004/09/16/bleep_2/, retrieved 8/26/17.

99. *Box Office Mojo.* http://www.boxofficemojo.com/movies/?id=whatthe.htm, retrieved 8/26/17.

100. Meyers, Royce J., III (July 24, 2017). "Former MUFON State Director Resigns, Cites Cult Leader Involvement." *UFO Watchdog.* http://ufowatchdog.blogspot.com/2017/07/former-mufon-state-director-resigns.html, retrieved 8/28/17.

101. Ibid.

102. Chilton, Martin. "The War of the Worlds Panic Was a Myth." *The Telegraph*, May 6, 2016. http://www.telegraph.co.uk/radio/what-to-listen-to/the-war-of-the-worlds-panic-was-a-myth/, retrieved 8/6/17.

103. McCaffery, Larry. "An Interview with Jack Williamson." July 1991. http://www.depauw.edu/sfs/interviews/williamson54interview.htm, retrieved 8/6/17.

104. *Astounding Science Fiction*, April 1950, p. 132.

105. Lovecraft, H. P. "At the Mountains of Madness." *Astounding Stories*, 16, No. 6 (February 1936), 8–32; 17, No. 1 (March 1936), 125–55; 17, No. 2 (April 1936), 132–50. http://www.hplovecraft.com/writings/texts/fiction/mm.aspx, retrieved 8/8/17.

106. The title of one of Dr. Heiser's presentations at the Modern Challenges to the ET Hypothesis Conference at the 2017 UFO Festival in Roswell.

107. Prophet, Elizabeth Clare. *The Seven Chohans—On the Path of the*

Ascension: The Opening of the Retreats of the Great White Brotherhood (Teachings of the Ascended Masters). Malibu: Summit University Press, 1973, p. 193.

108. Knowles, Christopher, and Joseph Michael Linsner. *Our Gods Wear Spandex: The Secret History of Comic Book Heroes.* San Francisco: Weiser Books, 2007, p. 18.

109. Graham, Robbie. "SETI Astronomer says We're Ready for Alien Contact… Thanks to Hollywood." *Mysterious Universe*, July 19, 2017. http://mysteriousuniverse.org/2017/07/seti-atronomer-says-were-ready-for-alien-contact-thanks-to-hollywood/, retrieved 8/6/17.

110. Levenda, Peter (2005). *Sinister Forces—The Nine: A Grimoire of American Political Witchcraft.* Walterville, Oregon: TrineDay. Kindle Edition, Kindle Location 5562.

111. Orleans Parish Grand Jury Testimony of F. Lee Crisman, 21 Nov 1968. https://archive.org/details/OrleansParishGrandJuryTestimonyOfF. LeeCrisman21Nov1968, retrieved 8/11/17.

112. Ibid.

113. Knight, Peter (2003). *Conspiracy Theories in American History: An Encyclopedia.* Santa Barbara, Calif: ABC-CLIO, p. 690.

114. Best, Emma. "FBI's Real-life 'X-Files' Documents Strange Connection between UFOs and the JFK Assassination." *Muckrock*, December 5, 2016. https://www.muckrock.com/news/archives/2016/dec/05/fbis-real-x-files-documents-strange-connection-bet/, retrieved 8/11/17.

115. Thomas, Kenn (2011). *JFK & UFO: Military-Industrial Conspiracy and Cover-Up from Maury Island to Dallas.* Feral House. Kindle Edition, p. 13.

116. Ibid., p. 32.

117. Levenda, op. cit. Kindle location 5636.

118. Levenda, op. cit. Kindle location 5667.

119. "5 Discs Sighted by United Flight." http://www.nicap. org/470704emmett_dir.htm, retrieved 8/11/17.

120. Levenda, op. cit. Kindle locations 5569–5678.

121. Best, op. cit.

122. Gulyas, Aaron John (2015). *The Paranormal and the Paranoid: Conspiratorial Science Fiction Television.* Lanham: Rowman & Littlefield, p. 30.

123. Thomas, op. cit., p. 15.

124. Ibid.
125. Ridgeway, James and Vaughan, Doug. "The Last Days of Danny Casolaro," *The Village Voice*, October 15, 1991, p. 34 ff.
126. "Jury Says Guilty—Man Claims Frame-Up but Faces 20-Year Term after Verdict on Seven Drug-Related Charges." *The Seattle Times*, January 19, 1992. http://community.seattletimes.nwsource.com/archive/?date=1992 0119&slug=1471110, retrieved 8/11/17.
127. Best, op. cit.; Levenda, op. cit., Kindle locations 5682–5683.
128. Kelly, William. "The Houma Bunker Raid Revisited." *JFKcountercoup*, May 20, 2009. http://jfkcountercoup.blogspot.com/2009/05/houma-bunker-raid-revisted.html, retrieved 8/11/17.
129. "Guy Banister." http://spartacus-educational.com/JFKbannister.htm, retrieved 8/11/17.
130. Levenda, op. cit., Kindle location 5699.
131. Which is a plausible scenario. See "The 1947 Roswell UFO Crash," http://www.roswellufocrash.com, retrieved 8/11/17.
132. Carrion, James. "Human Deception at Play during the UFO Wave of 1947." August 20, 2016. http://historydeceived.blogspot.com/2016/08/human-deception-at-playduring-ufo-wave.html, retrieved 8/11/17.
133. Ibid.
134. "AAF Drops Flying Disc Probe for Lack of Evidence." *The Waco News-Tribune*, July 4, 1947, p. 3.
135. Carrion, op. cit.
136. Coppens, Philip. "Driving Mr. Bennewitz Insane." http://philipcoppens.com/bennewitz.html, retrieved 8/23/17.
137. Redfern, Nick (2012). "UFOs: The Project Beta Scandal." *Mysterious Universe*. http://mysteriousuniverse.org/2012/04/ufos-the-project-beta-scandal/. Retrieved 8/22/17.
138. Donovan, B. W. (2011). *Conspiracy Films: A Tour of Dark Places in the American Conscious.* Jefferson, N.C.: McFarland, pp. 104–105.
139. Vallee, J. (1991). *Revelations: Alien Contact and Human Deception.* New York: Ballantine Books, p. 53.
140. Brewer, Jack (2016). *The Greys Have Been Framed: Exploitation in the UFO Community*, Kindle Edition. Kindle location 378.
141. Ibid, Kindle locations 210–212.
142. http://www.alienresistance.org/ce4.htm, retrieved 8/13/17.
143. Redfern, Nick (September 18, 2013). "Feeding the UFO Phenomenon."

Mysterious Universe. http://mysteriousuniverse.org/2013/09/feeding-the-ufo-phenomenon/, retrieved 8/26/17.

144. Ibid.

145. Heiser, Dr. Michael S. (November 27, 2010). "Review of Nick Redfern's Final Events." http://drmsh.com/review-of-nick-redferns-final-events/, retrieved 8/26/17.

146. Ibid.

147. Redfern, Nick (October 1, 2011). "A Religious Deception?" *Mysterious Universe.* http://mysteriousuniverse.org/2011/10/a-religious-deception/, retrieved 8/26/17.

148. Pilkington, Mark (November 3, 2010). "RAND, Superstition, and Psychological Warfare." *Mirage Men.* https://miragemen.wordpress.com/2010/11/03/rand-superstition-and-psychological-warfare/, retrieved 8/26/17.

149. http://www.talk2action.org/comments/2010/10/2/142824/582/9?mode=alone; showrate=1#9, retrieved 8/26/17.

150. For a further examination of that idea, we recommend the books *Saboteurs* by Tom Horn and *The Deeper State* by Lt. Col. Robert Maginnis (U.S. Army, ret.).

151. Levenda, Peter (2005). *Sinister Forces—The Nine: A Grimoire of American Political Witchcraft.* Walterville, Oregon: TrineDay. Kindle Edition, Kindle Locations 7603–7604.

152. Melanson, Terry (2001). "The All-Seeing Eye, the President, the Secretary and the Guru." http://www.conspiracyarchive.com/NWO/All_Seeing_Eye.htm, retrieved 8/14/17.

153. For that we recommend Peter Levenda's *Sinister Forces: The Nine.*

154. Levenda, op. cit., Kindle Locations 7734–7737.

155. Levenda, op. cit., Kindle Locations 7765–7769.

156. Levenda, op. cit., Kindle Locations 7809–7815.

157. Puharich, A. (1974). *Uri; a Journal of the Mystery of Uri Geller.* Garden City, NY: Anchor Press, p. 18.

158. Penre, Wes (1999). "The Council of Nine." *Fortean Times.* Republished at UriGeller.com: http://www.urigeller.com/plan-nine-outer-space/. Retrieved 8/22/17.

159. Ibid.

160. Ibid.

161. Ibid.

162. Ibid.
163. Christiane, Zivie-Coche, (2004). *Gods and men in Egypt: 3000 BCE to 395 CE*. Cornell University Press.
164. Penre, op. cit.
165. Ibid.
166. Ibid.
167. John 14:6.
168. "UN Secretary-General appoints high-level panel on post-2015 development agenda." United Nations Development Programme. July 31, 2012. Retrieved January 17, 2014. www.undp.org/content/undp/en/home/presscenter/pressreleases/2012/07/31/un-secretary-general-appoints-high-level-panel-on-post-2015-development-agenda.html.
169. United Nations Millennium Development Goals website, retrieved July 7, 2017. https://www.un.org/millenniumgoals/bkgd.shtml.
170. https://www.un.org/sg/management/pdf/HLP_P2015_Report.pdf.
171. http://fortune.com/2012/09/18/bad-to-the-bone-a-medical-horror-story/.
172. Shipman, Tim (November 30, 2008). "UFO Enthusiasts Call on Obama to Release X-Files." *The Daily Telegraph*. London, UK. Retrieved July 7, 2017. www.telegraph.co.uk/news/newstopics/howaboutthat/3536229/UFO-enthusiasts-call-on-Obama-to-release-X-Files.html.
173. Norman, Tony (December 2, 2008). "Change Is Coming (But Not for Space Aliens)." *Pittsburgh Post-Gazette*. Retrieved December July 7, 2017. www.post-gazette.com/pg/08337/932038-153.stm.
174. http://www.conwaydailysun.com/newsx/local-news/123978-clinton-promises-to-investigate-ufos.
175. http://www.cnn.com/2016/01/04/politics/hillary-clinton-area-51-aliens/.
176. https://www.nytimes.com/2016/05/11/us/politics/hillary-clinton-aliens.html.
177. https://www.youtube.com/watch?v=R95X8rwYD9o.
178. https://www.nytimes.com/2016/05/11/us/politics/hillary-clinton-aliens.html.
179. http://noetic.org/about/overview.
180. "Edgar Mitchell on the UFO Cover-Up." *UFO UpDates*. October 11, 1998. Archived from the original on January 28, 2007.
181. http://www.edgemagazine.net/2008/07/edgar-mitchell/.
182. http://www.terrimansfield.com/terri/.

183. Ibid.

184. http://www.terrimansfield.com/2017-year-of-justice/.

185. The exchange can be read on WikiLeaks here: https://wikileaks.org/podesta-emails/emailid/15052.

186. http://rebeccahardcastlewright.com/2016/10/18/wikileaked-was-edgar-mitchell-planning-to-meet-with-podesta-then-obama/.

187. https://wikileaks.org/podesta-emails/emailid/58918.

188. https://wikileaks.org/podesta-emails/emailid/6983.

189. https://wikileaks.org/podesta-emails/emailid/12127.

190. The word "contiguous" here seems to refer to what we might think of as "parallel" or "higher," such as regarding a parallel universe or higher dimension.

191. https://wikileaks.org/podesta-emails/emailid/32833.

192. https://wikileaks.org/podesta-emails/emailid/35713.

193. https://wikileaks.org/podesta-emails/emailid/1766.

194. https://wikileaks.org/podesta-emails//fileid/1802/608.

195. https://wikileaks.org/podesta-emails/emailid/1802.

196. 1 Corinthians 15:39–40 (KJV).

197. For an excellent examination into the ancient Near-Eastern idea of celestial flesh, check out the Naked Bible Podcast episode 88, hosted by biblical scholar and ancient languages expert Dr. Michael Heiser, here: http://www.nakedbiblepodcast.com/naked-bible-88-what-is-the-spiritual-body-paul-talks-about-in-1-cor-15/ or for the transcript, here: https://www.nakedbiblepodcast.com/wp-content/uploads/2016/02/Transcript-88-Spiritual-Body.pdf.

198. https://wikileaks.org/podesta-emails/emailid/33713.

199. https://wikileaks.org/podesta-emails/emailid/18724.

200. Ibid.

201. https://www.wikileaks.org/podesta-emails/emailid/30433.

202. https://wikileaks.org/podesta-emails/emailid/2125.

203. https://wikileaks.org/podesta-emails/emailid/3099.

204. http://www.worldufoday.com/is-it-time-for-the-truth-about-ufos-to-come-out/.

205. richarddolanpress.com.

206. *UFOs and Disclosure in the Trump Era*, Richard Dolan, Kindle Location 1162.

207. Ehman, Jerry R. (February 3, 1998). "The Big Ear Wow! Signal. What

We Know and Don't Know About It After 20 Years" www.bigear.org/ wow20th.htm.

208. "Humanity Responds to 'Alien' Wow Signal, 35 Years Later." www.space. com/17151-alien-wow-signal-response.html.

209. http://www.independent.co.uk/news/science/aliens-proof-evidence-facts-stars-scientists-extraterrestrial-life-et-intelligence-a7377716.html.

210. https://phys.org/news/2016-10-stars-strange-aliens-contact.html.

211. https://arxiv.org/abs/1610.03031.

212. https://arxiv.org/pdf/1210.5986v1.pdf.

213. https://www.space.com/27737-comet-song-rosetta-spacecraft.html.

214. http://www.cnn.com/2016/08/30/health/seti-signal-hd-164595-alien-civilization/index.html.

215. http://www.cnn.com/2016/08/31/europe/ seti-signal-hd-164595-not-alien-civilization/.

216. http://www.sci-news.com/astronomy/ross-128-signals-05052.html.

217. http://www.sci-news.com/astronomy/weird-signal-ross-128-extraterrestrial-intelligence-05064.html.

218. https://www.nasa.gov/press-release/ nasa-confirms-evidence-that-liquid-water-flows-on-today-s-mars.

219. https://www.nasa.gov/press-release/nasa-s-hubble-spots-possible-water-plumes-erupting-on-jupiters-moon-europa.

220. exoplanet.eu.

221. http://exoplanet.eu/catalog/.

222. https://www.seeker.com/alien-life-exoplanet-wolf-1061c-astronomy-biomarkers-habitable-zone-2204049638.html.

223. http://www.spaceflightinsider.com/missions/space-observatories/ james-webb-space-telescope-delayed/.

224. https://www.seeker.com/there-could-have-been-life-on-venus-1999229426.html.

225. http://www.trappist.one/#about.

226. *Monthly Notices of the Royal Astronomical Society*, Volume 468, Issue 3, 1 July 2017, Pages 2803–2815, https://academic.oup.com/mnras/ article/468/3/2803/3059153/Bayesian-evidence-for-the-prevalence-of.

227. https://planetplanet.net/2013/09/25/ where-did-earths-water-come-from/.

228. All seven tablets, translated to English, can be read here: http://www. sacred-texts.com/ane/enuma.htm.

229. http://www.ancient.eu/article/225/.

230. Pardee, Dennis. "Ugaritic," in *The Ancient Languages of Syria-Palestine and Arabia* (2008) (pp. 5–6). Roger D. Woodard, editor. Cambridge University Press, ISBN 0-521-68498-6, ISBN 978-0-521-68498-9 (262 pages).

231. Yon, Marguerite (2006). *The City of Ugarit at Tell Ras Shamra*. Singapore: Eisenbrauns. p. 15. ISBN 978-1-57506-029-3. Retrieved 16 May 2015.

232. Tubb, Jonathan N. (1998), "Canaanites" (British Museum People of the Past)

233. For more information on this, refer to the Chaos to Restoration Lecture Series by Dr. Michael S. Heiser at https://youtu.be/xUspLJjSjqo?list=PL5 2EgTwZYdvWlIxnSQphmeI8dDgE1mNde.

234. Psalm 68:4 and Daniel 7:13, for example.

235. Mark 14:61–62.

236. "A Prophetic Letter of Adad to Zimri -Li m" (A.1968). English translations in J. J. M. Roberts, *The Bible and the Ancient Near East. Collected Essays* (Winona Lake, IN: Eisenbrauns, 2002), ch. 14, pp. 157–253, "The Mari Prophetic Texts in Transliteration and English Translation," and in M. Nissinen, *Prophets and Prophecy in the Ancient Near East*, with contributions by C. L. Seow and R. K. Ritner (ed. P. Machinist; *Writings from the Ancient World*, 12; Atlanta, GA., Society of Biblical Literature, 2003), pp. 21–22 (A. 1968).

237. John N. Oswalt, The Book of Isaiah, Chapters 40–66, *The New International Commentary on the Old Testament*, Grand Rapids, MI: Wm. B. Eerdmans Publishing Co., 1998), 341–42.

238. For more information, watch *Could Christianity Accommodate a Genuine Extra-Terrestrial Reality?* By Dr. Michael S. Heiser, PhD: https://youtu. be/uOZ0KaUBkoU.

239. Jeff Levin, "Revisiting the Alexander UFO Religious Crisis Survey (AUFORCS): Is There Really a Crisis?" *Journal of Scientific Exploration*, Vol. 26, No. 2, pp. 273–284, 2012, http://www.baylorisr.org/ wp-content/uploads/2012-JSE-UFO-Levin.pdf.

240. American high schools have 752 students per school on average, https:// nces.ed.gov/pubs2001/overview/table05.asp.

241. C. Maxwell Cade, *Other Worlds Than Ours*; Taplinger Publishing Company, N.Y., 1967; 1st publ. in G. Britain in 1966.

242. Ernst Fasan; Relations with Alien Intelligences; (Berlin Verlag Arno Spitz, I Berlin 33, Ehrenbergstraße 29; 1970).